T0384194

"This beautifully clear guide to dreams and about dreaming shows both beginners and experts many ways to understand them. The book celebrates the sense of surprise we often feel when encountering the gifts dreams bring from the unconscious to the conscious mind. The latest discoveries in neuroscience are linked to contemporary issues in depth psychology, politics, and religion. An essential read!"

**Professor Andrew Samuels**, author of *Persons, Passions, Psychotherapy, Politics*

"We all dream, too few pay attention to their dreams. Despite the countless recipe books for decoding dream symbols, few understand them. *Dreams: the Basics* is a definitive dream book. It includes a discussion of dream history, theoretical controversies (Freud vs. Jung), neurological hypotheses, and the role of dreams in creativity. Practical techniques for remembering and exploring dreams are included. It is a book which had to be written. A must read for all—clinicians and lay alike."

**Melvin E. Miller**, co-editor of *Creativity, Spirituality, and Transcendence: Paths to Integrity and Wisdom in the Mature Self*. Psychoanalyst, Montpelier, Vermont, USA

# DREAMS

*Dreams: The Basics* presents introductory and accessible information about what dreams are, where they come from, what they do, and how to understand and work with them.

This book demythologises dream interpretation, with each chapter inviting the reader to ask questions about their own dreams and try exercises. Chapters explore social dreaming, how culture impacts dreams, and their use in counselling, therapy, and analysis. They offer suggestions about how to engage with and develop a skill set to work with dreams. This book summarises the latest thinking and research on this subject, as well as exploring key analytic theorists, such as Freud, Jung, and their successors. A glossary is included, along with useful diagrams and images. The book is aimed at high school and A-level students, undergraduate students, counsellors, therapists and analysts, and anyone interested in dreams.

**Dr Dale Mathers** is a psychiatrist, humanistic psychotherapist, and Jungian analyst in the United Kingdom.

**Dr Carola Mathers** is a Jungian analyst and formerly a consultant psychotherapist at the Southwest London and St. George's NHS Trust, United Kingdom.

# The Basics Series

*The Basics* is a highly successful series of accessible guidebooks which provide an overview of the fundamental principles of a subject area in a jargon-free and undaunting format.

Intended for students approaching a subject for the first time, the books both introduce the essentials of a subject and provide an ideal springboard for further study. With over 50 titles spanning subjects from artificial intelligence (AI) to women's studies, *The Basics* are an ideal starting point for students seeking to understand a subject area.

Each text comes with recommendations for further study and gradually introduces the complexities and nuances within a subject.

**ART HISTORY**
Grant Pooke and Diana Newall

**ARTIFICIAL INTELLIGENCE**
Kevin Warwick

**ATTACHMENT THEORY**
Ruth O'Shaughnessy, Katherine Berry, Rudi Dallos and Karen Bateson

**BEHAVIORAL ECONOMICS (second edition)**
The Basics

**THE BIBLE**
John Barton

**BIOPSYCHOLOGY**
Philip Winn and Madeleine Grealy

**DREAMS**
Dale Mathers and Carola Mathers

# DREAMS

# THE BASICS

**Dale Mathers and Carola Mathers**

Routledge
Taylor & Francis Group

NEW YORK AND LONDON

Designed cover image: 'Sea of Dreams' by Carola Mathers

First published 2025
by Routledge
605 Third Avenue, New York, NY 10158

and by Routledge
4 Park Square, Milton Park, Abingdon, Oxon, OX14 4RN

*Routledge is an imprint of the Taylor & Francis Group, an informa business*

ISBN: 978-1-032-33442-4 (hbk)
ISBN: 978-1-032-32735-8 (pbk)
ISBN: 978-1-003-31969-6 (ebk)

DOI: 10.4324/9781003319696

Typeset in Bembo
by SPi Technologies India Pvt Ltd (Straive)

To Joe and Rosie

# CONTENTS

List of figures                                         x
About the authors                                       xi
Preface                                                 xii
Permissions                                             xiv
Acknowledgements                                        xv

1  Introduction                                          1

2  Dreams are a bridge                                   15

3  Empathy – culture, religion, and politics             34

4  Dreams, reflections, memories                         52

5  The natural philosophy of sleep and dreams            67

6  Depth psychology and dreaming                         85

7  Dreams and therapy                                    102

8  Dreams and creativity                                 117

9  Social and cultural dreaming                          133

10  Play and the transcendent function                   150

Glossary                                                165
Neuroanatomy glossary                                   169
Selected bibliography                                   175
Index                                                   176

# FIGURES

| | | |
|---|---|---|
| 2.1 | The iceberg map of the psyche | 25 |
| 4.1 | Memory circuits | 58 |
| 5.1 | Neural pathways of sleep | 71 |
| 5.2 | How dreams are made | 75 |
| 5.3 | The salience network | 79 |
| 5.4 | The executive network | 79 |
| 5.5 | The default mode network | 81 |
| 7.1 | The triangle of person | 106 |
| 7.2 | The triangle of conflict | 106 |
| 7.3 | Victim, persecutor, rescuer | 107 |

# ABOUT THE AUTHORS

**Dr Carola Mathers** MB, BS, retired psychiatrist, former training analyst, supervisor, and teacher with the Association of Jungian Analysts. A certified social dreaming host, she hosted dream matrices in the United Kingdom, Europe, and Russia. During the 2020–2021 pandemic, she hosted online dream matrices for various Jungian groups. More recently, she has hosted online dream matrices for Ukrainian Jungians and for other Jungian groups. Her publications include 'The Symbolic Constrainer' in *Vision and Supervision* (2009, London: Routledge, ed. Dale Mathers), 'The Queen and the Servant' in *Alchemy and Psychotherapy* (2014, London: Routledge, ed. Dale Mathers.)

**Dr Dale Mathers** MB, BS, retired psychiatrist, former training analyst, and supervisor with the Association of Jungian Analysts. He was a member of the Russian Society for Analytical Psychology and a humanistic psychotherapist. He teaches analytical psychology in the United Kingdom, Ukraine, and Russia. Dale is also interested in creative writing. His publications include *An Introduction to Meaning and Purpose in Analytical Psychology* (2001, London: Routledge), *Vision and Supervision* (2009, London: Routledge (ed.)), *Self and No Self* (2009, London: Routledge (ed.)), *Alchemy and Psychotherapy* (2014, London: Routledge (ed.)), and *Depth Psychology and Climate Change* (2019, London: Routledge (ed.)).

# PREFACE

This book is a simple guide to dreams. It shows how they are made, what they are made with, and what they are made for. Dreams are a natural product of the unconscious mind as it goes about its nightly task of helping us understand the world and our place in it, making bridges between conscious and unconscious. We are social beings. We cannot exist on our own. Dreams are an essential part of a culture's psychological ecosystem. They are not a personal possession.

Dreams evolve memory, which has a predictive function, letting us guess what is next up. Memory is prospective, as well as about what has happened. Dreams are creative play spaces. They have a transcendent function, moving between and beyond ego and self. I have not capitalised self – though some analysts do. Sometimes, dreams are the source of religious, political, and spiritual insights. However, most are not remembered.

Many of the dreams in the book are mine not because they are especially remarkable; rather, the opposite, but because of confidentiality. People whose dreams appear helped to disguise themselves. The dreamers are fictionalised; their dreams are not.

You can read the chapters in any order, but it is easier to start at the beginning because the concepts build on each other. I cross-refer to sections like this: [3.2] means Section 2 in Chapter 3. There is a glossary of technical terms at the end and a separate one for neuroanatomy. Please don't be put off by this. It's hard to give an up-to-date account of dreaming without referring to the latest research. Some chapters have quite simple maps of the brain, enough to give you a rough idea of where the structures are. Notice the mind does not equal the brain: this is discussed as we go through the book.

There are also questions marked [Q]. They do not have 'right answers' because there is still so much we don't know about how the mind works, so there are no answers at the back of the book. The questions are more like 'stop signs' to encourage you to pause and reflect. At the end of each chapter are suggestions for further reading which lead to accessible books and articles, and a list of references which lead to more complex material, including original research. Much of the detail about 'the three network model' – a best guess at how the mind works – is still evolving. You can find many helpful videos on YouTube – though these tend to go out of date quickly, and you need to be discerning about who put them up.

Take your time. Write all over the book. Write 'NO!' in big letters if you don't agree and 'YES!' if you do. Don't be reverent with the text. Think of new and awkward questions to ask. And don't expect this book will teach you how to interpret dreams or 'work' with dreams. Personally, I feel 'work' is the last thing a dream ever needs. They are gifts from your unconscious for your conscious to play with. The less solemn you are in your approach, the more you'll discover from their ever-changing symbols.

Dale Mathers

# PERMISSIONS

# ACKNOWLEDGEMENTS

This book was made possible thanks to the generous help of family and friends.

A special thanks to my wife, Carola, for her help, support, and encouragement; for her chapter 'Social and Cultural Dreaming,' careful editing, and cover illustration – 'Sea of Dreams' (www.alternativeartsales.com).

To Ewan Mathers for the cover photography (www.ewanmathers-photography.com).

To our daughter, Rosie, for advice about anthropology and editorial suggestions. To our son, Joe, for the music. To Rachel Hartzell for the illustrations.

A special thanks to those friends, patients, and colleagues who kindly gave consent for their dreams to appear. Their identities have been fictionalised with their help.

To Katie Randall, Sarah Rae, Pragati Sharma, and all the editorial team members at Routledge.

My thanks to the many people who read drafts, commented, and suggested improvements and simplifications:

Peter Afford, Carolyn Boyes, Jack Bierschenk, Dr Joe Calabrese, Dr Sarah Hall, Dr John Erskine, Rabbi Helen Freeman, Philippe Jacquet, Richard Jenkins, Dr Elena Liulena, Dr Bridget Lock, Dr Jennifer Low, Megan Lewsey, Erin Lewsey, Dr Will Longden, Vreni Osterwalder-Bollag, Prof Christian Roesler, Prof Mel Miller, Chris Robertson, Prof Andrew Samuels, Dr Susan Schwartz, Keith Silvester, Jan Tiro, Dr Konstantin Vakhitov, Andy White, Jack White, Marilyn Williams, and Ruth Williams.

And thank you to the Institute of Psychoanalysis for the Maudsley Lectures on Dreams, Autumn term, 2023, which were invaluable.

# INTRODUCTION

## 1.1 DREAMING IS STORYTELLING

This book tells stories about dreams: what they are, where they come from, and what their functions may be. Two primary functions are developing empathy and evolving memory. I look at the natural history of dreams and their place in our lives and in our culture. This is not a book about how to interpret your dreams because, as I'll show, each dream is as unique as its dreamer. Understanding their meaning depends on the context – you, the dreamer, are the context. All stories need a language. I'll use a few specialist terms from philosophy, psychology, psychoanalysis, and neuroscience to tell the story, explaining them as I go. You can look them up in the glossary at the back, and there is an appendix summarising the neuroanatomy.

Finding meaning in dreams is like learning any language, except that in this one, the words – symbols – continually change their meaning, so it's about finding patterns rather than reading symbol dictionaries, where you may learn that if you dream of a cat, it means you will have good fortune. If you wish to read a symbol dictionary for inspiration, then classics are by J.E. Cirlot (1962) and Tom Chetwynd (1982).

A sign, like a road sign, has one meaning. A symbol has multiple meanings [2.3]. Sometimes the meaning is less important than the work a dream does in building memories, practising actions, trying things out, and choosing future actions in a safe place (sleep). Though analysts are supposed to have unique skills in 'interpretation,' what we really do is help people learn to use their own natural

DOI: 10.4324/9781003319696-1

dream-language skills (Mathers, 2001, pp. 116–138). Our minds tell stories all the time. Dream stories are intriguing, mysterious, sometimes annoying, often insightful, occasionally terrifying. They are stories about things which matter to us.

Dreaming is a natural activity. All mammals dream. If you know a cat or a dog, you can watch them dream. Their whiskers twitch, their bodies shiver, they make low purrs or soft growls, and they have rapid eye movements – REM sleep is a sign of dreaming. What do you suppose they dream about? What do *you* dream about? What do you dream *for*? We spend about 10 per cent of our lives dreaming, 7 years if you live to 70, so it's highly likely it has a meaning and a purpose; otherwise, why burn so much energy doing it? My aim is to help you look for answers to these questions and to ask better questions about your own dreams rather than to give answers. There are no 'answers,' there are only better questions.

Arrange the 'facts' in this book into patterns which have meaning for you – question everything. When you look at one of your own dreams, question each part – the details matter, as well as the big story. Danish Jungian analyst and scholar of dreaming Ole Vedfelt (2017, pp. 40–41) lists ten core qualities of dreams, and his book gives an excellent detailed review of the topic.

---

### Box 1.1   Core Qualities of Dreams

- Deal with things which matter to us
- Symbolise
- Personify
- Are a trial run in a safe place
- Are online to unconscious intelligence
- Recognise patterns
- Are high-level communications
- Condense information
- Are experiences of wholeness
- Are psychological energy landscapes

---

Developing skills to be with our dreams needs far more effort than looking up a symbol in a dictionary or using an internet search engine, but it's more fun and relates you to your personal reality. Just as we talk about 'playing' music rather than 'working at' music, playfulness is a better word to use than 'dream work' – which is a technical psychoanalytic term for the work the mind does to form a dream. The results are playful, often humorous, and the best way to understand them is to play with them. Chapter 10 suggests ways to do this and what you could try if you don't easily remember dreams.

Dream-language skills are essential in daily life. We can look at life as if it were a dream or a dream as if it were life or both. This binocular vision includes inner and outer worlds, encourages dialogue between them, and helps us learn how to separate fantasy from reality, as dreams are fantasies which contain reality. However, as I discuss later, reality is itself a creation rather than a 'truth' because we predict what we're going to perceive. We don't see 'things as they really are,' we see them as *we wish and expect* to see them. Dreams help us to do this.

Any meanings we find – and not all dreams are full of deep meaning – relate to the dreamer. If I dreamed about blue elephants, it won't mean the same as if you did – and it won't mean the same for me today as it did 30 years ago. I'd have to talk to the blue elephants to find out who they are and what they want – today. Dreams can be deeply emotional experiences which reshape our lives. Equally, and commonly, they are our minds reacting to inner events noticed while asleep. I might dream of a waterfall in my bathroom; this could mean, 'Wake up and go to the toilet.'

Q: How do you imagine this happens? Is this the mind at work, or the body, or both? Is there a difference between mind and body?

When I ask questions like this, it is not because I know the answers. Sometimes, there aren't any, or they are a paradox. To find a meaning, we start from where we are, like this:

*As a boy in Ireland, my friends and I went on a long bike ride. We got lost. We asked an old man, 'What's the way to our village?' He scratched his head and said, 'Well boys. If I were you, I wouldn't start from here.'*

The paradox is that as we are *here, now,* there is nowhere else to start from. Dreams often talk in paradoxes. To find what they're about, start from where you are. What do you wish? What is your conscious attitude? Analysts study meaning by separating a dream into its elements [1.4]. The word 'analysis' comes from Greek, 'ana,' throughout, and 'lysis,' to loosen. Dream stories loosen the grip of fixed meanings, process feelings, and change meaning by connecting past experiences to present (and sometimes future) events.

Any good story asks questions: 'Will the hero complete the quest?' Or, 'Will the princess fall in love with the prince?' Dreams are us asking *ourselves* questions. They give ambiguous answers. To test this out, try writing down a question about something important to you before you go to sleep. If you remember a dream in the morning, how do you find the answer within it? First, you suppose that the dream – whatever it is – answers the question. Analysts explore dreams in several ways.

One is called 'free association' – lie down, relax, and say the first thing which comes into your mind about the dream, then the next, and keep going. Associations include sensations, feelings, thoughts, and memories; some will be nonsense. Dreams have layers of meanings: there may be overwhelming feelings or a lack of feeling where we'd expect there to be one.

When my bladder was full, the symbols – waterfall and bathroom – predicted what could happen if I didn't wake. This isn't precognition; it's physiology. Dream symbols give clues as to what the dream is for and its purpose, as well as its meaning. Big dreams certainly can be a *Portal to the Source* – a book on dreams by American Jungian analysts Ed Whitmont and Sylvia Pereira (1989, pp. 1–4). However, most dreams never cross the threshold of awareness into consciousness. We wake half aware that we've dreamed but can't remember much – because we don't need to. Most dreams are the mind doing the filing. We add, delete, reorder, evolve, and integrate daily events. Jungian analysts, like me, use a concept, 'self,' to organise our thoughts about life's meaning and purpose.

Q: What do you think the word 'self' means?

I'll expand on the many possible answers throughout the book, but I will leave a space here for you to make your own meanings. In analysis, one person actively listens while the other tells stories about themselves. Together, they re-edit the stories to make better sense: a 'director's cut' rather than 'the family version.' Over time, a tangle of narratives – stories scripted by others, negative stories (and lies) we tell ourselves – disentangle. This dream was my first in analysis:

### The blue elephant dream

*I'm on my first analyst's couch, looking at her garden. There is a rockery of Alpine plants and a miniature Venetian canal, a foot wide. In it swim tiny blue elephants, one behind the other. Each one's trunk holds onto the tail of the elephant in front. Slowly, they let go and disappear around the corner.*

I often felt sad then. The analysis worked; I don't feel this now. Not because my analyst 'interpreted' this – or any other – dream. She said, 'If I interpret your dreams, it's like you ask me for guitar lessons, but I take your guitar and play it for fifty minutes. How much would you learn? – not much.' What she did was listen, observe, and be curious. The word 'interpretation' does not mean translate – it means what a musician does with a piece of music, a dancer with a dance, an actor with a role. There are endless interpretative possibilities; some more beautiful, others more moving. None are 'right.' Dreams can never have a 'right' interpretation.

You might take one of your own dreams and play with it as you go through this book. If you don't remember dreams, use a film, play, or your favourite online show *as if it were a dream.* This works best when you can strongly identify with the hero. All these stories came from their creator's unconscious minds. They were dreams, once upon a time. You could ask, 'What's the blue elephant dream about?,' and 'Why start with a dream? Why not just give us the facts?' Well, 'the facts' are as hard to catch as the blue elephants: slippery, heavy, and all linked together. I will try to separate them.

An insight from analysis is dreams can hide important feelings. Not to 'preserve sleep' but to help us ask better questions. So, when looking at a dream, look at what is *not there*, as well as what is. In the blue elephant dream, the remarkable thing is – it wasn't remarkable. It felt quite natural for there to be a Venetian canal I'd never noticed in my analyst's garden. I wasn't curious about how the line of blue elephants got there. So, one thing the dream is about is my lack of curiosity.

Slowly, eventually, I realised a canal is a waterway going somewhere for a purpose. It's an image for self as a container for interconnected memories. The dream began to suggest its own interpretations – imagine the canal talking, *'I'm your dream. I'm going somewhere for a purpose. I link things together for you.'* This chapter is about linking. Dreams are stories which link things together. We usually use 'self' as if it was a noun. Suppose it is a verb, an action word – the actions include coherence (these are parts of me) and continuity (this is who I was, am now, and might be). So, in a dream, we see self in action.

Adults dream about two hours a night; children, about three. We dream more in late adolescence as we become adults. We dream most, around 40 per cent of the time, just before we're born, when we're rehearsing movements and behaviours – like suckling, smiling, wriggling. Dreams are where we create self – feeling coherence (the wholeness of our experience) and continuity (continuing over time). Two other actions of self are agency (having a choice about what we do) and relating to others.

Creative story writers say, 'Show, don't tell,' and this is what dreams do. The blue elephant dream came back strongly as I wrote this. Thirty-five years ago, I thought 'elephants never forget' – and 'blue' means sad, so 'I've got the blues.' The dream suggested linking together old memories which led to sadness and then letting them separate and go away rather than holding on. Today, the dream means 'link things together.' Tomorrow, it may mean something else.

Dreams always change meaning over time. This is why you can't have a 'dictionary of dream symbols' – a lexicon where one image has one meaning; symbolic meanings constantly change. If I say, 'Right!' – I could mean turn right, or 'correct,' or I could be being sarcastic – it depends on the context. Dreams range in scale from 'postcards' – a single image or sensation, hardly remembered – to 'blockbuster fantasy trilogies' (in seven volumes, like *Game of Thrones*) which explore a theme for nights, months, or through our life.

Listening to dreams is an ordinary part of analytic work. The skill in analysis is not *doing things to the dreams* but *being with the dreamer* – this is what to do when you wish to learn from a dream. Spend time with it. They are, as Sigmund Freud, a pioneer of psychoanalysis, said, 'the Royal road to knowledge of the unconscious mind.' So, what's that, and why would we wish to go there?

First, simply, the unconscious is everything going on in our body and mind of which we are unaware: like our blood pressure, heart rate, and blood glucose level. Our unconscious automatically keeps these optimal for whatever we're doing and reminds us when we need to do something about them – like eat. It holds our perceptions, reflections, memories, and feelings. We don't need to be conscious of our heart rate second by second, though part of our mind knows exactly what it is. Similarly, we don't need to be conscious of almost all our memory. We select what matters in this moment, here and now. Consciousness is attention. Dreams select unconscious themes for our attention.

Second, our unconscious overlaps with the unconscious of those around us – friends, family, society, culture. These, in turn, shape how we experience the world: what we deal with and what we ignore. What we regularly dream about depends on what we do. Writers dream of words; actors dream of feelings; sports people and dancers dream of body position; fishermen dream of fish. It takes years to learn to do these things 'unconsciously.' For example, in tennis, the ball moves so fast no conscious mind could ever hit it. And we can't maintain focussed concentration for more than about 20 minutes before we drift into daydreams. These arise in the same way as night dreams and from the same part of the brain, the default mode network, so-called because it's the 'default,' what we do when we're not doing anything [5.5.4]. Dreaming goes on during waking as 'daydreams.'

Dreams are perceptions of events in the mind. They are us looking at ourselves. I'll explain more about what conscious and unconscious are in the next chapter, but you could start to work this out yourself. How do you know when you are conscious and when you aren't? How does your mind watch itself – not, '*does* my mind watch itself,' but '*how* does it …?'

## 1.2 DREAMING HAPPENS IN THE MIND

This is not a statement of the obvious. To understand what is going on in our mind, we need to discover what a mind is – an elephant-sized question. Psychology studies the mind. In ancient Greek, *psyche* means spirit (and butterfly); *logos* means knowledge. The question is bigger than psychology. Answers – opinions – about the mind come from all parts of any culture, including its religion and politics. Each society has its own views about what the mind is, who has one, and what they can or can't do with it. So, the answers you choose about what a mind is depends on what you want to do with the answer.

Mind is sometimes supposed to exist in the brain alone, and the 'mind/body problem' has always intrigued philosophers. Once, the Christian religion shaped the dominant discourses in the Western world. It was a big deal whether the mind was something which existed separately from the body (like a spirit or an immortal soul) or was 'simply' a result of physical processes [5.7]. However, as our anatomy professor joked when our group of medical students was especially dim – 'I can see bodies without minds, but I've yet to see a mind without a body.' Dream language includes the body – a sensation shown, a feeling felt. So, where does the mind begin, and where does it end?

Does it extend to the tiny nerves around the blood vessels at the tips of your fingers? Unconsciously, yes, it does. Is your mind separable from the mind of another? How much of what we suppose are our minds, our thoughts, is just going along with a story from our family or our culture – or advertising? How would we know? What would we know *with*? Well, with the mind. This is an 'if I were you, I'd not start from here' – a paradox. Using the mind to study the mind is like standing between two mirrors: the images go on forever. Philosophers call this an infinite regress: the question has no answer because the answer has no limit.

Let's try this another way. What are the functions, the purposes, of a mind? The mind 'does' perception, thinking, feeling, sensation, intuition, and will – the ability to make choices and carry them out, quite how nobody knows. All I can do is give you best guesses. Likely, these guesses will soon turn out to be wrong. Our minds are not the same as our brains. The mind extends through the whole body, into our social environment, and across the world. Throughout the book, I will look at where the two overlap. Because dreams are not just 'personal' – not just about 'me!' They link us to our social network.

A key concept is 'neural networks.' We have millions of overlapping paths between brain cells, always connected to and responsive to input from the body. The cortex, the outer layer of our brain, folds like a walnut and has around 16 billion nerve cells (out of about 90 billion in the whole brain). In the cortex, the neurons are arranged in six layers. Imagine six Amazon rainforests stacked on top of each other. Now, imagine each tree can talk to any other tree. How many connections are possible?

Nicholas Rashevsky (1899–1972) from Kyiv, professor of mathematical biology at Chicago University, modelled neural networks to better understand how they work. The number of potential interconnections is named 'the Rashevsky number.' It's larger than the number of atoms in the universe, says neuroscientist Gerald Edelman (2005, p. 14). Our minds contain and create infinite possibilities.

Before birth, dreams help make paths through the neural jungle. They are whisperings in the forest as emerging minds make test runs in a safe place. Once born, minds adapt, change, and upgrade as we sleep, when they don't have to concentrate. I could use IT analogies here, like 'we install new software in sleep.' This would be simple, uncomplicated – and wrong. It's hard to imagine anything less like a computer than a brain. They are complex adaptive systems which change organically, like any ecosystem. Edelman describes how neurons compete and 'the fittest survive,' which he calls neural Darwinism (1987). As parts of a neural network die, others are born. If you learn a thing but don't use it, the pathways wither. I can't remember how to do calculus. I knew, once. Dreams help us let go of feelings and ideas, too, as memories are reconstructive imagination [Chapter 4]. We make them up anew each time.

## 1.3 DREAMS HAVE A PURPOSE

Your purpose in reading this book shapes how you read it. You could go from cover to cover, or search the index, or be intrigued by something and follow it up by doing your own research. (There are suggestions for further reading at the end of each chapter.) You could write a poem or do a drawing. Or dance it or write a song. Or you might put the book down and daydream. You could wonder, 'What's the purpose of a dream?'

A philosophical term for purpose is *teleology* from the Greek *telos*, which means end. Teleology is explaining a thing in terms of its goal. For example, the purpose of an acorn is to become an oak tree. Asking about the purpose of our lives is a big question. Religion, politics, family, and friends offer suggestions from the outer world; dreams offer suggestions from the inner world. But if you don't check out what they say with external reality, there's trouble. A good historical example is when Hannibal, the leader of the army of Carthage, was ready to lead his elephants across the Alps and conquer Rome in 218 BC.

He dreamed the God Jupiter appeared and said, 'If you cross the Alps, a great Empire will fall.' Hannibal did, and the Romans destroyed the Carthaginian Empire. The dream did give him a big clue. Jupiter is the Father God of *Rome* – not Carthage, where Baal Hammon is 'Sun Father,' and Tammit, his wife, is 'Moon Mother.' Hannibal found in his dream what he wanted to find. He turned a dream narrative (a story) into a discourse (a story with a political purpose) – an easy mistake.

Dreams help us separate *discourses* from *narratives*. How? Discourses are about power. Political propaganda, advertising, marketing, and internet 'influencing' are examples. Discourses are when one person or group wants another to do something – give them power or buy their soap. A narrative is a story. When there are strong feelings in a dream, they give clues to where power conflicts are – inside us or between ourselves and others. The blue elephant dream is a narrative, a *myth* made up by my unconscious to show me something about linking. We mythologise our lives any time we tell anyone a story about ourselves. Dreams which persist become personal myths. A myth is a story a culture uses to explain things which matter to it – like a 'myth of origin' – 'Our people are special because God chose us,' or 'We are the Sons and Daughters of the Sun and Moon' [3.4.2].

Q: What myths of origin does your culture have? Do you believe them? Are they discourses or narratives?

You don't need the 'facts' about Hannibal; you need the idea that conscious desires (wishes) interfere with comprehending a dream's meaning and purpose. Which is usually not to reveal great spiritual truths about 'the soul's inner healing journey,' or be a 'portal to the source'; their ordinary purpose is to link thoughts to feelings and feelings to thoughts; memories to possible futures – elephants to elephants.

## 1.4 DREAMS USE ORDINARY STORYTELLING TECHNIQUES

A dream, like a novel, play, or film, has five basic elements: *story, plot, character, world, and voice.* The story is a summary of the narrative, 'boy meets girl' or 'hero slays dragon.' The plot is how they do it. The characters are who does it, the world is where they do it, and the voice is how the story sounds – how it sings. For example, in the Harry Potter books, the story is 'defeat the monster' (Lord Voldemort); the plot – in seven volumes – is about growing up and learning how to do this. Harry, Ron, and Hermione are the main characters; the world is the intersection of the real and the magical, and the voice beautifully changes from a children's story into young adult fiction.

As dreams are stories too, you can use these five elements to navigate them. In 'the blue elephants,' the story is 'stop going round in a circle'; the plot is about 'holding on and letting go'; the dreamer is *all the characters*; the world is the analyst's garden; the voice is comedy – a compensation for the sad feelings. The dreams we remember are like plays or films we've written for ourselves. Use the same critical skills you use when talking about a film: include the musical score, casting, and cinematography. It's not necessary to learn a whole new language to understand dreams or any of the dialects of 'psychoanalysis.' Humans have listened to dreams for longer than we can imagine. We do this before we're born. We're born knowing how to.

## 1.5  WHY THIS DREAM NOW?

What we do with a story depends on the context. Telling a 10-year-old person a hero story might aim to inspire them to be a hero; telling the same story to an 80-year-old might lead to their reflections on the futility of sacrifice. In my clinical work, a key concept is, 'Your unconscious is always on your side right now.' Who else's side would it be on? Who else is there inside our minds? Because usually there are others. Think of your mind as an inner village with its internal politics. Your family, friends, and enemies 'live' there, as well as cultural characters with meaning for you – perhaps Harry Potter and his crew. The characters in a well-made story are 'archetypal images' – symbols standing for an archetype: the Blessed Virgin Mary, the Hindu Goddess Lakshmi, the Buddhist saint Kwan Yin, and the Greek Goddess Demeter are versions of a 'great Mother archetype.'

Suppose an *archetype* is an inborn, genetically inherited pattern for a psychological behaviour found in all humans (and mammals) at any place and at any time. All mammals mother and father, breed and raise children, age and die. These are the commonest archetypes. Which one matters most to us here and now depends on where we are in our lives: hero is important in young adulthood; parent is important later. Dreams often show which archetypal patterns are emerging from the unconscious. A dream can never bring you something you can't manage because it is from your own psyche. It may be challenging. But it comes at this moment because this is 'the right moment' for a particular change. If we miss the opportunity, then the story will come back with a minor plot change, or be recast, or set in another location, or with a change of voice until we attend (listen) to it. Dreams are our unconscious asking our conscious to pay attention.

## 1.6  DREAMS: LINKING AND NOT LINKING

Playing with dream meanings is like doing a jigsaw without the picture on the lid of the box. Usually, we start by finding the edges – they stick out; they make a frame. Unless it is a circular puzzle, then you start in the middle. To find a dream meaning, start with edges, the boundaries, with what feels 'edgy.' Dreams don't have a picture on the lid. Sometimes there are blank pieces, images of absence. Though a sequence of dreams may tell us the same story a hundred ways, no dream ever has one meaning. It's like putting a jigsaw together and then finding the picture on the box has changed. Multiple focuses are possible, necessary, and wise – they can all be true at the same time. When you look at a dream, any object in it offers a point of view, a voice. Imagine what the elephants might say the blue elephant dream meant, or the canal, the water in it, the garden. Try this with one of your own dreams.

Dream symbols have situational meanings. If you dream about an elephant, it won't mean the same as if I do or if you are an elephant driver. This is because of the type of conjunctions dreams use – a technical term (from computing) is 'logical operators.' These are the links, the connections between trunk and tale – like 'and,' and 'or.' For example: {*if* x is greater than 3, *then* do y} uses the operator {*if / then*}. A common one we use as children is {*either/or*}; as in {*either* friend *or* enemy} {*either* right *or* wrong}, {*either* good *or* bad}. As we grow older, we discover things can be good, bad, and both good and bad at the same time: {*both/and*}. This is called ambivalence. It's a sign of mental health.

And then there is {*both/and / neither/ nor*}: like this, dreams are conscious {*both/and / neither/nor*} unconscious. In the Harry Potter books, the change from {*either/or*} thinking to {*both/and*} is seen in Harry's changing relationship with Professor Snape: first a villain and then, finally, both a villain and a hero. Dream stories try to move us on from {*either/or*} to {*both/and*}. Frequently, dreams use {*both/ and / neither/nor*} as logical operators. The blue elephants are both thoughts and feelings, neither thoughts nor feelings. If you can, use one of your own dreams, and try working out what the links are. Are there any? What if there aren't? What if you remember a dream where nothing happens? Here is an example.

### The Port Ban dream

*I'm on the island where I lived as a little boy, Iona, at my favourite beach, Port Ban. (Gaelic for ' white beach.') It's empty. It's peaceful.*

I learnt to swim here. When I was older, I'd sit here and daydream. A beach is a *between* space – both land and sea, neither land nor sea. Dreams are events in a '*between space*' in our minds – both conscious and unconscious, neither conscious nor unconscious. Try standing in a doorway. Are you in the room or outside? You're both inside and outside, neither inside nor outside. The Latin word for a threshold is *limen*. Dreams are *liminal* experiences. They are a space within which we create, which means managing uncertainty and being able to be with *not knowing*. The English poet John Keats called this negative capability. We can't create from a discourse when there is a power issue. Fundamentalism of any kind is a refusal of dialogue. It is about holding onto power. This is why it is dangerous – fundamentalists feel threatened by change, creativity, and questioning. Theirs is an 'it's my way or the highway,' attitude.

Q:  Do you know any fundamentalists? Are there similarities to any part of your mind?

We can only create from a narrative, not from a discourse. Dreams don't give commands, they offer suggestions – useful to know when you have nightmares. They may show a catastrophe, but they are not predictions. Dreams can have meanings which are images of empti-ness, like a beach. These often occur when we're working with a new idea. Potential meanings are tried out and dumped until we find one which fits.

The Port Ban dream showed me how essential emptiness is when approaching a dream. If we already know what it's about, there's no space to find anything. We can't learn anything if we already know everything (are omnipotent). This is why dialogue with fundamen-talists is so challenging, and this is most particularly true for the fun-damentalist parts of our own minds. The Port Ban dream contains an image of absence. Have you had images of absence in your dreams? Be curious about what is *not* there, as well as what is. In jigsaws, we use the shape of a space to find where a piece goes. Dreams can show a feeling by not showing it.

This dream might be saying, 'You're at home with these ideas. Dive in and swim around.' In the following chapters, I look at how dreams bridge between conscious and unconscious; how the dreamer's cul-ture and context mutually influence each other; the links between dream and memory; their natural philosophy (science); dreams in depth psychology; their use in counselling, therapy, and analysis; their role in creativity; how sharing dreams leads to new thoughts; and how to play with dreams – play is where we try out new ways of being. Play is a transcendent function: that means it bridges spiritual and material ways of understanding the world. We can {*both/and / neither/nor*} understand a dream each way.

## KEY CONCEPTS

**Dreams:**

- tell stories using symbols which have multiple meanings
- are a natural product of the mind
- happen in the daytime as well as at night
- have a meaning related to the context

## FURTHER READING

Mathers, D. (2001) *An introduction to meaning and purpose in analytical psychology*, London: Routledge.

Vedfelt, O. (2017) *A guide to the world of dreams: an integrative approach to dreamwork*, London: Routledge.

## REFERENCES

Chetwynd, T. (1982) *A dictionary of symbols*, London: Paladin.

Cirlot, J. E. (1962) *A dictionary of symbols*, London: Routledge and Kegan Paul.

Edelman, G. (1987) *Neural Darwinism: theory of neuronal group selection*, New York: Basic Books.

Edelman, G. (2005) *Wider than the sky*, London: Penguin.

Whitmont, E.C., and Pereira, S.B. (1989) *Dreams, a portal to the source* London: Routledge.

# DREAMS ARE A BRIDGE

## 2.1 DREAM LANGUAGE

In dreams, we talk to ourselves about things which matter to us. This chapter looks at the language used – symbols – which make bridges between conscious and unconscious, self and ego, and two different experiences of time. To look at what a dream means needs a little philosophy to help work out what has meaning, what doesn't, and how to tell the difference.

What is a language? It's a pattern of communication in speech, gesture (body language), writing, or signs. The structure is the grammar; the freely moving parts are the vocabulary. We all use symbols and are strongly influenced by cultural symbols yet are hardly aware of this (Siegelman, 1990, pp. 13–16, 31–34, 159–185). Dream symbols are spoken by the unconscious to the conscious. Like words, symbols have a range of meaning depending on the accompanying feeling, personal and cultural context. This ambiguity is how they help us solve problems (Robb, 2018, pp. 81–101). In waking life, our vocabulary changes depending on context. Think of words you might use (or not use) with friends, teachers, or parents. For example, as a Scot, if I say, 'Aye, right,' this means anything from 'I totally agree' to 'what nonsense!' depending on the gestures and voice tone. In dreams, the vocabulary is complex because the symbols keep shifting meaning. The grammatical patterns are similar [2.9].

When we learn a new language, at first, we don't know what we don't know. Then, we know what we don't know. Next, we know we know something. Eventually, we find limits to what can be

DOI: 10.4324/9781003319696-2

known and discover knowledge isn't enough. We need wisdom to know which words to use, when, and how to say them. To understand dream language, look for patterns, explore the structure of the whole dream, and use the feelings it contains to guide you. You, the dreamer, are always on the same side as your dream – even a nightmare. There's no special magic to dream language. It is a system which opens and closes on meanings.

Anything made of parts forms a system: whether it's a single cell in the body, neural networks making up the brain, a crowd of people, a society, or a rainforest. Cybernetics is the study of how systems are organised and controlled (self-organise and self-control). It comes from two Greek words – 'cyber' meaning governance and 'naut' meaning navigation (as in astronaut). In a simple system, central heating, the boiler goes on and off depending on a thermostat measuring room temperature. This is a feedback loop. The idea of dreams as feedback loops is explored by Danish analyst Ole Vedfelt (2017, pp. 35–42). He says the mind is a parallel processing system – thousands of different information processing networks run simultaneously, monitor each other, interact, and continually change.

Living systems have boundaries, adapt using positive and negative feedback, tend to self-regulate towards an optimum condition – called homeostasis (same state) – and do this by opening and closing the boundaries. Neurons change the permeability of their membrane (boundary) when they send messages. Our minds are complex emergent systems [Box 3.1] continuously opening and closing to perceptions from the inner and outer worlds. Open systems have permeable boundaries; closed ones have firm boundaries. A game of 'ultimate Frisbee' has an open field, no uniforms, and as many players as you like: professional baseball and cricket are played on closed fields, with rules, uniforms, and a fixed number of players.

Open thinking allows and includes new ideas and is curious about difference. But, if we're too open, we can be flooded by thoughts and feelings which are not our own. Closed thinking consolidates and organises what is already known, drawing a boundary around it – sometimes as if it were the only possible truth – this is fundamentalism (whether artistic, scientific, religious, or political). Open thinking can be indecisive, as there are so many possibilities, or depressing, as there is always more to find out, and everything changes. Change *always* means loss – of the safe and familiar. Change for the better is difficult emotionally because you regret not having made the change earlier.

Q: Because you didn't do what?
   To find answers, remember when this happened to you.

Closed thinking easily becomes paranoia, as in conspiracy theories – *'they'* (whoever *they* are) are inevitably out to get *us*, 'the little guys.' Both types of thinking are essential, or we would not have them. Neither is right or wrong. The question is, 'Which is appropriate, here and now?' It is important not to be judgemental about this. In the politics of the inner world, liberal (open) is not necessarily better than conservative (closed), and vice versa. A system needs both to form feedback loops and govern itself, whether the system is a mind or a society.

## 2.2 SIGNS AND SYMBOLS

Signs are a closed, simple system; symbols are an open, complex system. The study of how signs and symbols make meanings and who gets to name the meanings is called semiotics (from the Greek: *observing signs*). In medicine, we use clinical signs to make a diagnosis: a runny nose, cough, headache, and sore throat could be a cold or COVID-19. We do tests to see which it is. We can't do tests with dream symbols to prove what they mean, but we can amplify them, turn up the volume, and see what other images, memories, and reflections they suggest using free association.

Imagine dream symbols are made of 'meaning concentrate,' like fruit cordial. They need diluting to be drinkable. Associations dilute the symbols, giving them space and time to expand. If the signal is too quiet, they may need amplifying – adding a fairytale, a myth, a legend – or using active imagination (talking to the monster).

A symbol is not a sign. Signs usually mean one thing. Road signs have a clear meaning – a red light means stop. Symbols have many meanings. Dreaming of a cross doesn't only mean 'I'm at a crossroads,' it could mean, 'I am cross,' or Christ's crucifixion. If it means that for you, then it has a transcendent (bridging) meaning about God's love. For Christians, this is a life-defining image, a statement of core identity. For non-Christians, a cross may mean 'the Christian's religion' rather than, say, Islam or Hinduism. Or it may mean nothing at all.

The word 'symbol' comes from classical Greek. A 'symbolon' (*sym* – together, *bolos* – to throw – a 'thrown together') was a clay tablet marked with their personal seal by someone wishing to send a message later and then broken in half. One half went to the person who'd receive the message; the other half went with the messenger boy. When he arrived and the halves matched, it proved the message came from the sender (Stein, 1958). Symbols can be proof of identity, like wearing a crucifix or having a tattoo.

Q:  What identity symbols do you use – clothes, hairstyle, body language?

No identity statement is right or wrong; they're different. They mark boundaries so we know who we are – they are about persona: the mask we wear for others and for ourselves – most of us have several. They help us know who we are. Unknowns are uncomfortable, especially when they threaten our identity. Strangers are a threat until they're known. Symbols, however, always contain an unknowable. And that is threatening.

An unknowable is *not* an unknown – an 'x,' which we could find if we knew how – (like the weather on Neptune) but a thing which cannot ever be known. In maths, equations often 'solve for x' (find out what x is). However, sometimes 'x' can't be known. In maths, '$x^2 + 1 = 0$,' is the formula for the square root of minus one. No real number solves this equation, so mathematicians invented a symbol 'i' (meaning $\sqrt{-1}$ ) as a 'placeholder' in certain calculations. Equations which combine real and imaginary numbers make complex numbers. Like dream symbols, they combine the real and the imaginary – like finding a dragon in a supermarket (see p. 19). Dream symbols may show what analysts call a complex – a highly emotionally charged tangle of memories, feelings, and behaviours often related to childhood trauma. Here, the dream's aim is to open a dialogue with the distressed part of our mind rather than to close it down. And sometimes, the aim is to close, not open.

Q:  Can you remember a dream which helped you close something down and move on? What feelings did they contain? What did you do after the dream?

---

### Box 2.1    Sign and symbol

| **Sign** | **Symbol** |
|---|---|
| • Signs always have the same meaning | Multi-level communication |
| • Meaning can be fully known | Meaning can't be fully known |
| • Time bound | Time free |

---

Symbols do not translate 'word for word.' And the meanings change over time.

### The blue flowers dream

*I'm in a meadow full of blue flowers, playing in a stream. My Mum sits on one bank, knitting a blue baby jersey. I feel safe.*

This is the first dream I remember. What is the first one you remember? Why did it stay with you? I dreamed this at age three, shortly before my first brother was born. We lived on Iona, a small, remote island off the west coast of Scotland. It has no meadows like this. Blue baby clothes are for boys. In the 1950s, no one knew an infant's sex before birth, so perhaps this was precognition. Then, it was a dream about a big change and safety. In analysis, 30 years later, it symbolised safety with my analyst – 'playing in the presence of the mother/analyst' while we knitted feelings and thoughts together. The meadow might mean her blue consulting room, the stream might be my 'stream of consciousness' as I free-associated. Now? I wonder about 'blue' – a common symbol in my dreams, but I'm not sure of what. The next example is a dream I had about a patient:

### The dragon in the supermarket dream

*I'm in a supermarket. In the next aisle, a dragon wearing a headscarf pushes her shopping trolley. A little dragon walks beside her. It feels quite normal to see them. At the check-out, the dragon is in front of me in the queue. The little dragon pesters her for sweets. Mummy dragon breathes fire.*

In the dream, a dragon in a supermarket feels ordinary; in real life, it wouldn't. Dreams have a context. The previous day, I listened to a young person describing painful conflicts with their mother. They called her 'the dragon.' The dream came that night. When I went shopping the next day, by chance, the patient and their mother were in the next aisle, arguing. In the next session, the patient talked about the argument. They'd not seen me in the supermarket. This is a symbolic experience, bridging between the personal and the collective (Gordon, 1977).

Free-associating to 'dragon' led to the myth of St. George. I wondered if they had to be a hero, a dragon slayer, battling to escape a 'terrible witch mother' and win a prince/princess. Did confrontational patterns appear in other relationships? They did, including their relationship with their partner and with me. I asked if they feared they'd be treated like a whining child if they asked for something – I didn't tell them my dream; I used it. Patients may find being told their analyst's dream about them is – all kinds of things: they may feel special or intruded on. My dream shows a negative feedback loop between a mother and child – mirroring one between me and this patient at that moment.

A 'dragon in the supermarket' became, for me, a shorthand phrase for an extraordinary thing appearing ordinary in a dream. They are useful keys. The dream could mean this patient saw me as a dragon, or I saw my mother as a dragon, or using a 'heroic' attitude in every situation is a mistake. There are more meanings. You could find them yourself.

Q:  What would it mean for you if you had a dream like this? Try telling the dream from the point of view of each dragon, the cashier, or the supermarket trolley.

As with gesture and speech, we decode meaning depending on context, practice, and patience. We have a conversation *in* the dream and then *with* the dream. Conversations are between two or more people, or two or more parts of the same person. Imagine we have a village in our minds. Our Self is a multiplicity (Redfearn, 1985, pp. 88–100). Some are 'the dreamer who dreams the dream,' some 'the dreamer who is in the dream,' and others 'the dreamer who understands the dream' [2.6]. Of course, there are no people sitting in our skulls. There are overlapping neural networks with differing points of view, sometimes different languages. Let's call them 'subpersonalities.' They make up an inner village whose population is not always the dreamer: other people live there too.

Q: Who lives in your inner village?

If you are bilingual, you may dream in either language or both – or neither. If you're learning a new language, dreaming in it means it's become unconscious – you're getting it. Sub-personalities have their own language: one might speak like a frightened child or a critical parent, or a close friend. These sub-personalities don't speak the same emotional language. Their misunderstandings create closed systems/ complexes – in which time becomes a loop: what happened before will happen again, as in the film *Groundhog Day* (Ramis, 1993). The hero relives the same 24 hours over and over again.

## 2.3 CONSCIOUS AND UNCONSCIOUS

The riverbanks bridged by dreams are the conscious and uncon-scious. Try defining these yourself before reading on. If you wish, close the book, relax, and imagine a symbol for each. You could draw it. Or do this later. If you try it, be curious about what sym-bol you found and how you found it. Did you answer like an artist, a scientist, a sports player, a religious, or a political person – or all of them? Is your answer from personal experience, or was it found online?

Defining consciousness is not easy. It raises philosophical problems about how we know, *epistemology*, and what's real, *ontology*. How do we know we're conscious, alert, and awake, and how do we know we're dreaming?

### 2.3.1 *What is consciousness?*

If you are alert, awake, attentive, and focussed, as well as able to make choices – you're conscious. You may be distracted (your mobile goes off), your attention wanders, you lose interest, daydream, or fall asleep. There's a continuum between full alertness and deep sleep. Sometimes, we can't be conscious – we're intoxicated, anaesthe-tised, delirious with fever, or in a coma. Doctors assess this with the Glasgow coma scale. Full consciousness means we have normal ocular, verbal, and motor responses. But consciousness gets harder to define the closer we look.

Q: How would you define consciousness?

### 2.3.2 *The psychology of consciousness*

This topic needs a book to itself. Dreams are {both/and / neither/nor} conscious. Consciousness is essential for reality testing – who am I, where, when, who with, what has just happened, and what's likely to happen in the next few minutes. These ego functions are suspended in dreams. There are big debates about when consciousness begins – maybe around 23 to 30 weeks after conception. All human minds have the same basic properties:

---

**Box 2.2  Properties of a mind**

- Senses
- Emotes
- Feels
- Thinks
- Imagines
- Intuits
- Remembers
- Intends
- Predicts

---

## 2.4 THE PHILOSOPHY OF CONSCIOUSNESS

Once, the mind was imagined as a thing poured into the body when life began, which left when it ended. In the Christian West, this was called 'the Soul.' Other religious traditions have similar yet subtly different ideas. The seventeenth-century French philosopher René Descartes imagined 'the soul' lived in the pineal gland. His view is called 'Cartesian dualism' – here's the mind, there's the body – they are not the same. But where is consciousness? This problem puzzled philosophers for thousands of years. It still does. Are we 'conscious' in dreams [8.6]? Is this different from waking consciousness? Western philosophers have diverging views.

Aristotle (Athens, 384–322 BC) wondered whether there were not only 'natural things' but also 'independent things' existing outside the natural world, like Platonic 'forms' [3.2]. He guessed they overlap. He said dreams replay sensations from our day (day residues). We are in an altered state in which our secret wishes can be fulfilled.

Freud took some of his ideas from Aristotle [6.3]. Creating dreams is imagination rather than a communication from Gods or Spirits.

Like Aristotle, David Hume (Edinburgh, 1711–1176) wanted to discover the 'natural philosophy' of mind rather than accept religious speculations. He said knowledge comes from experience rather than being inborn. Passions (feelings) rule us, not reason. We are what we sense – rather than what our Soul tells us (because there isn't one). Consciousness is a by-product of sensation and doesn't have a purpose or a goal – it just is. In his *Treatise of Human Nature* (1739–1740), Hume argues we can only know a mind's subjective experience. Minds create illusions about the world, who we are, and how we work. So, consciousness is an illusion.

The eighteenth-century philosopher Immanuel Kant (Konigsberg, Prussia, 1724–1804) was inspired by Hume, challenged by his scepticism, and wrote *The Critique of Pure Reason* (1781), proposing 'percepts without concepts are blind.' Concepts come first (are *a priori*). Again, he echoes Plato's idea of 'forms.' His ideas are basic to social sciences, including anthropology. We see what we can conceive of rather than what's there. Minds continually respond to their culture and find it difficult or impossible to 'see things' outside cultural patterns. Kant saw dreams as a 'between' state – neither conscious nor unconscious, both conscious and unconscious. They bridge between everyday reality and an 'eternal' world.

Henri Bergson (Paris, 1859–1941), winner of the Nobel Prize for literature, continued this argument. Immediate experience and intuition are *'a priori'* – sensation comes first. Reality is made from change. Nothing exists in and of itself but only in a flow state (which he calls duration). In his book *Dreams* (2023), he mentions five functions of dreams (Box 6.1) based on observing his own dreams.

Contemporary Australian philosopher David Chalmers (1966–) wonders how can we know we have an experience – this is the 'hard problem' of consciousness. It's like explaining an ocean to a whale. How can we be conscious of being conscious? This is an infinite regress, like looking at yourself when you're standing between two mirrors. And an infinite regress is a philosophical dead end because it goes on forever. It is, partly, a problem of definition and relates to your worldview – if you suppose there are 'transcendent realities' (angels, fairies, nature spirits, spiritual worlds, heavens, and hells), you'll need to explain what happens when such realities appear in the mind and how the mind recognises them, because 'extrasensory perceptions' are still perceptions.

First Cultures often say, 'The spirits talk to us in dreams. We dream so we can hear them.' Our culture said this too, till recently. I've shown this to support the view dreams are real psychological events on the borders of consciousness. The natural science of dreaming depends on the philosophy – not the other way around. Dreams put together alternative realities against which we test reality [5.2]. When we use the body to strengthen the body, it's called calisthenics, so dreams are like mental calisthenics. In Chapter 10 [10.6], I look at another mental exercise which affects consciousness: meditation.

Conscious and unconscious are concepts, not things. A concept is an idea, thought, or belief: a thing is a material object, like a table. To mistake a concept for a thing is called reification. It's a philosophical error – common in dreams. The concept 'Mum behaves likes a dragon' becomes 'mother dragon.' Freud calls this condensation.

Consciousness tends to be a closed system; the unconscious tends to be an open system. There is a vast difference in scale: if the conscious is an island, then the ocean is the unconscious. If a surfer is consciousness, then the board is the 'here and now,' the wave is the object of attention, and the ocean is the unconscious. Dreams are sandcastles built between the high watermark and low watermark, where the boundary always moves. The conscious has limits: the unconscious is, effectively, infinite. And not all of it is personal.

Vital body processes (breathing, maintaining heart rate) are unconscious. 'Conscious' suggests control; 'unconscious' suggests the opposite. It is 'not controllable' (because not in need of control) rather than 'out of control.' This subtle difference may be why people find the idea of an unconscious mind troubling; indeed, some deny it exists. They fear loss of control. To them, control *seems* natural. This usually means, 'I want to be the boss!'

Analytical psychologists (like me) suppose there is both a personal and a collective unconscious (Box 3.2), which contains patterns for psychological behaviours humans and animals share – how to give birth, how to make love, how to grieve. All people, everywhere, at any point in history, draw on these genetically inherited patterns, just as all cats know how to pounce. Jung called these patterns archetypes – like the Great Mother, the Great Father, Hero, Shadow, Trickster. They live in the 'inner village.' But we can't see an archetype; we only see 'archetypal images,' a set of symbols representing it. Myths, legends, and religious beliefs form around archetypes, shape the stories in cultures, and regularly appear in dreams.

It is possible to make 'psychological maps' of the conscious and unconscious. The one in Figure 2.1 is based on work by Jolande Jacobi (1973), one of Jung's close colleagues. I call it 'the iceberg' model:

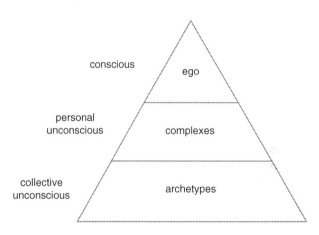

*Figure 2.1* The iceberg map of the psyche

It looks as though there are layers of consciousness and that it's hierarchical. It isn't. There is no 'Great Leader' at the top. The ego is not in control. Do maps like this have value? Or are they like medieval maps with helpful signs that say, 'Here be dragons'? A map is not the territory. Relying on maps like these is like using a subway map to find a friend's house if you've never been there. You might get to the right part of town, but after that, you're lost.

---

**Box 2.3   Conscious and unconscious**

| Conscious | Unconscious |
| --- | --- |
| • What we are aware of here and now | Everything else |
| • Explicit knowledge ('the facts') | Implicit knowledge |
| • Small | Vast |
| • Has limits and boundaries | Unlimited |
| • Looks at the immediate experience | Looks at physiology |
| • Feelings and perceptions | Memories |
| • From drowsy to highly focussed | From sleep to coma |
| • Assumed to have 'control' | Beyond control |
| • Reality testing | Creativity |
| • A function of ego | A function of self |

## 2.5 EGO AND SELF

Ego and Self are concepts – technical terms used in psychology and analysis. They aren't things – you can't open a brain and find them. Nor have any neural pathways so far discovered shown any correspondence to them. Confusingly, mental health professionals don't always mean the same thing by them. It won't surprise you to know different groups of analysts and psychologists argue passionately about what each of these terms means. People always argue about things which matter to them.

We long to be right; our ego demands it! It wants to be *in control*. In everyday speech, ego means, 'me, me, me!' An egotist is someone who considers only themselves. However, ego names essential functions of the mind which test reality: who am I, where am I, what's going on, what's just happened, what may happen next? Self means 'the wholeness of me,' what I was, am now, and might become. For some, the concept 'Self' includes soul or spirit. People with this concept suppose dreams are messages from the spirit world, from angels or 'the transcendent' [3.4.3, 10.4] – which means beyond the usual range of perception, above the ordinary. Sometimes, dreams give us a sense of being in the presence of a higher awareness – analytical psychologists call this a numinous (spiritual) experience. But usually, a dream leaves hardly a trace.

---

**Box 2.4    Ego and self**

| **Ego** | **Self** |
|---|---|
| • Latin word for 'I' | From Middle English 'sulf' (self) |
| • Reality tests | Gives a sense of wholeness |

**In psychoanalysis**

- negoitates between Id (primitive animal-like needs and desires) and superego
- (primitive, animal-like needs and desires)
- and 'superego'
- (critic, makes moral judgements)

**In analytical psychology**

| • Ego orients us | Archetype of wholeness |
|---|---|
| | • Centre of the psyche |

**In psychology**

| • Cognitive functions, identity | Individual as their own object |
|---|---|
| | • Integral to motivation |
| | • Shaped by the culture |

Ego is time bound; Self is time free. Let's look at what 'time bound' and 'time free' mean – because dream language makes bridges across time.

## 2.6 TWO KINDS OF TIME

Conscious and unconscious navigate time in two separate ways (Wiener, 1996). Time is hard to define (Callender and Edney, 2001, pp. 3–21). St Augustine said he knew what it was until asked to define it. A good account is given by the Italian quantum physicist Carlo Rovelli (2019, pp. 118–124), who explains, in science, a quantum of time is $10^{-44}$ of a second. What's interesting is there is a quantum, the smallest possible amount of time – and how incredibly small it is. Messages in neural networks travel at between a tenth and a hundredth of a second. On a quantum scale, a thought takes aeons. Maybe we have plenty of time.

French philosopher Henri Bergson, writing at the start of the twentieth century, contrasted the eternal present (*la durée* – 'here and now') with time as a series of moments (scientific time). Jung was familiar with Bergson's work and borrowed many of his ideas (Gunter, 1982).

To make this easier, let's call the first kind of time Kairos and the second Chronos. As Chronos time is more familiar, I describe it first. Chronos is a Greek god, the father of the Olympian gods. He ate his children until his wife Rhea gave him a stone and saved Zeus, the youngest. Chronos is 'Old Father Time.' He is Saturn in astrology, often depicted as an old man in a cloak carrying a lantern and a scythe because he is a god of the Harvest, of death, and of rebirth. This is 'ego time,' measured in seconds, as a series of events – yesterday, today, and tomorrow – sequential time.

Kairos is a youthful Greek god, 'god of the fortunate moment' – 'the right time' – like the right moment to let an arrow fly from a bow. Or the right moment for a first kiss. In consciousness, time is successive. In the unconscious (dreams, daydreams, and active imagination), all time can be one time; any time can be a fortunate moment. We are in such a time during a creative reverie, whether we're diving into the ocean of the unconscious or paddling in the mind's rock pools. Dreams express a transcendent function: 'beyond limits,' it does not just mean sacred.

In maths, transcendent functions include logarithms, exponentials, and trigonometry. In analytical psychology, it names a bridge between conscious and unconscious [10.4].

In analysis, a dream can be read several ways. You could start at the end and read it backwards, or begin at any point and go either forwards or backwards (reversing the dream 'time'). Try this with one of your own dreams and see what happens. This time-kaleidoscope produces variations on the dream's theme. It's liberating. It lets us stop trying to make 'clock time' sense from time-free symbols.

Ego tends to close things down, looking for 'the right answer' – sometimes, 'the perfect answer.' This is its job – selecting what matters to us in the here and now. But there can never be one answer about the meaning of any dream. Now let's look at who is the dreamer, who is the storyteller, and who is the audience.

## 2.7 DREAM EGO

For a dream to reach consciousness, part of consciousness must be watching it. American psychoanalyst James Grotstein, analysed by British analyst Wilfred Bion [6.5], explored this in his paper 'Who Is the Dreamer Who Dreams the Dream and Who Is the Dreamer Who Understands It?' (1979). He wonders who writes the script, designs the set, chooses the cast, acts, directs, and produces it. When we see ourselves in a dream, this is the 'dream ego.' So, who is the audience? Grotstein argues with Freud's idea that dreams function as guardians of sleep – wish fulfilments made to satisfy desires (including sexual desires). He suggests our sub-personalities form a scriptwriting team. They explore, explain, and expand our daily experience, connecting it to memories and possible futures – bridging time.

Dreams are problem-solving stories, projected like a movie by an infant-like part of the mind (the contained) onto a mother-like part (the container). The idea of container and contained comes from Bion. Dream content is edited by the container, written by the contained – as in the blue flower dream [2.3] – and draws on an infinite set of themes to produce a wholeness, a healing experience. Dream narratives put pieces back together, connecting them to the dreamer who understands the dream. They re-edit the past, bringing closure to painful experiences. Dreams synthesise rather than analyse.

## 2.8 PHILOSOPHICAL QUESTIONS

Philosophy is where theology and science overlap, according to English philosopher Bertrand Russell (1996, p. 1). It examines the validity of arguments on topics about which people have always argued – what is life for; is there a right way to live it; how do we know what something means? Such questions are common topics in dreams. Philosophers might ask, 'How do you know a dream image is real?' and 'What if you are only dreaming you are dreaming?' This becomes an infinite regress, shown in the film *Inception*, where Leonardo DiCaprio plays a dream hacker. He becomes trapped inside a dream, inside a dream, inside a dream (Nolan, 2010).

Here are some questions philosophers ask:

i. Are dreams hallucinations during sleep?
ii. How could you prove any psychoanalytic ideas about dreams? Would this proof be scientific, or felt, or both?
iii. What are we remembering when we 'remember' a dream?

Answers might be:

i. A hallucination is a conscious perception without an external stimulus; we see, hear, taste, smell, or touch something which is not there. Dreams are perceptions of the 'inner world,' sometimes caused by an external stimulus– like Salvador Dali's dream of a buzzing bee becoming a roaring tiger [8.3.1].
ii. Philosopher Karl Popper (2002) suggested falsifiability is necessary for scientific proof: being able to prove a thing is not so is more important than proving it is. It's called 'the null hypothesis.' Suppose you do an experiment to prove toast always lands butter side down. Two outcomes are possible: one supports your hypothesis, and the other doesn't. If both outcomes occur equally often, the null hypothesis holds, and your theory is wrong. The experiment is repeatable by any scientist interested in the aerodynamics of toast. But dreams are unique, individual communications whose meanings change over time. What hypothesis could test the idea that 'all dreams have no meaning?' Any 'proof' of theories about dream meaning will be felt rather than scientific.
iii. We remember symbols – projections from one part of the mind onto another – because of the feeling (or lack of it) attached to them.

And from philosophy come three simple ideas which help make meaning from dream symbols. The first is a *category error* (a dragon in a supermarket). The second is *ontology*. The third is *epistemology*. The words look far scarier than they are.

In Greek, 'ontos' means *being*, so ontology is *knowing about being*. 'Episteme' means *knowledge*, so epistemology is *knowing about knowing*. When exploring a dream, what is it like to be with it; what is it like to know it? What's it like to be a dragon in a supermarket? What's it like to know the dragon?

Category errors often point to what is significant in a dream. Oxford philosopher Gilbert Ryle (1900–1976) gives a classic example (1949/2000, pp. 17–18, and pp. 74–80). Tourists are being shown around Oxford; they see the colleges, the Radcliffe Camera, and the Bodleian Library. One asks, 'But where is the University?' They've mistaken a concept (university) for a thing (a building). Ontology helps us work out how we know what exists. In an ontological error, a particular object becomes a universal idea: 'my mother is a dragon' becomes 'all women are dragons.' Similarly, the concept 'my mother is a dragon' becomes a thing called 'mother dragon.' Ontology, in plain English, is, 'OK, what's in this picture?' (or 'What's wrong with this picture?') This question helps to reveal a hidden feeling.

Epistemology asks, 'How do we know what we know?' When we meet a dream symbol and then free associate, we're asking this. How do I know it's a dragon? What else does my unconscious know about them? Here's an example of these concepts in action:

### The (ex) PM at Glastonbury festival dream

*I am at Glastonbury festival with my friends, in a refreshment tent, having a beer and waiting for a band. The (ex) Prime Minister Boris Johnson appears, dishevelled, in mud-splattered evening dress, drunk, and shouting 'champagne, champagne! Party, party!' We say, 'But we don't have any champagne.' He staggers off, finds a bottle of port in an antique chest, and drinks it all – by himself.*

Here, the ex-prime minister is out of context (a category error), and so are the champagne, the antique chest, and the port. They are 'what's wrong with this picture.' The epistemological mistake is I know the ex-PM would never *be* there. The dream could be saying, 'Sharing is better than being selfish'; the feeling could be amusement or sadness at seeing his sad display of pathological entitlement. If everything in the dream is the dreamer, then it might be warning me not to behave as if I'm entitled. As the dream happened during the Pandemic, it could be a wish to be at Glastonbury again with my friends. It might be many things.

Q:  What else is out of place? If this were your dream, what could it mean?

Epistemology helps us separate true from false and asks whether a behaviour is justified and whether the beliefs behind the behaviours are consistent. Category errors conceal feelings. Curiosity about categories, about being, and about knowing helps work out what's hidden (or censored). Curiosity is the best tool for opening dreams. If their meaning and language are a can of worms, philosophy is a can opener.

## 2.9 DREAM GRAMMAR

Symbols are the vocabulary. The grammar is metaphors, puns, similes, word plays, and surreal images. Dream grammar is a paradox – the logical operator [1.6] is often {*both/and / neither/nor*}. A common part of dream grammar is a *rebus* when a picture stands for a word or idea:

### The KGB dream

*A good friend visited Russia in the 1970s. He dreamed a bee kept trying to enter through his bedroom window but cautiously stopped each time.*

On waking, he wondered what this meant. Then he realised, 'It's a cagey bee,' (cagey means cautious). The KGB were the Russian secret service. He'd feared he'd be arrested and accused of spying.

Dreams often use dreadful jokes. Here, the feeling is anxiety. The dreamer could be 'the bee' – as in 'bee careful!' The window could mean 'opening' – 'bee careful who you open up to'; an internal fear (paranoia) is projected onto the outside world, where *'they'* are out to get the dreamer. Or, if I'm scared and dream about sucking up chicken soup: 'chicken' could mean 'a coward' or 'being in the soup.' It could mean 'suck it up' or the opposite: 'Don't be a chicken!' Metaphors can't be reduced to a single meaning.

'*It is as if ...*' is an essential part of dream grammar, much like '*once upon a time ...*' is for a fairytale. The dream ego – the dreamer in their dream – is asked to suspend judgement and say '*as if*' to whatever happens and accept it as ordinary.

The 1950s film director Alfred Hitchcock liked to appear in a tiny cameo role in his thrillers. The dream director does the same. Noticing the extraordinary thing we've taken for granted in a dream is as though the dreamer has appeared, like Hitchcock. This helps work out who wrote the dream, from their language. In the KGB dream, the joke is a pun. My friend, an analyst, guessed the frightened child in him (the contained) projected the 'cagey bee' onto the parental part of him (the container), making a symbol he could translate into action – being cagey (careful) himself.

A 'dream is a bridge' is a metaphor. Dreams link symbols together *because* their meaning is indefinite – 'I know what it means,' and 'I don't know,' and 'I don't know if I know or not.' Knowing and not knowing, certainty and uncertainty, go around in a circle. Symbols link past, present, and future; possible and impossible; real and imaginary; concrete and abstract; particular and universal. When playing with a dream, analysing it, taking it to bits, it is useful to put it together again afterwards. You'll find this happening when you write or draw a dream. It's seldom exactly what you dreamed. See what new patterns and what creative solutions to problems appear as you improvise with your translation. Like playing jazz, any interpretation is worth trying – some will work better than others.

## KEY CONCEPTS

**Dreams:**

- Tell stories about things which matter to us
- Bridge between conscious and unconscious, ego and self
- Speak in symbols, not signs
- Range in scale from a postcard to a blockbuster movie
- Differ in intensity, from hardly remembered to unforgettable
- Dream time is 'timeless'
- Feeling is a guide to meaning
- Meaning depends on context

## FURTHER READING

To find more about dream language, the following are useful guides:
Robb, A. (2018) *Why we dream*, London: Picador.
Rycroft, C. (1996) *The Innocence of Dreams*, New York: Jason Aronson.
Stevens, A. (1995) *Private myths: dreams and dreaming*, London: Penguin.

## REFERENCES

Bergson, H. (1914/2023) *Dreams*, Uxbridge: Lushena Classics.
Callender, C., & Edney, R. (2001) *Introducing Time*, Cambridge: Icon books.
Gordon, R. (1977) 'The symbolic experience as bridge between the personal and the collective' *J. Analytical Psychology* 22(4), 331–342.
Gunter, P. (1982) 'Bergson and Jung', *Journal of the History of Ideas*, 43(4), 635–652, Pennsylvania, PA.: University of Pennsylvania Press. https://www.jstor.org/stable/2709347
Grotstein, J. (1979). 'Who is the dreamer that dreams the dream and who is the dreamer who understands it?' *Contemp. Psychoanal.*, 15, 110–169.
Jacobi, J. (1973) *The psychology of C. G. Jung*, London: Yale University Press.
Nolan, C. (2010) *Inception*, Los Angeles: Warner Brothers.
Popper, K. (2002) *Conjectures and refutations: the growth of scientific knowledge*, London: Routledge.
Ramis, H. (director) (1993) *Groundhog day*, Los Angeles: Columbia Pictures.
Redfearn, J. (1985) *My self, my many selves*, Library of Analytical psychology, vol. 6, London: Academic Press.
Rovelli, C. (2019) *The order of time*, London: Penguin.
Russell, B, (1996) *History of Western philosophy*, London: Routledge.
Ryle, G., (1949/2000) *The concept of mind*, London: Penguin.
Siegelman, E.Y. (1990) *Metaphor and meaning in psychotherapy*, London: Guilford press.
Stein, L. (1958) 'What is a symbol supposed to be?' *J. Analytical Psychology* 2(1), 73–84.
Vedfelt, O. (2017) *A guide to the world of dreams*, London: Routledge.
Weiner, Y. (1996) 'Chronos and Kairos: two dimensions of time in the psychotherapeutic process,' *Journal of the British Association of Psychotherapy* 30, 1, 65–85.

# EMPATHY – CULTURE, RELIGION, AND POLITICS

## 3.1 WHAT IS CULTURE?

Our culture is where we grow and live, held and contained by a network of relationships. Culture can be defined in many ways, depending on who is doing the defining and what they are doing it for (Maitra and Krause, 2015, pp. 83–101). It is not a neutral word. We usually mean, 'my culture' and define this by its differences to others, assuming 'ours is the best.'

In the unconscious, there are no 'high net worth' individuals or cultures. Any human being is neither better than me, worse than me, or the same as me. No one can be human alone, and each of us has equal value – one unit of 'human-beingness.' So, this chapter is about empathy (Greek *em* – at, towards, and *pathos* – feeling): sharing in the feelings of others accepting, no matter how different they are, that their rights and feelings are as valid as ours. Some religious and political traditions claim they believe this, but the reality they deliver is different, probably because they are organised by humans rather than angels. Humans naturally bicker and argue.

Dream symbols reshape the religious and political stories which may set unnatural boundaries to empathy by 'othering': *They* (whoever *They* are) are not like *Us* (whoever *We* are). Dreams are a safe place to learn empathy. This is a primary function of dreaming – as is evolving memory, discussed in the next chapter. We can't have one without the other because memory and feelings inter-depend. For example, we have 41 muscles in our faces. They continually express emotions. How we interpret a face depends on our culture. We unconsciously read the feeling state of those around us – face, voice

DOI: 10.4324/9781003319696-3

tone, and body language – and re-process this in sleep. Try noticing how often you see faces in dreams and their expressions. And how troubling it is when there is a person in a dream without a face.

Let's turn the usual questions about dreams upside down. What if what matters is not '*what does the dream mean for the dreamer?*' [Chapters 6 and 7], but '*how does a culture create and use dreams?*' [Chapter 9]. Suppose they are not just about 'Me!' they are about 'Us.' Religion and politics are social networks which tell stories and unfold dominant discourses – about power and what 'the right thing to do' is. Often, these discourses are consciously unquestioned, maybe because we usually don't question our own internal discourses. However, our unconscious always questions dominant discourses in dreams.

Q:  Find an example of one of your own dreams which questions 'social values.' What did it question? How?

Boundaries between politics and religion are fluid. In Ancient Egypt, the two were, sometimes, identical. Pharaoh was a living God – Ra on Earth, eternally reborn. In Medieval Europe, Kings claimed to rule by Divine Right – a few contemporary politicians share this delusion. And in some models of mind, self is seen as a 'living' inner God (a soul or spirit) which 'knows,' directs, and speaks to us through dreams.

Q:  Do you think this is true or false? Is this a belief or an experience? What consequences follow if it's true – and if it isn't?

Where a culture places the boundaries between inner and outer worlds has religious and political implications (Samuels, in Singer and Kimbles, 2004, pp. 124–144). In George Orwell's dystopian novel *1984* (Orwell, 2021), the hero Winston Smith is guilty of thought crime. He dared question 'Big Brother' – the 'Great Leader' who created the dominant discourse. Dreams are naturally subversive because they compensate for our conscious attitude – and the conscious attitudes of our society.

## 3.2 REALITIES CHANGE ACROSS TIME

Here is an example of a place and time where the boundaries between inner and outer, politics and religion were different: and dreams were accepted as a natural source of healing.

In Ancient Greece, Asclepius, son of Apollo, was the God of healing. He learnt the art from the Centaur, Chiron.

*The temple of Epidaurus, in a beautiful olive grove, has a hot spring, guest rooms, and a theatre. We spend our nights hoping for a dream to guide us back to health. Our dreams are acted out for us by the resident theatre company and interpreted by a Priest.*

Understanding a symbol needs a context. Epidaurus gave a context – a healing village. Contexts are personal, familial, and social, like this:

*culture shapes dreams > dreams shape dreamers >*
*dreamers shape culture > culture shapes dreams*

This feedback loop between inner and outer worlds probably always existed. Once, we were hunter-gatherers. We lived in small groups. Culture meant 'what our tribe does, knows, and believes.' It's a good guess we saw ourselves as coming from a spirit world and going back to it after death – to become ancestors. Maybe we came and went many times? Such ideas were common 5,000 years ago, perhaps much earlier. They are still central to lots of religions.

Many First Cultures share this worldview. 'First' is a truer description than 'primitive,' a colonialist term based on overvaluing material technology, as if wearing a certain style of clothes and owning guns measures cultural success. There is also spiritual technology. This includes engaging with the natural world – not *apart from*, but *as part of* – an act of imaginative, creative empathy. Dreams supply this every night, free, to everyone.

Once, there was no split between the spiritual and the material. Plants and animals had spirits, so did rivers, the land, the stars. They talked to us in dreams, visions, trances, rituals, sacred plants, and sacred spaces. Dreams were advice from the spirits. As Western materialist-based science evolved, it questioned the discourse of medieval Christianity and wondered if what went on in the mind was from 'the spirits' (angels or demons). The 'spirit world' subtly became 'the unconscious.' Both have dangers.

In 1936, Jung gave seminars on Bailey Island, Maine, USA. A participant asked, 'Dr. Jung, how should we approach the unconscious?' Laughing, he said, 'Look. If there were a cave of hungry bears on the island, how would I advise you to approach it? Just don't.' It is deeply unsettling to discover our sense of self, of who we are; it depends on a thing we can never know or control – our inner world. This is equally true if we believe in a spirit world – even the best shaman can't *know* it. However, we can know some aspects of the cultural setting of an inner world:

### The whale dream

*I'm deep in the ocean. There are whales, all around. We're singing.*
*I'm singing too, and I realise I'm a whale.*

Whales sing across oceans. Mother whales coo to their babies, adults court and exchange news. In analysis, we listen to songs from deep in the unconscious. I was born in Dundee, Scotland, formerly a world whaling centre. There's a whale skeleton in the city museum; this dream came as I began analysis. As my unconscious swam into analytic culture, it chose familiar images from my childhood culture.

Q: What would a dream symbol be like if it didn't come from your culture? Where else would it come from? How would it get there?

When I was 8, we moved to Northern Ireland. Going to play 'Cowboys and Indians' (as an Indian), I met Pat, a Belfast Cowboy. We became best friends. But, before we could begin, he asked if I was Protestant or Catholic. I'd no clue. I'd never heard either word before. For him, these words truly were matters of life and death. His country was in the grip of a culture war. To me, the two communities looked identical. Both felt threatened by change – and the lack of it. Change means loss of the familiar, the secure. It creates nostalgia. Idealising the past is a defence: like imagining a 'happy childhood' when there was none.

Cultures have fuzzy boundaries. Whale cultures have boundaries too. Perhaps they have politics and religions – they certainly have empathy. Cultures hold individuals, families, friends, social (and anti-social) networks. They have myths, legends, and histories; music, dance, art, and science; laws and customs; sports and games; religious and political systems. Dreams draw on their symbols, particularly around rites of passage (birth, initiation, courtship, marriage, parenting, age, and death).

Symbols explore the fractal boundaries between self and culture, and between 'our' culture and everyone else's. A fractal is a natural

---

**Box 3.1    The Collective Unconscious**

- Common to anyone, anywhere, at any time in history
- Contains archetypes
- Developmental archetypes unfold over a lifetime
  - (birth, infancy, childhood, adolescence, parent, elder, death)
- Relational archetypes make bridges to others
  - (shadow, hero, trickster, animus, and anima)

---

pattern with self-similarity at any scale – like ferns, trees, lungs, coastlines, the edges of clouds, or galaxies (Lesmoir-Gordon, Rood, and Edney, 2000, pp. 8–47). Cultural fractals are easy to see in a city where many cultures overlap. There are 'day' cultures and 'night' ones. The city children live in is not the same as the one we live in as adults. Each collective (child and adult) has its own collective unconscious: a concept Jung introduced in 1916 [Box 3.1].

Jung suggests it underpins all cultures at any time – a universal form. He took the idea of forms from the Greek philosopher Plato's notion of eternal models (1987, pp. 59–60) called archetypes (Greek for 'old forms'). These exist independently of the material world, in a world of spirit or 'pure essence.' To be used, an archetype has to be downloaded and installed – like a zip file. How it does this depends on the culture. But, like describing the ocean to a whale, how can you observe the collective unconscious if you are always inside it? We don't know how dreams emerge, but we can study how they arise from a culture rather than simply from a dreamer's mind. You may say, 'I thought dreams arose in the mind?' Well.

Q: Where are the boundaries of your mind? What are they made of? How do you know? If you buy something after seeing an ad or an online 'influencer,' is it *your* idea?

The nineteenth-century Irish writer Oscar Wilde said, '*Most people are other people. Their thoughts are someone else's opinions, their lives a mimicry, their passions a quotation.*' Here, Wilde names a boundary problem. Minds are not just an event in our brains. They are part of our bodies too. Minds depend on the space/time around them and are like waves – fluent forms – individual parts constantly change, but the shape remains similar, like a waterfall or a candle flame. Every dreamer is different, yet the patterns in dreams are similar. This allows 'structural analysis' (finding common patterns). As we're immersed in a culture before we're born and (often) strongly committed to it, can we stand back and see it rather than see what we project?

Q:  Could dreams do that? Could anyone?

## 3.3 ANTHROPOLOGICAL VIEWS

Anthropologists are professionally curious about how humans relate. They know they can't stand outside their own culture. At best, they are participant-observers, as we are in our dreams [2.7]. Similarly, no therapist can stand outside their emotions or culture (Maitra and Krause, 2015, pp. 32–47). Our feeling responses to dream symbols give clues about the meaning: what attracts us, what upsets us, what do we reject or find rejecting?

For example, American anthropologist Joe Calabrese learns and studies with the Navajo people in Arizona. Formerly a psychiatrist working with addiction, he grew curious about how young Navajo addicts were helped by the Native American church and its peyote ritual. He felt troubled when a research assistant tried the hallucinogenic cactus, and Joe dreamed:

### The drug dealer dream

*I'm in a smart bar with my assistant when Shaft appears (the black private detective from the '70s film about a drug gang-busting private detective).*

Joe realised he felt like a drug dealer. Reflecting, he saw he had a white person's mistrust of religious rituals involving drugs. Unconscious prejudices had influenced his observations (Calabrese, 2013, pp. 195–202). He uses dreams – his own, those of colleagues, and the people he studies – to gain insights. Dreams are part of anthropological practice: inner worlds are a research tool.

Anthropologists understand culture as a lived and felt experience: overlapping sets of concepts and values, languages and symbols, beliefs and ideas, fantasies and realities. To survive, a culture has to adapt. As we live in time, change is inevitable. But what if the rate or direction of change becomes stressful – when facing climate change or in war? Then we use the three primitive defences of the self: splitting (it's their problem), denial (what problem?), and projective identification (my mind unconsciously shoves the problem into your mind, then it's your problem!) Empathy fails. Culture wars become real wars. When they do, everyone's dreams flood with war images.

I supervise analytic colleagues in Ukraine and Russia. Before February 2022, few patients from either country brought dreams of guns and bombs. Now, everyone does. Colleagues in the Holy Land are having the same experience. War, a severe cultural dysfunction, imposes on the dream world.

What happens when we are pushed back by our culture? If you're LBGTQ+, or from a minority group, or have a disability – do you try to fit in, stay true to who you are, try doing both, or deny the problem? How do we negotiate this outer boundary? Dreams help. They suggest negotiations at outer boundaries and continual negotiations at inner boundaries between different aspects of our personalities. Let's call them 'sub-personalities.'

We all have an internal politics. Some sub-personalities seek social acceptance; others don't. Some sub-personalities imagine they are kings or queens with Divine Rights; others imagine they're eternal victims. Dreams can be like a parliament where our sub-personalities bicker and argue. And seldom reach consensus, as in the outer world.

### 3.3.1 Senoi dreaming

American anthropologist William Domhoff (1936–), professor of psychology and sociology at the University of California, is an expert on dreaming (Domhoff, 2022). In the '80s, he studied a First People in the remote Malaysian mountains – the Senoi. They seldom meet outsiders but meet 'insiders' every night. In the morning, they share their dreams. They may find solutions to individual problems – 'X could make up with Y' – or group activities – 'It's a good day to hunt.' Dreams give practical guidance direct from the spirit world (Domhoff, 1985, pp. 13–34). This is common among First Cultures.

In the '60s, drawing on fieldwork done in the '30s by anthropologist Kilton Stewart (1902–1965) (Domhoff, ibid., pp. 35–64), the Esalen Institute in California promoted Senoi group dream sharing as a way to encourage lucid dreaming. This was supposed to bring about life-enhancing well-being and personal growth. 'Senoi Dream Work' became a popular brand amongst the Human Potential movement. Domhoff revisited Stewart's original research and contested many of Esalen's claims. There were 'fair and frank' exchanges of views, which continue.

Q:  What is your view? Is this a cultural appropriation (stealing from someone else's culture) or a 'rehoming' of a spiritual technology?

In certain circumstances (controlling persistent nightmares), lucid dreaming is helpful [8.6]. But for me, the joy of dreaming is we don't have to have 'control.' Western cultures overvalue control – along with hard work, conspicuous achievement, power, and status – yet at the same time assume each individual has 'free choice.' We're responsible. We feel guilty if we make the wrong choices. Cultures like the Senoi are collective-based, as Westerners often imagine Eastern cultures to be. This may or may not be true. It could be projection – as we project 'Ancient Wisdom' onto 'the Noble Savage' (a colonialist fantasy) and 'Mystic Spirituality' onto Easterners (a West-is-best fantasy).

Q:  What do Easterners project onto Westerners?

You can find some answers in the Kyoto philosopher Keiji Nishitani's book *Religion and Nothingness* (1982, pp. 46–76) and experiential answers in Jan Willem van de Wetering's description of trying to be a young Zen monk (1973, pp. 110–118) or the probably mistaken idea that Japanese culture is 'shame based' and Western culture is guilt based (Lebra, 2010, pp. 102–110).

### *3.3.2 Japanese dreaming*

Westerners imagine individual choice counts less for Easterners. If they don't 'get it right,' they feel shame (Lebra, pp. 102–112 in Le Vine, 2010). This is a projection, an example of 'othering.' The Japanese Jungian analyst Hayao Kawai wrote about Japanese dreams (1995, pp. 19–27, 107–110), using the idea of 'polyphony' of meanings. In Japan, there are choices of religious images, drawing on Buddhist and Shinto traditions. It's common to follow both – Shinto for weddings and births, and Zen for funerals. The spirit world is close, as shown in films by the Japanese Studio Ghibli like *Princess Mononoke* (1997) and *Spirited Away* (2001). The heroes go into the spirit worlds; the spirits come into ours.

The same theme underpins the ancient art of Noh theatre. A bridge leads to the stage. There's a curtain at one end of the bridge, behind which is the spirit world. The troubled hero is on stage. A spirit (an angel) comes to give guidance. The plays were traditionally performed at sacred shrines and enacted sacred myths and dreams with burlesque breaks (Keene, 1966, pp. 28–45).

Researchers in Germany and Japan compared dreams from analytic patients in both countries using structural analysis (Roesler et al., 2021). They found statistically significant differences. German dreams tend to be about individuality, autonomy, and ego identity; in Japan, about social exchange, harmony, and cooperation. This reflects cultural values. However, they recognise an investigator effect is a problem. Did they find this because it is what cultural stereotypes predict, or is it 'real?' It's the whale and the ocean problem again: you can't objectively see something you are inside.

## 3.4 RELIGIOUS DREAMS

Not being objective from the inside is especially true for religious experience. It's a boundary problem – where does a religion end or begin? Who gives out the labels? What seems perfectly reasonable in one tradition may seem crazy in another (like worrying whether bread and wine really turn into the body and blood of Christ in the Mass, or who is the true successor of Mohammed, or how 'Orthodox' is 'Orthodox enough' in Judaism). Religious differences create huge conflicts – (wars) – internally and externally. Empathy is forgotten: 'Yes! We love your immortal soul so much we'll burn you alive.'

Every religion has stories about revelations, dreams, and visions brought by angels (Ancient Greek for messenger) or spirits. The Angel Gabriel spoke to Mohammed and visited Mary, the mother of Jesus. An angel spoke to Moses from a burning bush. Angels taught Joseph Smith (founder of the Mormons). Buddha's mother dreamed a white elephant entered her side and she became pregnant. Hinduism has many similar stories. The Mahabharata (Vyasa, ed. Smith, 2009) is full of them. Angels inspired Christian saints like Teresa of Avila. Angels are 'other.' The intensity of the experience of meeting one is a unifying thread. The form of the spirits may vary, but the life-changing effect is the same.

Q: Are angels and spirits real, dreams, visions, or imagination? None of these, or all of these? How would you know?

This dream/reality boundary problem is one where people have the strongest feelings. For some, religious beliefs are foundational to their identity. Others don't care. Arguments about beliefs quickly become arguments about who has the dominant discourse – the power to name. Changing a dominant discourse is the theme in the 4,000-year-old *Epic of Gilgamesh* [3.4.1]. And a contemporary Western myth about 'culture wars' is actually about who has naming power – meaning political power. One side – those afraid of change – use the three primitive defences of the self. You can work out how they do this.

We have the same problem in our minds. We may conservatively resist inner change and only be able to name a dream symbol in one particular way: a monster *can only be* a monster, never a helper; an angel *can only be* an angel, never a demon. To let a symbol have more than one meaning, maybe opposite meanings at the same time, means being able to tolerate uncertainty and empathise with two opposing views. Belief systems often deny change to avoid uncertainty. Long term, this never works because everything naturally changes. No one argues about Ra and Osiris anymore. People and their beliefs are complex emergent systems. Dreams are essential for empathic change management.

### 3.4.1 Complex emergent systems

---

**Box 3.2    Complex emergent systems**

- Self-organise
- Show collective behaviours
- Network
- Evolve and adapt
- Make patterns
- Are similar but never identical
- Are non-linear: a change in output does not depend on a change in input

---

Dreams are complex emergent systems. In climate change, tiny shifts in global temperature have huge effects. In maths, this is called 'the butterfly effect' – a butterfly flapping its wings in a rainforest creates a hurricane elsewhere. Dream symbols do the same in our mind/psyche (*psyche* is Greek for butterfly). As they emerge, they create ripples. Symbols are also complex emergent systems. Other examples are hydrogen clouds which become stars, and tree seeds which become forests. Pre-thoughts become patterns, become dreams, become actions. Mind is a set of complex emergent neural networks.

Cultures filter meanings, encourage some and discourage others. They may promote 'a dream' – like the American dream: 'the right to life, liberty and the pursuit of happiness.' But this is not a dream. It's a wish. Dreams may find symbols no one dreamed of before, borrow from other cultures, or make new symbols – drawing on the collective unconscious, which can rearrange fixed cultural ideas into anything. Dreams cannot be censored by the dreamer's culture.

## 3.5 POLITICAL AND RELIGIOUS DREAMS FREELY ASSOCIATE

It's hard to tell where religion ends and politics begins. The word 'religion' comes from the Latin, meaning 'to bind back' (*re* – about, concerning: and *ligare*' to bind,' as in 'ligature'). We may feel ties to a religion or tied up by it, as it is a primary identity definer:

'Yes, I am a (*insert name of preferred religion and / or political party here*).' These marks of belonging can be inclusive, tolerant, and empathic or defined by greed, hatred, and delusion. They are seldom emotionally neutral. Religion and politics are forms of belief requiring faith, but as the nineteenth-century American author Mark Twain said, 'Faith is believing in what you know ain't so.' Dreams routinely question beliefs. Jung had an unforgettable dream of God dropping a turd on the roof of Basel cathedral – the dream helped him question his family's religious values.

The word politics comes from the Greek 'polis,' meaning 'the city' (rather than politics). As analytical psychologist Andrew Samuels says, 'We have a political psyche' (1993, p. 56). We can't not. Even if we claim not to be interested in politics (the people), they are interested in us. We mythologise this. Did democracy begin in ancient Athens where the people were allowed to vote? No. Only rich male property owners could vote. Women couldn't. Slaves, a third of the population, couldn't. Did communism suddenly appear to Karl Marx in the reading room of the British Museum? No. His ideas would be long forgotten if he hadn't given words to the dreams (wishes) of poor, oppressed people around the world.

Q: How do you arrange the politics of your inner world? How do you govern yourself? How do dreams help you answer this question?

Around 400 BC, In *The Republic*, Plato named four types of government, all imperfect (1987, pp. 356–420). They are timarchy (Ancient Sparta: rule by a small, rich, militaristic elite, now called fascism), oligarchy (rule by the superrich), democracy (rule by the people), and tyranny (rule by the 'Great Leader'). All exist 'out there' because they all exist 'in here' – in our minds. When we're scared, we want 'Big Daddy' (the 'Great Leader') to get rid of the monsters. This never works, as they quickly turn into monsters themselves, like the emperor in *Star Wars*.

Cultures are a collective. We have choices about what kind of collective we live in, how it cares for the young, the ill, the old, and whether it can reality test. Or where it puts the boundaries. Or what to do if we don't agree. Some cultures do not give their members these privileges. However, the things we eat and use are there because someone else made them. There is a strong survival incentive to engage with politics and with other people.

This is even truer in our inner world. Each sub-personality has conflicting needs, views, and opinions. Inside every hippie lurks an inner fascist (and vice versa). We all have a Shadow: someone we would least wish to be. Shadow does not go away. It can sometimes change but is not necessarily 'healed' or 'transformed by being brought into the light.' It is not there because something is broken. Dreams compensate for the conscious attitude to maintain emotional balance. Shadow may be our inner 'Darth Vader' – a 'Great Leader' who takes over our inner world. Or 'Leader of the Rebel Alliance.' A bully or an angel?

Q: Is your Shadow a perfectionist? An inner critic? A saint? How do they appear in your dreams?

### 3.5.1 The Epic of Gilgamesh

Here's a story about a 'Great Leader,' possessed by his Shadow. It's the oldest-known written (fictional) dream – central to the *Epic of Gilgamesh*, a Sumerian story at least four thousand years old. Gilgamesh, the lustful young king of Uruk, is an anti-hero. He's meant to shepherd his people, but he preys on them like a wolf. The people beg the Gods for help. Ani, the Father God, asks Anu, the Mother God, to create a man to stop him. She makes Enkidu – an innocent shepherd lad living wild, befriended by animals. The Gods send Gilgamesh a dream. He asks his mother, the Goddess Ninsun, to interpret:

### Gilgamesh's dream

*I saw a bright star, it shot across the morning sky, it fell at my feet and lay before me like a huge boulder. I tried to lift it, but it was too heavy. I tried to move it, but it would not budge. A crowd of people gathered round me, the people of Uruk pressed in to see it, like a little baby. They kissed its feet. This boulder, this star that had fallen to Earth, I took it in my arms, I embraced and caressed it the way a man caresses his wife. Then I took it and laid it before you. You told me that it was my double, my second self.*

(Mitchell, 2004, pp. 72–75, 81–84)

This fallen star becomes Enkidu. The lads fight, then become lovers. Their first mission is to kill Humbaba, the monster defending the Land of Cedars (Lebanon), which Gilgamesh wants for his city. But this leads to Enkidu's death. Gilgamesh goes on a quest to find his beloved in the underworld. In the end, grief tames him. He becomes a better king.

Lust, pride, and arrogance were a common problem among political leaders 4,000 years ago – as they are today. This story is a collective response. In Sumerian culture, a king is meant to shepherd his people. Here, a young shepherd tames a wolf-like king. The storyteller shows us the meaning of his story *in the dream* – a plot device still used today. Dreams often have a similar 'key' – an 'aha moment.' In 'the dragon in the supermarket dream [2.3], it was that the dragon was not a surprise.

### 3.5.2 Joseph and Pharaoh

This is a typical 'Myth of Origin.' They are a discourse used to explain a tribe's beginning, like 'Freud "discovered" the unconscious.' But Shamans knew about the unconscious forever. Or Pharaoh saying, 'Egypt is mine because I am a God!' He replaced experience with a wish (a 'dream'). In this myth, Joseph, the 12th, youngest, and best-loved son of Jacob, is a dreamer (Genesis, Chapter 41) with an amazing technicolour dream coat. His brothers are envious. He dreams:

### Joseph's dream

*Eleven sheaves of corn the brothers harvested bow to the sheaf he harvested. In another, the sun, the moon and eleven stars bow to him.*

Angry, his brothers sell him in Egypt. Joseph is a slave to Potiphar, captain of Pharaoh's guard. His wife tries to seduce Joseph. He refuses, so she accuses him of rape. Joseph ends up in jail, where he interprets the dreams of his cellmates. Word reaches Pharaoh, who'd dreamed:

### Pharaoh's dream

*Seven fat cows are followed by seven starving ones.*

Joseph says seven years of plenty will be followed by seven years of famine. Pharaoh builds grain stores (Pharaohs always built grain stores – and kept them full, as the Nile floods were not predictable). Egypt survives. Joseph's brothers bow to him. He's a friend of 'the Great Leader.' Pharaoh gifts the family Goshen, a fertile corner of the Nile delta. A political purpose of the story may have been solving conflicts between the rulers and their subjects. It is interpreted in different ways by Jewish, Christian, and Muslim groups. What it means depends on who is viewing it, what for, and to whom they are re-telling it.

Q:  What interpretation would you create? How are they influenced by your culture?

A perennial problem with dreams and visions is only seeing the meanings we wish for – feel entitled to, or our cultural beliefs say it ought to have, like a politician 'giving you the facts' (which support their view) rather than all the facts. Suppose, like Hannibal, you have a problem and fall asleep, hoping to find a solution [1.3]. This happens in Iceland, [9.2]. For the Senoi [3.3.1], it's the default setting. These cultures encourage dreams to develop community empathy and contain social, political, and religious differences.

## 3.6 DREAMS AND 'RACE'

Dreams mark boundaries and appear when boundaries are approached, crossed, or challenged. 'Exam anxiety dreams' are about failing a rite of passage. 'Going naked in public' dreams are about social anxiety. If you're a naturist, this may not be a problem, or if your culture lacks a concept of clothes. Any culture has stereotypes about itself; these, too, are boundary markers. Some are self-mockery; others are marketing – like 'the shortbreadification' of Scotland. Edinburgh, our capital, is festooned with biscuit tins swathed in fake tartan.

What happens when two cultures clash? Black people in the West face discrimination and repression and are victims of assault and murder by forces of law and order – the police, the criminal justice system, the prisons. Does this affect their dreams? Yes. New York Jungian analyst Fanny Brewster in *Race and the Unconscious* (2023, see pp. 130–165) explored African dreams in West Africa, then looked in detail at the dreams of three black women in therapy with her, using structural analysis. She gives detailed personal backgrounds and explores their family and relational settings. Symbols relating to relationships (empathy) formed the largest set of dream images. All the women used their dreams to help with daily life decisions. All had dreams relating to their African ancestry – particularly their matrilineal traditions.

However, she notes the archetypal symbols they brought could be found in women from any culture. There were no dreams about slavery but many about fear of the police. All had experienced racism, though it was not a specific dream theme. 'Race' itself is a Western colonialist fantasy because there are no significant genetic differences between human groups. Like cats, we have different coat colours, that's all. To enslave, American colonialists needed to 'other' their victims. This was not done in Ancient Greece or Rome, nor in Africa. A West African patient told me their family still own slaves. When offered freedom, they were upset: 'But then we'd have to ask the State for the schools and hospitals your family provide. Our "Great Leaders" are so corrupt! You've owned us and cared for us for many generations.'

Here's a clinical example of racism: Jay, a young, mixed-race artist, was in analysis with me twice a week for six years. Early in our work, he brought:

### The white zombie dream

*I'm chased by a crowd of white zombies into a house made of glass. I feel sure they can't get in, but they do. They eat me alive.*

He linked this to racist bullying as a child: being 'too black' for the white kids but 'not black enough' for the black ones. He's careful around white people (including me). He felt the art world has a 'glass ceiling' – a level black people can't get above. We wondered if, for him, the archetype of the Shadow was white – as, for some white people, it's black. His dream contains images of exclusion, being put in a glass box. This reminded me of 'the Glass Illusion' – a psychiatric condition seen in the seventeenth century. Sufferers believed they were made of glass and would break if you touched them. It's a form of paranoia; the word means 'to be beside one's self' (in Greek, *para* – beside, *noios* – self). But, as the joke says, 'I'm not paranoid. They're really out to get me!' For Jay, it felt as though everyone was. The dream led to discussing how to manage 'the glass ceiling' – including having the courage to point it out.

Q: How does your culture shape your dream landscape?

When change threatens our comfort zone, a normal response is to use the primitive defences of the Self – denial, splitting, and projective identification. Socially conservative people don't join liberal online chat groups (or vice versa). We use 'othering,' so *they* carry our Shadow. Then we find ways to get *them* to behave badly (like bullying). Refusal of dialogue defines fundamentalism (whether religious or political), premature mind closure, and denial of empathy. When this happens in our inner world, it's called a complex. If we close our minds to new possibilities, we can't adapt. Dreams challenge this.

As the '60s rock musician Frank Zappa (1940–1993) said, 'A mind is like a parachute. It only works when it's open.' Dreams are an open system in the inner world, where internal religious and political negotiations take place. In the next chapter, I look at how dreams evolve memory, which depends on empathy because memory is feeling-led.

## KEY QUESTIONS

- What are the boundaries of your culture? Who says?
- How do your dreams have social and political consequences?
- Do cultures have dreams? Or do dreams have cultures?

## KEY CONCEPTS

- Dreams are complex emergent systems.
- Dreaming aids adaptation to change, rehearsing new ideas and behaviours in a safe place (sleep).
- Dream symbols arise from a cultural context.
- Dreams give a culture new symbols and find new meanings in old ones.

## FURTHER READING

Domhoff, G.W. (1985) *The mystique of dreams: a search for utopia through Senoi dream theory*, Berkeley: University of California Press.

Domhoff, G.W. (2022) *The Neurocognitive Theory of Dreaming: The Where, How, When, What, and Why of Dreams.* Cambridge, MA: MIT Press.

Le Vine, R. A. (2010) *Psychological Anthropology*, London: Wiley-Blackwell.

Mageo, J., Sheriff, R. E. (2021) *New directions in the anthropology of dreaming*, London: Routledge.

## REFERENCES

Brewster, F. (2023) *Race and the unconscious: an Africanist perspective on analytical psychology and dreaming*, London: Routledge.

Calabrese, J. D. (2013) *A different medicine: Postcolonial healing in the Native American church*, Oxford: Oxford University Press, Ritual Studies Series. No. 2.

Kawai, H. (1995) *Dreams, myths, and fairytales in Japan*, Einsiedeln, Switzerland: Daimon Verlag.

Keene, D. (1966) *Noh: the classical theatre of Japan*, Tokyo: Kodansha International.

Lesmoir-Gordon, N., Rood, W., Edney, R. (2000) *Fractal geometry*, Cambridge: Icon books.

Lebra, T. (2010) *Shame and guilt in Japan* in LeVine, R., *Psychological anthropology*, Oxford: Wiley – Blackwell.

Maitra, B., & Krause, I-B. (2015) *Culture and madness*, London: Jessica Kingsley.

Mitchell, S. (2004) *Gilgamesh*, London: Profile Books.

Miyazaki, H. (dir.) (1997) *'Princess Mononoke'* Tokyo: Studio Ghibli.

Miyazaki, H., (2001) *Spirited away*, Tokyo: Studio Ghibli.

Nishitani, K, (1982) *Religion and Nothingness*, Berkeley, CA: University of California Press.

Orwell, G., (2021) 1984, London: Penguin Classics.

Plato, (trans. Lee, D.) (1987) *The Republic*, London: Penguin.

Roesler, C., Konakawa, H, Tanaka, Y. (2021) 'Differences in dream content and structure between Japanese and Western dreams', *International Journal of Dream Research* 14, No. 2 195–202.

Samuels, A. (1993) *What does it mean to be in the West?* Chapter 9. London: Routledge.

Singer, T., and Kimbles, S.L. (2004) *The cultural complex, contemporary Jungian perspectives on psyche and culture.* London: Routledge.

Van De Wetering, J. (1973) *The empty mirror: experiences in a Japanese Zen Monastery,* London: Routledge and Kegan Paul.

Vyasa (trans: Smith, J. D.). (2009) *The Mahabharata* (abridged) London: Penguin Classics.

4

# DREAMS, REFLECTIONS, MEMORIES

## 4.1 INTRODUCTION

Lets consider what memory is – and isn't – and the role of sleep and dreaming in evolving memory. The previous chapter explored empathy, which links us to our community. Memory also does this, and this moves the viewpoint from 'dreams are about me' to 'dreams have a social function.' If we can't remember who we are, where we are, or who others are, we become anxious and isolated, as when a child has to move home or when we're old and gradually lose our mind and self-understanding [4.9.2].

Memory is feeling-based rather than thought-based. Memory problems are not about storage; they are about retrieval. This is still true in the earliest stages of dementia. Emotional 'flags' attached to an experience enable us to recall and re-imagine. We don't store memories – there is nothing at all like a library in the brain. We 'store' patterns as complex neural pathways.

I will introduce you to the neural networks which imaginatively re-construct memory and help turn memory into 'mind.' The salience network decides what to attend to and what to ignore; the executive network decides whether or not to recreate a memory; the default mode network is responsible for empathy and dreaming, which sculpts memories. I discuss them in detail in Chapter 5.

These networks are not 'the mind'; they are where thoughts and feelings are put together. Twentieth-century neuroscience was rather like 'old-school' geography. We'd learn 'copper is the chief export of Zambia,' as if that were all there was to know about Zambia. It's a simplification, like the three-level model of the brain, introduced

DOI: 10.4324/9781003319696-4

by neuroscientist Paul McLennan in the 1960s [see 'neuroscience' in the glossary].

He divided the brain into the reptilian (the hindbrain, responsible for body maintenance), the old mammalian brain (the limbic system, responsible for emotion), and the new mammalian brain (the cortex, responsible for thinking). There are multiple overlaps and multiple feedback loops between them. 'Bits of the brain' do not 'do things.' No part ever acts in isolation. We need all of the brain, all of the time, to make a mind. Memory is not just recall of the past – it predicts possible futures. Dreams help us guess what is next up by retelling old stories in new ways, which I explain later [4.10].

Jung retold his story in his autobiography *Memories, Dreams, Reflections* (1986). Dreams mattered to him, especially those from early childhood. These dreams became memories on which he reflected all his life. Dreams, reflections, and memories co-create each other. A reflection means both seeing in a mirror and reconsidering events. I will look at pattern recognition before explaining how memory works and how we continually rebuild the networks involved. We consolidate memory in sleep and dreams; without them, we wouldn't have one.

A basic function of the mind deeply embedded in our unconscious is the need to meet survival demands – for oxygen, water, fuel, safety, and company (Barrett, 2021, pp. 4–12). The first is easy – we can't help breathing – the rest need plans and actions. Our survival economy, like any other, depends on the two laws of economics: supply and demand and diminishing returns. 'How much energy will it take?' The more energy a survival strategy takes (like going hunting when prey is scarce), the less worthwhile it is. Our minds balance cost against predicted benefit by processing information and comparing it across time.

Much research into memory was done by cognitive psychologists. To me, though I love this subject, it's like taking a piano apart to find where the tune is. A tune is a pattern. So is a memory. Dreams weave patterns, making new memories, sometimes of things which haven't yet happened – memories of the future. Jung called this 'the prospective function.' Dream researchers Zadra and Stickgold call this NEXTUP: the sleep-dependent memory evolution function.

## 4.2 REFLECTION AND MIRRORING

Memory begins with reflection on both internal and external perceptions, reconsidering events. Reflection could mean a face in a mirror, the moon on a lake, or the name of an early infant experience. When a baby sees Mum, they smile, and she smiles. They frown, and she frowns. We all do this tens of thousands of times. A 'good enough' Mum reflects her baby's emotions, mirrors them, and names them. This grows awareness of 'me' and 'my feelings' in the baby. The couple digests these together: a baby can *have* a feeling rather than be *had by* them, which creates stress. As babies gradually discover other people have feelings too, they develop empathy. This mirroring process grows many neural networks.

The default mode network helps enable empathy [5.5.4] (see Anon., *Psychology Today*, 2023). Newborns do not have one, but 8-year-olds do. It's not fully formed till our late teens or early 20s – and upgrades constantly, as long as our minds are open to change. As we age, our minds tend to close – we prefer safety and sameness to experimenting. In the nursery story, the young explorer 'Goldilocks' complains the three bear's things are too much or too little. She wants them 'just right.' Nothing is ever 'just right.' 'Good enough' parents don't love us too little or too much. 'Just right' means there are failures of mirroring. Our feelings are not reflected accurately. We get upset. We might never forget this. We might dream about it for the rest of our lives. This is quite normal.

Upset infants can feel, to their parents, like an Evil Doctor trying to take over the world. But parental failures are inevitable and essential. Without them, we could imagine 'Mum is under my control! When I smile, she smiles' – an infant's omnipotence fantasy – and 'everything in the world happens because of me!' This is called primary narcissism. Fortunately, most people grow out of it. Narcissism is named after the mythical young Greek lad who fell in love with his own reflection. The narcissist's world is 'me, me, me!' There is an almost complete failure of empathy. Others are forgotten before they are even noticed. Narcissists lack a sense of belonging and may be unable to tell the difference between truth and fantasy. Dreams grow our sense of emotional belonging to our family and society by reflection.

So ... when you finish reading this sentence, stop. ...

Q: Why am I being asked to stop?

## 4.3 PATTERN RECOGNITION

… because when we read, we stop to reflect all the time, for fractions of a second. This is why I'm asking you to stop, to remind you that reading is a most complex pattern recognition task. When learning to read, we slow right down, maybe trace the shape with a finger, and say the sound aloud. Pattern recognition also happens continuously in our emotional lives. We may ask, 'Why do I always make a mess of relationships?' We're wondering about patterns: what are they? Can we change them and, if so, into what? Can we step back and notice them? Well, yes. That's what we do when we dream.

If I reflect on learning the alphabet from building bricks at age 2, I always see coloured bricks with letters. The feeling is joy at recognising how shape and sound went together. And my Mum's joy I could read. If you had a highly anxious Mum who lost it with you whenever you tried to read, then the feelings associated with reading will be fearful. So, memory depends on feelings rather than 'facts.' This has survival advantages.

As hunter-gatherers, like any predator, we patrolled a territory, checking out where prey might be. The landscape always subtly changed, so we'd reflect. If there was a lion on the usual path, we'd feel fear and learn to go another way. We'd remember the fear and maybe give that path up in the future. Memories are 'the usual paths' shaped by family and culture [Chapter 3]. It comes as no surprise that we often dream about friends and family. We try out different versions of the family stories: a bullying mother might be symbolised as a dragon [2.3]. Fear and anxiety create highly emotional memories, which form the core of any complex – a repeating dysfunctional pattern.

For example, a big childhood loss may later become a fear of abandonment by anyone we are close to. This then becomes a self-fulfilling prophecy – I failed before, so I will fail again. Memory loops like these drive post-traumatic stress disorder (PTSD) – endlessly trapped in a frozen moment.

A young man spent his late teens in active front-line combat. Most of his comrades were killed. One day, walking down a London street, he heard a loud bang. Immediately, he threw himself to the ground and reached for his rifle. He didn't have a rifle; a car had backfired. This distressing incident brought him to analysis.

We can also imagine patterns where none exist. This is called 'apophenia' (from Greek – 'to appear'). Everything *seems* meaningfully connected. This can occur in pathological disturbances of the mind like delirium, early schizophrenia, acute psychotic states, or the clouding of consciousness in cannabis intoxication. Cannabis reduces perceptual skills. We are far less aware of what's going on, but we imagine the opposite to compensate. This is called 'effort after meaning' – like this:

I admitted a young patient on Christmas day. Ben was brought in naked by the police. He *knew* he was Jesus, 'the Voices' told him. He stopped, staring at dropped chewing gum, and gave me a huge smile. 'Look!' he said. 'The chewing gum makes the letter B. B is for Ben. I'm safe!'

Intoxicated by risk, gamblers imagine seeing patterns in the cards when none exist. They are 'reconstructively imagining.' Beliefs encourage us to see what we wish to see rather than what's there. Religious people may see the face of the Blessed Virgin Mary (or deity of choice) on a piece of toast or in the clouds. This is how prejudice works: once *they* (whoever *they* are) have been othered, then *their* behaviour (whatever it is) can only be read as negative [3.6]. We make up memories to fit our opinions [4.8].

## 4.4 WHAT IS A MEMORY?

Re-constructing the past lets us predict the future. Dreams 're-organise' the past so we can do this. They can re-organise bad memories too – PTSD begins to be resolved once the traumatic event can be dreamed about.

A hospitalised person with severe depression couldn't remember any dreams. Using active imagination, they gradually began to and told me a dream of watching a crab on a beach walk into the sea. They began to cry. I asked why. 'My father died of cancer a few months before I got so ill,' they said. They'd not told anyone this before. This dream was an essential part of their recovery, as was re-imagining their father.

There are several models which explain how memory works. You may have read about the 'classic' information processing model, dating from the 1950s. Memories can be explicit and implicit – also called declarative and non-declarative. Explicit memory is when we start to learn words in a new language, a 'fact memory.' This needs conscious effort. Riding a bicycle needs effort and produces big emotions – joy and frustration. After lots of practice, we no longer think about it. If you go ride a bike, at first you struggle – after a few years, it's not a problem, you 'just know.' What was explicit has gradually become implicit and unconscious.

The memory model from the '70s, was, roughly, like this. First comes a sense experience, a perception. This stays in a 'flash memory' for a few seconds and then transfers to short-term memory for a few minutes. If selected for survival, it moves into long-term memory. Psychologists once imagined we soaked up any incoming information and they imagined separate parts of the brain processed it. The auditory cortex heard, the visual cortex saw, and the olfactory cortex smelt.

The pathway is actually like this – sense organ (ear, eye) = > cortical area => thalamus => hippocampus, as each perceptual system uses multisensory integration. Every sense is involved in any perception. You can observe this in cats and dogs. When they listen, look, or sniff, all three senses together adjust their body position. When cats go into 'kill mode,' they enact remembered, instinctual patterns – implicit memory. We do this too when we intensely attend – using the executive network [5.5.3]. This happens in play and in flow states; when we concentrate so hard, we lose all sense of time [10.7].

The classical model from the 1950s was simple and uncomplicated, and it had problems. There is no hierarchy in the mind, with a chief executive who gives orders and decides what we're going to remember or forget. The executive network is only one part of three networks which make up our sense of 'me' (like the Christian idea of the trinity). But the executive network is not 'in control' of everything all the time. Our minds do not have a 'Great Leader.' The mind is a natural anarchy. And we don't process random information. We deliberately, unconsciously, choose what we're going to attend to or ignore as we switch between the three networks very quickly, all the time – none are ever off.

Q:  Can there be unconscious choices?

Yes. We habituate (tune out) things of little or no interest – attention is never random. This also becomes implicit. Our salience network [5.5.2] continually seeks things which matter to us ('salient' means 'sticks out'). If you are not a bird watcher, you won't give a bird a second glance. If you are, you love each thrilling, tiny detail. If you're a cat, you plan how to kill a bird and re-imagine past hunting experiences before you pounce. Memories are actively built up depending on their usefulness, probably like this [see Figure 4.1].

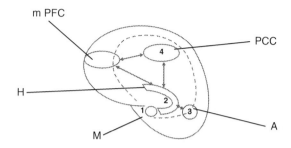

*Figure 4.1* Memory circuits

Let's look at the integrated pathways which collaborate to make memory. Any pre-selected perception enters 'flash memory' in the mammillary bodies (M) at the bottom of the hippocampus (H). They hold it for minutes and then move it to a short-term 'working memory' in the rest of the hippocampus.

The hippocampus is the source of theta waves (slow brain waves between 4 and 10 a second) associated with slow-wave sleep interrupted by sudden bursts of high amplitude waves called 'sharp waves.' A suggestion is these sharp waves are associated with changes in how easily neurons connect – more connections grow on the pathways which become long-term memory. This is a guess because it is not easy to study. However, it is certain sleep deprivation seriously impairs attention the next day and reduces the ability to learn. It allows 'false memories' to form – and false forgetting.

Understanding what the hippocampus does comes from lesion studies – the changes which occur if it is damaged or removed. In the '50s, this happened to H. M. – a young American man with extremely severe epilepsy. All treatments failed. A neurosurgeon decided to remove his hippocampus and surrounding parts of the temporal lobe, where the seizures began (Squire, 2009). The fits stopped, but H. M. could never form any new memories or imagine possible futures. He could not care for himself and lived the rest of his life in hospital. H. M. couldn't report dreams, though electroencephalogram (EEG) studies showed he still had rapid eye movements (REM) sleep. He dreamed but couldn't process them into a conscious memory. It was hard for him to name feelings.

Transfer to long-term memory depends on feeling. The hippocampus and amygdala are part of the salience network (A, in figure 4.1).

If a red balloon has no emotional salience (we don't care), then we forget it. If it is heart shaped and a special gift from someone we love on Valentine's Day, we may remember it always. And it's more likely to become a dream symbol.

The emotional 'labelling' of memory uses (amongst other areas) the posterior cingulate cortex (PCC). This part of the brain is always 'on,' uses the most fuel (glucose) of any brain area, and belongs to the default mode network as does the mPFC, the medial pre frontal cortex. The amygdala is involved too. It is responsible for fear and its opposite: ecstasy. Curiously, it's where the recreational drug 'ecstasy' (E) works. An 'E' causes almost all the neurons in the amygdala to release their neurotransmitter (serotonin), so there is not enough left for it to work and make fear with. People become 'loved up' – they may feel emotionally 'flat' when they come down.

The hippocampus and amygdala consolidate memory. This does not mean our eyes take a picture and store it like a photo in a drawer. A vast neural network is needed for any perception. The emerging 'pattern networks' are kept going by something the hippocampus does. Perhaps it 're-fires' the network at regular intervals; perhaps it is linked to its role in spatial awareness. Because when we 'revisit the scene of the crime,' spatial awareness brings forward intense emotional memories. This spatial and sensory component of memory is usually overlooked – it's implicit – and it's essential to making dreams.

These models are ideas in evolution [see Box 4.1] – they are not definitive. It appears complex because it is complex, and no one has worked it out yet. We reconstitute experience, and this is highly energy intensive. This may be why we do it during sleep because we're doing nothing else. We need to be free of perceptions, as building memory needs 'all the bandwidth' we have. This is why dreams matter.

Any learning needs repetition, both awake and asleep. We remember better after a nap. Given a simple task (remembering a list of

---

**Box 4.1   'Classical' stages of memory**

- Acquire, store, and retrieve the latest information
- Consolidate during sleep and in dreams
- Recall in consciousness

words), people who nap perform better at recall than those who don't. When learning a new language, one day, we find we're dreaming in it – it has moved from explicit to implicit memory. Musicians, learning a new piece, will rehearse it during sleep. In many 'rehearsal' dreams, the dreamers let go of what they knew to discover something they haven't yet remembered [see the naked dancer dream, 8.3.4].

## 4.5  MEMORY IS RECONSTRUCTIVE IMAGINATION

Memories are a whispering, randomly moving, chaotic crowd, like leaves murmuring in a forest. They are not a bookshelf or 'stored' anywhere. We have no 'libraries' of sounds, images, feelings, or sensations. This would take too much space and be far too slow. Instead, patterns are recreated through millions of interconnected neural networks. These networks are located across the brain and shift continually as neurons grow, die, or change connections. Like body growth, this change happens at night.

The brain is completely unlike a computer. There is no 'hard wiring,' no processors, no data storage. Any time we actively re-imagine anything, the neurons we use are different. For example, to read the letter 'S' needs the visual, auditory, spatial, and motor cortex, as well as the cerebellum. It balances our muscle tone and body position so our eyes stay focused when reading. The cerebellum is crucial to body memories. We can't recreate a word without it, as we learn the tongue, lip, and vocal chords movement at the same time as we learn the breathing to make a sound. Muscle memory is essential for both emotion and thought, and it is rehearsed in dreams. The role of the cerebellum in memory is underestimated, except by sports people.

Q: Do we really use different neural pathways each time for the *same* letter?

Yes! After a neuron fires, it takes fractions of a second for it to be able to fire again. So, one pathway per task is hopelessly slow. If there were only one pathway for S, we'd have to stop every time we met one on a page. Our memory, like truth, is plastic – there are so many ways to do what looks like the same thing. Older people have seen similar situations many times and can explore several possible viewpoints and outcomes, especially in dreams. Memory can be shaped and bent. Dreaming is essential to make, shape, consolidate, change, delete, and amend memory. They reflect what we remember in new ways to adapt to the current situation. We 'fill in the gaps' and tell dream stories which fit our expectations or those of our culture.

Q: What happens if we can't do this?
A: We create false memories [4.6.1].

## 4.6 SLEEP AND MEMORY

In slow-wave sleep, the hippocampus replays some of a day's events – easy to say, but it's not at all certain how this happens. The medial prefrontal cortex (mPFC) – now known to be a part of the default mode network – seems to initiate this and aid the selection process (Buzsaki, 1989).

We know the hippocampus is involved in spatial awareness. Let me give you an example of 'whole-brain memory' where the situation itself is a learning experience. Most actors use spatial awareness to learn their lines: 'I walk over there and say that, and then turn around and say the next thing.' Traditional mnemonic (remembering) systems use an imaginary landscape, which we walk around placing things we need to recall in the space. When learning neuroanatomy, our professor regularly took us on guided tours around the brain:

> *And here we are standing on the floor of the fourth ventricle. Behind you, that huge tunnel is the way down to the spinal cord.*

Explicit memory improves during slow-wave sleep, and implicit memory improves during REM sleep – in dreaming. Any new learning is dreamed about, though we usually don't remember it when we wake. The saying 'sleep on it' is true. If learning a list of random names in a cognitive psychology experiment, a short nap immediately after the task increases success. A night's sleep increases recall even more.

## 4.7 DREAMS AND MEMORY

As we reflect on what we've done or are doing, we review the feelings and the physical events. Can we think about our actions with empathy for ourselves, or do we do this in a critical way? Let us consider, as a simple example, 'What do you do when you lose something?' What do you feel? Can you learn to change what you do, like putting your keys in the same safe place every time?

Making a memory and keeping it means using it. Dreams can draw on any memory or any part of one; they are how the unconscious evolves memory. They are multimodal sense-based events which retell us the stories we imagine about the past.

As an analyst I noticed how, at first, patients have a 'made-up' biography. They are trying to live up to, or down to, what *someone else* told them their story is. They may have stories about parental abuse and neglect but often believe the abuser's version and identify with the persecutor. A natural function of dreams is to put the dreamer back into their own story and to retell it [see the footballer's dream, 7.4.1].

## 4.8  FALSE MEMORY AND EYEWITNESS

Let's consider noticing and its relation to memory. This involves the salience network. Here is an example. Do we remember our dreams, or do we make them up as we try to remember them? Both. We are unreliable witnesses. A friend taught the law of evidence to new students at the London School of Economics. In her first lecture, she always asked a second-year student dressed in a striped T-shirt, a black face mask, and carrying a large bag marked 'swag' to ostentatiously tiptoe in and steal her briefcase. She ignored this. Later, she asked if anyone had seen anything unusual. At least a third of the students hadn't. Why?

By not noticing, my friend misled the observers. They saw what they expected rather than what happened. We remember what we predict rather than things as they 'really are.' Perceptions are strongly determined by expectations, and this distorts memory. It may create a false memory, and sometimes these begin in dreams. As Freud said, dreams fulfil wishes. So, if we wished we'd said some smart put-down to a person we can't stand, we might dream we had and then prefer the dream to the reality.

Dreams often imagine a result before we've got there, like downloading anxiety from the future. Anxiety dreams occur in those who care about their performance rather than in those who don't. Whilst most memories of abuse which resurface in therapy are, sadly, true, some are not. Sometimes, we mistake a dream for reality. Or take a fantasy to be real, particularly if this boosts our self-esteem.

There is a difference between concealed and revealed memory, as seen in the (rare) false memory syndrome. A person is convinced a terrible thing happened (like being sexually abused) – but it didn't. This is a complex and controversial area. I mention it because any evidence based on a dream is no evidence at all. As mentioned, a dream can be a wish-fulfilment. Even of abuse? Yes. If we can consciously make up a false story deliberately to hurt someone, we can also do this unconsciously and/or delete the memory of making it up.

### 4.8.1 Losing memory

People with severe memory loss confabulate. This means they make up stories to fill in for their absence of recall. Confabulation is like shouting 'electoral fraud' when there is no evidence. Like 'fake news,' this is an example of 'wish = > dream = > reality.' The more contrary evidence appears, the more strength the 'unshakeable false belief' (delusion); it's become a delusion [like Ben and the chewing gum, 4.3]. Here is an example of severe memory loss.

Jim, 21, lived in a long-stay ward. Severe alcoholism caused catastrophic vitamin B1 deficiency. This destroyed two tiny areas at the base of the brain, the mammillary bodies – the flash memory store. Jim has no idea at all who he is, where he is, or how he got here. He remembers nothing for years before the hospital (retrograde amnesia). No new memories ever form (anterograde amnesia). I'd say, 'Hi, Jim,' and come back a few minutes later, and he'd have forgotten who I was. He always chatted but could never start a conversation. Jim has Korsakov's syndrome. I often asked Jim if he dreamed, but he couldn't understand the question. He'd say – yes, no, maybe, not sure at random.

### 4.8.2 Losing memory – dementias

In dementias (loss of mind), our neural forest gradually dies either from lack of blood supply (vascular dementia), build-up of abnormal proteins (Alzheimer's disease), or from other pathologies as yet unclear. Generally, the memory losses are not specific or diagnostic.

In Alzheimer's, the hippocampus is severely affected. The most active part of the brain, where coordination of emotion with thought takes place (the PCC), is likely the first part damaged. As people become demented, they become increasingly anxious about their loss of cognition. Anxiety makes recall far harder.

The PCC is part of the default mode network which is like our emotional suspension. Infants haven't yet grown one, which is why any tiny thing becomes a total catastrophe – they have meltdowns.

As the default mode fails, older people can no longer benefit from their previous experience.

As the dementia progresses and the frontal lobes begin to fail, the executive network fails. We can't think logically or work out that actions have consequences. We lose the predictive functions of memory and may leave the microwave on for hours or run the bath till it floods.

We lose the ability to learn and may become disinhibited. When dementing people report dreams, they are full of anxious images. Nightmares become common again.

In a rare dementia (Lewy body dementia), there are visual hallucinations and troubling nightmares, part of a REM sleep disorder. The dreamer flails about or tries to run whilst asleep as if trying to escape an attack. Usually, in sleep, we can't move (sleep paralysis), but the part of the brain responsible for this is failing – so we move. Recent research (The Guardian, September 2022) shows links between frequent nightmares in older adults and an increased risk of future cognitive impairment. But this isn't diagnostic: this science is very much in evolution.

Sleep deprivation, on its own, upsets cognitive processing, and impaired cognitive processing causes anxiety, which disrupts sleep. It's a vicious circle. We lie awake trying to remember what it is we've forgotten. And then forget why we woke up. Older people tend to dream far more about past events, as they are making sense of a lifetime. In dementia, it is harder and harder to recall dreams, which is, in itself, distressing. We're losing an essential cushion to ordinary anxieties as the default mode network fails.

## 4.9 THE NEXTUP THEORY

Let's move on to the evidence for dreams processing memory. This theory of dream function is backed by extensive research by Antonio Zadra, professor at Montreal, and Robert Stickgold, professor at Harvard (Zadra and Stickgold 2021, pp. 108–129, and 264–266). They began by showing how weak associations to words are better recalled than strong ones after REM sleep.

A strong association might be 'left – right,' a weak one might be 'left – thief' (maybe like this: left > lift > steal > thief: it's like doing a cryptic crossword). Dreams seem to use weak associations rather than strong ones. These free associations are created by the default mode network. This is why dreams are often bizarre, like the dragon in the supermarket [2.3], or use awful puns like 'cagey bee = KGB' [2.9]. Dreams use 'what if?' – the counterfactual – *all the time* to bring forward hidden feelings, and they strengthen reality testing by using divergent rather than convergent thinking. Here is an example:

As a kid, I loved playing 'Cluedo,' a board game. Each player is a detective trying to find who murdered Dr Black. Murder cards show a person, an implement, or a room. You say to other players, 'I suspect Prof. Plum is in the library with the dagger'; if they have a card, they show you. Then you record it on your detective notes. This uses convergent thinking: you continue till all possibilities are eliminated. Divergent thinking is like starting with the detective notes and working backward to find out who had which 'murder cards.' Going away from 'the answer' towards 'the question' is how dreams help us ask better questions.

This involves the default mode network – you can watch this on a functional magnetic resonance imaging (fMRI) scan. Give someone a task, and it goes quiet. As soon as the task ends, it will almost immediately start up, connecting the parts which had done the task; this is called 'learning.' And it happens when our minds are wandering. William Domhoff and Kieran Fox (2015) suggest the default mode network is where dreaming occurs. Asleep, there is nothing to distract it from linking anything to anything else, which allows us to reconstructively imagine things which could be NEXTUP – what could happen next.

Interestingly, this strongly supports how essential 'downtime' is to learn anything at all and to process new information. 'Downtime' means what it says – not doing anything. We are unconsciously re-constructing experience, daydreaming. Downtime is truncated by using 'mobile devices.' Downtime then becomes 'uptime.' This contributes to insomnia – because at the end of the day, there is far more micro-processing of day events to do – the cost of being able to find out anything and talk to anyone whenever we like is we stop talking and listening to ourselves. This deprives us of sleep and dreaming.

We need to reflect, to daydream, or we can't reconstructively imagine what has happened or what will happen next.

## KEY CONCEPTS

- Memory is reconstructive imagination
- A memory is made anew each time, using different neurons

- Dreams evolve memory
- The purpose of memory is prediction, not recall

## FURTHER READING

Barrett, L. F. (2021) *Seven and a half lessons about the brain*, London: Picador.

## REFERENCES

Anon. (2023) https://www.psychologytoday.com/intl/basics/default-mode-network

Buzsaki, G. (1989) Two stage model of memory trace formation. *Neuroscience*, 31 (3): 551–570.

Domhoff, G. W., and Fox, K.C. (2015) 'Dreaming and the default network: a review, synthesis and counterintuitive research proposal.' *Consciousness and cognition* 33: 342–53.

The Guardian. (2022) https://www.theguardian.com/society/2022/sep/21/bad-dreams-in-smiddle-age-could-be-sign-of-dementia-risk-study-suggests.

Squire, L.R. (2009) The Legacy of Patient H.M. for Neuroscience. *Neuron* 61(1): 6–9. https://www.ncbi.nlm.nih.gov/pmc/articles/PMC2649674/

Zadra A., and Stickgold, R. (2021) *When brains dream*, New York: W.W. Norton.

# THE NATURAL PHILOSOPHY OF SLEEP AND DREAMS

## 5.1 INTRODUCTION

This chapter is about the natural history of sleep and dreams. Science is sometimes called natural philosophy, and philosophy means 'love of wisdom.' So, this is not just 'the facts' about sleep and dreaming but also wonders … but also wonders what the wise things are to do with 'facts'.

One is to question them. In this chapter and the last, I sometimes say, 'A part of the brain does…'; this is 'old-school' neuroscience. It has a colonialist flavour, as if the mind had a hierarchy: the frontal lobes 'command'; the limbic system is 'emotional'; the medulla 'humbly serves,' taking care of the body. This is simply not true. We need all of our brain, all of the time, with all of our body to make a mind. And we need the minds of others too. Minds can't ever exist separated from their culture.

Another myth is brain areas are either *on* – doing something – or *off*, not doing anything. This is not true either. *All* of our brain is 'on' *all the time*, but the activity levels vary from part to part, as does the level of consciousness.

How do we know what consciousness is? [see 2.4–2.5] How do we tell if we are awake, asleep, daydreaming, having visions, intoxicated, or deluded? How do we test reality? This is what the 'ego' does [Box 2.3] – and it does this by referring to the self (the totality of who we are). But do these two psychological concepts, ego and self, have any neuroanatomical basis? Maybe not.

DOI: 10.4324/9781003319696-5

Q:  Do you think it matters if they do or they don't?

Dreams test reality by suggesting alternative realities – it's a paradox. Lawyers and detectives use the same paradox all the time. They call this 'the counterfactual': 'If X didn't commit the crime, then who did?' Or, 'What would have happened if?' Exploring alternate realities is essential to creativity [Chapter 8] and to creating a future, even if it is only seconds away. This keeps us alive when we're travelling: 'What if that lorry suddenly turns left? Can he see my bicycle?'

Do dreams select facts at random? No. They simply use different criteria, preferring sensations to feelings, feelings to thoughts, and weak associations to strong ones [4.10] almost as if dreams are a reversal of waking consciousness. Dreams may be 'portals to the source' of wisdom, but most dreams never reach consciousness. Perhaps wisdom is largely unconscious? Or maybe wisdom is a form of spatial/temporal awareness – an unconscious sensation rather than a conscious thought? Rather than 'the humble body' being 'servant of the mind,' they are inseparable. Bodily life and physical sensations, particularly balance, shape our dreams as much as our frontal lobes. The reality is the opposite of the old top-down hierarchical model of the mind.

Writing this chapter, I hoped for a helpful dream. I did not *ask for a dream* – this isn't necessary. Dreams happen anyway. When you need a dream's guidance, let the unconscious speak for itself and use whatever you get:

### The walk in the park dream

*I'm walking on Wimbledon Common, in South London, with Professor Arthur Crisp. He said, 'Just pass the trees in the right order,' and smiled.*

Waking, I realised if I put the trees (topics) in the right order, then *it's a walk in the park*. Prof. Crisp was chair of psychiatry at St George's Hospital, London, where I trained. He ran a sleep lab. Like other junior doctors, I helped there, waking people when they'd dreamed, to record what they'd dreamed – looking particularly at early morning waking, a symptom of depression. What follows is a walk-through about sleep, the how and the where of dreams. It introduces the 'three network' model, a present-day best guess at how minds make bridges between the cortex and the limbic system. Dreams are ways we process feelings and thoughts *together* during sleep.

### 5.1.1 *Sleep*

All living things sleep – including plants – and adapt to changes between light and dark. This is called a circadian rhythm. Some mammals are nocturnal, like hedgehogs; others wake at dawn and dusk, like cats. A human wake/sleep rhythm is around twenty four hours – but not exactly. Experiments letting people 'free run' (by living in caves) found that the natural human rhythm is around twenty seven hours. We resynchronise each day to adjust to seasonal changes. Light signals go from the eyes to the pineal gland, which releases melatonin (the same chemical as in skin pigment) to reset one of the body clocks (we have several). Small doses of melatonin help treat jet lag and some rare sleep disorders. Adolescents produce their 'sleep burst' of melatonin about two hours later than children: this is why they stay up late and sleep in later.

During sleep, growth hormone is released, particularly in childhood. When the body relaxes, maintenance takes place: muscles repair and organs regrow. Without sleep, in the extremely rare fatal sleep disorder, we dement and die in about a year (because a virus-like particle 'melts' the thalamus, a vital part of the sleep network.)

Sleep patterns change throughout life. The brain begins to appear around six weeks after conception, and then the neurons gradually migrate to their correct places. After sixteen weeks, the structures which allow sleep and dreaming are formed. From then on, a foetus sleeps about 40 per cent of the time. In the weeks before birth, we dream the most, for several hours a day, as we try out new things in a safe place whilst we dream ourselves into being.

Newborns sleep about ten hours, though for parents it doesn't feel like it. Infants are not able to sense time, as those networks have not grown yet. During the first 18 months, our time senses slowly emerge, and a wake/sleep cycle stabilises. By 2 years old, most of us settle into about nine to ten hours of sleep, with a nap, and about three hours dreaming. By school age, we sleep eight to nine hours and dream for two and a half. Adolescents need more sleep, between nine and ten hours; they dream more and start having sexual dreams. Educational research repeatedly shows we'd grow better physically, emotionally, and academically if allowed to start school at 10 a.m., but social and political pressures keep preventing this beneficial cultural change.

Each of us has our own circadian rhythm (chronotype). 'Larks' think dawn is wonderful. 'Owls' (like me) have heard rumours about dawn; we're still happily awake at two a.m. Although rare, some people have a circadian rhythm disorder. A young man I saw for analysis had wake/sleep cycles which 'slid forward' about two hours a day. By the end of the week, our day was his night. In adolescence, he was diagnosed with attention deficit hyperactivity disorder (ADHD). He had vivid dreams and often dreamed whilst 'awake.' This problem was helped by Ritalin, an amphetamine. It causes wakefulness in ordinary people but helps those with ADHD to sleep. Given at a regular time (a.m.), it creates an artificial rhythm. Later, sleep lab studies showed he had a rare asynchronous sleep disorder, which was helped by timed treatment with melatonin (however, most people diagnosed with ADHD do have ADHD).

Sleep begins partly by choice, partly because our body clocks tell us, and partly when blood levels of glycogen fall and adenosine levels rise. Glycogen is a long-term energy source stored in the liver. Adenosine is an amino acid, part of DNA, found everywhere in the body. It inhibits neuron activity. As the blood level rises, we become drowsy, can't concentrate, and get irritable. Caffeine sticks to the same receptors on neurons as those taken by adenosine and wakes us up. High doses of caffeine cause 'the shakes.' And like any other addictive drug, there's a withdrawal syndrome – sleep disturbance, tiredness, and irritation.

It will help you as we look at neuroanatomy of sleep and dreaming to imagine the structures are as big as a cathedral and then use higher magnifications. Make a neuron as big as a tree, a receptor the size of your front door, and a neurotransmitter molecule the size of a parcel. The story and the diagrams are deliberately as simple as possible. I've left out almost all of the story about neurotransmitters to keep this simple.

Once the conditions for sleep are met, the reticular activating system (RAS) in the medulla (brain stem) sends signals to the thalamus (T) (Figure 5.1). The RAS is a network of spread-out nuclei (collections of neurons) in the medulla. It looks like an old-fashioned lady's net handbag (called a reticule). It liaises with the cerebellum (which is responsible for balance), belongs to a network controlling the heart rate, and modulates pain. Some parts are concerned with arousal and alertness, others with sleep. Damage to either can cause an irreversible coma.

Both talk to the thalamus. The name means 'bridal chamber,' as it marries information from all over the body about sensations (especially pain), emotions, and whether to be alert or to relax. The

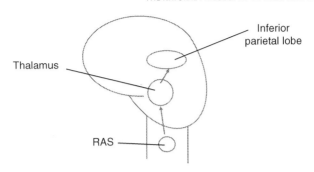

*Figure 5.1* Neural pathways of sleep

thalamus then signals the lower part of the parietal lobe (responsible for movement and sensation) to gradually withdraw attention, and we drift into sleep.

Sleep deprivation is dangerous and sneaks up on us unawares. Jet lag is a mild form. It's worse flying east because we adjust more easily to waking up early than to staying up late. Missing a night's sleep is a common cause of accidents. This is why pilots and others in the transport industries have strictly regulated work schedules. Deficits self-correct if we have time to sleep them off, which takes a few days. There will be 'dream rebound' too, as we need our two hours of dreaming. If people are woken each time they dream, they become emotionally unstable, and reality testing (ego function) breaks down. This is one of the most effective forms of torture, often used to obtain 'confessions.' Violence isn't necessary; just keep someone continuously awake for a week. Such unnatural experiments show that whatever else dreams do, they are essential to mental health.

### 5.1.2 *Stages of sleep*

Sleep follows drowsiness. There may be transient visual hallucinations on falling asleep (hypnagogic) or on waking (hypnopompic) – both are common. We may 'story tell' ourselves to sleep (this helps) or anxiously go over the day's events (this doesn't). Gradually, we slide deeper into unconsciousness. Our brain is continually electrically active – brain waves can be measured with external sensors on an electroencephalogram (EEG). In the old days, this threw out kilometres of paper a night and was a labour-intensive read. Now, it's done by computer. It's particularly used to discover whether someone has epilepsy – in which there are sudden big bursts of abnormal electrical activity accompanied by seizures. An EEG can tell where the seizures begin, whether they are getting better or worse, and if drug treatment is working.

During the day, the normal background resting rate of brain waves (alpha rhythm) is between 8 to 10 Hz (Hz = a hertz is one wave per second). During sleep, this slows (theta rhythm) to 4 to 8 Hz and gradually accelerates as we return to consciousness. During complex thinking (like maths), it increases (gamma rhythm) to between 30 and 50 Hz. Slow waves come from the hypothalamus and occur as memory 'uploads.'

### 5.1.3 REM sleep

In sleep, bursts of fast brain wave activity recur about every 90 minutes, accompanied by rapid eye movements (REM) and body paralysis. REM occurs in all birds and mammals. It was discovered in the 1950s by a sleep researcher watching eye movements in his sleeping baby as if they were looking at something. Cats and dogs dream with rapid whisker movements, as well as moving their eyes. Dreams only last a few minutes, though some seem to last for hours. Our ego functions (reality testing), including time perception, are temporarily suspended.

After the first two or three bursts of REM (two sleep cycles, about three hours), there are short moments of wakefulness. Here, dreams are 'shown' to consciousness, processed, and then we go back to sleep. In depression, we still wake after a dream and look for it, but we can't find it – so we become fully awake. Spells of REM happen more often nearer waking; dreams before waking are easiest to remember.

### 5.1.4 Right and left hemispheres

There are two sides to the cortex: the right and left hemispheres. They have different functions. 'Lateralisation' varies from person to person. In most right-handed people, the left hemisphere is dominant, and vice versa, but not always. Put simply, the left is more rational and mathematical, has language, and deals with sensation and motor control of the right side of the body. The right is more holistic, tends to look at the bigger picture, and deals with the left side. There are huge amounts of research about what happens where, often based on studies of people who have had the connection between the left and right hemispheres divided (Springer & Deutsch 2001, pp. 31–59, 102–116). This gave rise to popular cultural myths about 'right-brain' and 'left-brain' properties and personalities. The story is sometimes presented as if there were a power struggle – as if the left brain were 'masculine' and the right brain 'feminine.' To me, this looks like a projection of a social conflict onto the brain. There isn't any evidence to support this gendering.

Some propose the right hemisphere, which is more 'holistic,' takes over in dreaming because it's no longer dominated by the left, or the right hemisphere is 'the unconscious.' It certainly deals with non-verbal image-based thinking, so it is like Freud's idea of primary process thinking [Box 6.2]. EEG and fMRI studies do show the right frontal cortex is more active in dreaming, though this doesn't mean it 'makes' dreams (McGilchrist, 2009, pp. 187–188, 198).

### 5.1.5 Non-REM sleep

Sometimes sleep is so deep there are no dreams at all. But we spend at least an hour of sleep in non-REM dreams – possibly more in childhood. These dreams have a different quality – they're abstract; there may be kaleidoscopic patterns of shifting colour, or they may be like watching bubbles through water. They have sound and movement but no story– with strong, deep feelings ranging from oceanic oneness to nameless dread. Often, they are peaceful, like a meditation. They are hard to notice unless someone wakes you up (in a sleep lab). If you regularly attend to your dreams, you may occasionally catch a few:

#### A blue dream

*Blue, transparent, and opaque swirls, changing shades, falling upward into a light at the top of a well, music ... intense calm ... timeless.*

It is hard to put this into images, and the sensations are beyond (or before) words. An analytic patient reported:

#### A black dream

*Falling downward forever, towards a 'dark light' – deeper shades of black – peaceful.*

This was from a young woman in analysis who was dying of breast cancer on opiates. As she went deeper and deeper into this dream, she became calmer. This calmness stayed with her when awake. She shared this dream a week before she died.

### 5.1.6 How dreams are made

> 'We are such stuff as dreams are made on, and our little life is rounded with a sleep.'
>
> (Shakespeare: *the Tempest*, act 4, Sc 1)

Dreams are stories we tell ourselves: they are {both/and / neither/nor} conscious and unconscious: they're between them [Box 5.1]. They may be as short as a postcard or as long as a fantasy trilogy in seven volumes. They have different strengths and flavours.

(If neuroscience makes you dizzy, feel free to skip the next few paragraphs. To me, that we know any of this is a miracle: I find it beautiful. If the technical names seem strange, look at the neuroscience appendix. To make it easier to read, I use initials for the parts of the brain involved. When we appreciate what our mind does, we can use it better – and not try to make it do things it can't.)

Impulses to trigger dream making come from an area called 'the periaqueductal grey matter' (PAG). These neurons surround the channel which carries cerebrospinal fluid from deep in the brain to the spine. It is quite small and extremely important in sensing and modulating pain, and for our fight/flight responses. It coordinates with the reticular activating system (RAS). Both send signals to several places – the thalamus (T), amygdala (A), parts of the default mode network, especially the medial prefrontal cortex (mPFC), and the lowest part of the parietal lobe, called the parietal-temporal-occipital (PTO) junction. It's where the parietal lobe meets the

---

### Box 5.1    Sleep in adults

- Two hours of REM sleep a night
- An hour of non-REM dreams in a night
- Many minutes dreaming whilst 'awake'
- Fifty per cent of waking is spent in daydreams

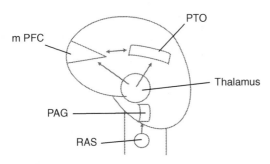

*Figure 5.2* How dreams are made

temporal and occipital lobes. This connects to the default mode network, and when we dream [see Figure 5.2].

The PTO is where abstract thoughts, sounds, and images are put together – no surprise because it joins the parts of the cortex responsible for spatial awareness to those responsible for sound and vision. If this area is damaged, then dreams don't have images. Notice how spatial awareness is built into the images. We make a 3D inner 'world' where we can move, as well as sounds and pictures. It's like writing a novel beginning with the world, not the characters or the plot. Then this connects with the default mode to 'make up a story.' So, the story comes last. The differences in timing are in fractions of a second. Dreams are sense-driven rather than arising from thoughts – the opposite of how it is commonly imagined.

The South African psychoanalyst and neuroscientist Mark Solms (2016, pp. 237–247) researched what happens in people who can't dream visually as a result of trauma, surgery, or strokes. They have 'abstract' REM dreams – spatial movements, swirly patterns, sounds, feelings. But if the connections from the PAG to the mPFC are destroyed (if a neurosurgeon does a frontal lobotomy), then we can't dream at all.

Hardly any of these operations are performed now. They didn't work. They did nothing for untreatable depression or schizophrenia (and made both conditions worse). Survivors are typically 'a-motivational' – they can't start things, and if they do, they can't maintain interest. They can't really reality test, and they don't care about their worlds either, probably because they can no longer tell themselves stories. The operation destroys their default mode network, so they can no longer connect thoughts to feelings.

Interestingly, connections to the prefrontal cortex are disrupted in schizophrenia (Selemon and Zecevic, 2015). The name of this serious mental illness is rather like saying 'rheumatism.' Which covers a range of joint disorders, as schizophrenia covers a range of mental disorders. An old name was 'oneirophrenia' from the Latin 'dream mind.' Common symptoms include loss of motivation, profound failure of reality testing, and being 'in a dream.' If you can't tell if you are awake or dreaming, then life becomes your worst nightmare. Try and remember your worst nightmare, and you will see how distressing this is. People with this condition truly are scared out of their wits. They project this fear into those they meet, which is why this mental illness scares others so much.

### 5.1.7 Sleep disorders

As this book is about dreams, I won't say lots about insomnia (lack of sleep), which needs a separate book. It's both a symptom and a condition in itself. Any physical or mental illness may cause insomnia. Anxiety is the most common cause, often accompanied by ruminating. But sometimes no cause is found. With age, we sleep less (in our 60s, about six to seven hours) and more lightly, and the content of dreams may change [4.9.2]. There are many good books about sleep hygiene (e.g., Littlehales, 2016). Have a quiet, comfortable, and safe bedroom; don't drink coffee at bedtime or use technology (mobile phones, computers) for *at least an hour* before sleep; and have a regular routine. The most important part of which is a regular wake time.

Sleeping tablets treat the symptom, not the cause. If insomnia is a persistent problem, see your doctor rather than self-medicate. Over-the-counter herbal remedies have a good placebo effect – this can be enough to make a difference. As sleeping tablets are addictive and suppress dreaming, when they're stopped, there is usually a dream rebound, and then the insomnia starts again.

Sleep changes are seen in every mental illness – anxiety, depression, bipolar disorder, and schizophrenia. Drug-induced changes in sleep and dreams occur with any recreational drug. Alcohol, cannabis, cocaine, opiates – all reduce REM sleep. Amongst the sleep disorders, narcolepsy is when people fall asleep for no external reason. Those affected go from consciousness to REM sleep with almost no interval and have vivid dreams and sleep paralysis. Narcolepsy has several causes, one of which is damage to the hypothalamus. This may be genetic, follow a viral illness, or be an autoimmune disease. The condition affected Mike (played by River Phoenix) in Gus Van Sant's film *My Own Private Idaho* (1991). Treatments include amphetamines to reset the wake/sleep cycle. It's rare, but it is an example of dreams suddenly intruding into consciousness. We usually call this daydreaming.

## 5.2 DAYDREAMING (PART ONE)

In daydreaming, we don't have sleep paralysis. We all micro-dream throughout the day, up to as much as 50 per cent of the time. A daydream is what it says on the tin – a dream during the day. It uses the same parts of the brain as a sleep dream, except for the RAS. We're in slightly lower states of arousal but can quickly go back to full alertness. I discuss daydreams in detail in Chapter 8.

### 5.2.1 *The three network model*

Advances in neuroimaging mean we can now watch the brain being a mind (Springer and Deutsch, 2001, pp. 61–96). Up till now, our knowledge of function mostly came from what happened when things went wrong – head injuries, strokes, surgery, mental and physical illnesses. From the end of the nineteenth century, we could use X-rays to see inside the skull. These became increasingly sophisticated by adding radioopaque dyes. EEGs began in the late '40s. CAT scans began in the '70s. They use computer assistance to take X-ray pictures of the brain – in slices. Studying function only became possible using fMRI scans in the last twenty years (Karahanoğlu and Van De Ville, 2017).

Simply, an fMRI works like this. Blood contains iron (haemoglobin). Iron is magnetic. When a part of the brain works harder, it uses more oxygen, like a muscle. If you measure the magnetic field per cubic millimetre of brain tissue, you get a good approximation of how much blood it's using, so you know 'which bit does what.' There are many technical issues, but it's better than anything available before. It is to neuroscience like the James Webb space telescope is to astronomy. We can see further and better, and find new questions.

At first, neuroscientists were excited to discover which 'bits' lit up when we 'did things' – people in fMRI scanners were given tasks. The visual cortex lit up when they looked at patterns, and when they closed their eyes and imagined them, the same thing happened. Everything seemed to fit with what anatomists predicted.

When we make decisions, a pattern of brain areas from both the cortex and limbic system lights up. They called this the executive network (when we are vigilant, another set of areas, also bridging the cortex and limbic system lights up). The salience network ('salient' means 'to stand out.' We notice this in our experience when we're in a flow state, completely focussed [10.7]). One day (or so legend has it) the guys running a scanner had a coffee break but left their subject inside. When they came back, they found another set of areas lit up when the subject wasn't doing anything. They called this the default mode network.

The salience network switches between the default mode network and the executive network. The two are anti-correlated – like 'the Weather People' (two little figures with two doors to their house. When Mr Sun is out, Mrs Rain is in, and vice versa). But neither network is ever 'off.' The salience network does risk assessment; the executive one plans actions; the default one is 'the storyteller.' None of them are 'consciousness' or 'unconsciousness.' Nor are any of them 'ego' or 'self.'

No part of any network ever acts alone. Each has a diffuse 'edge.' As the brain is the same consistency as thick yoghurt, it's hard to say where one part begins and another ends. Dreaming is an essential part of balancing the three networks – let's explain this by looking at each in more depth.

### 5.2.2 *The salience network*

The salience network includes the hypothalamus (responsible for hormonal control), the hippocampus (which helps build memory), and the thalamus (the switchboard, which monitors incoming sensations). This network stops us from putting our hands in a fire. Everyone does this – once. It includes parts responsible for reward, ethics, impulse control, and emotions. It gathers intelligence from inside and outside, does risk assessment *all the time*, and switches between executive network and default mode network. It's not the ego because it doesn't 'do' affect (feeling) regulation.

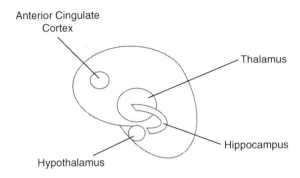

*Figure 5.3* The salience network

| **The Salience Network** | **RISK ASSESSMENT** | |
| --- | --- | --- |
| | Hypothalamus (Hy) | hormone regulation |
| | Hippocampus (H) | choice about what we remember |
| | Thalamus (T) | switchboard, for sensations |
| | Anterior cingulate cortex (ACC) | reward, ethics, impulse control, emotional awareness |

## 5.2.3 *Executive network*

The main parts are responsible for working memory and planning, visual imagination, and the feelings which go with images, especially with faces, and the parts responsible for compassion, empathy, and self-awareness. We don't just 'think' and then 'act' – we evaluate the likely emotional responses of others and of ourselves first before any action (and we are usually unconscious of this).

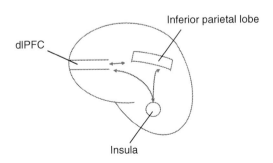

*Figure 5.4* The executive network

| The Executive Network | **FOCUSSED ATTENTION** | |
|---|---|---|
| | Dorsolateral prefrontal cortex (dlPFC) | working memory |
| | Inferior parietal lobe (IPL) | visual imagination and faces |
| | Insula (I) | empathy, self-awareness |

Notice the executive network includes parts involved in movement and sensation (the parietal lobe). So, when we do focussed thinking, we rely on patterns of movement and sensation. The parietal lobe always refers to the cerebellum (responsible for balance). This is how yoga, dance, and body-based therapies work and bring up strong feelings. It's where change happens when a memory trapped in the body emerges – like early abuse or post-traumatic stress disorder. Maybe these physical sensations are the 'pre-thoughts,' which the psychoanalyst Wilfred Bion called beta elements [6.5].

The executive network is not the ego either – it doesn't 'do' time perception, as you can see when you concentrate on anything creative and lose track of time in a flow state [10.7]. So making executive decisions is not like having a guy in a suit sat behind a big desk in our frontal lobe – it's far more like an improvisational contemporary dance company.

### 5.2.4 Default mode network

Like the other networks this never, ever works on its own (Davey, Pujol, and Harrison, 2016). One part, the medial prefrontal cortex (mPFC), re-organises and consolidates memory, and helps direct attention. It's concerned with the control of slow-wave sleep. This is when memories transfer from the hippocampus into long-term storage. And the mPFC wears out as we age. This is why older people can't remember what happened today but can remember childhood events which were attached to big feelings as if they happened yesterday.

The posterior cingulate cortex (PCC) is the back of the upper part of the limbic lobe. It communicates with almost every neural network and has a key role in awareness, alertness, and attention, especially to pain or painful experiences. It's essential to memory – particularly spatial memories, autobiography, and what matters most to us. This is where memory and emotion interface. If an event has no emotional meaning, we're not going to remember it for long. The PCC uses the most fuel (glucose) of any part of the brain and as much whilst we're asleep as awake.

The angular gyrus (AG) adds words to pictures; it is vital for understanding speech and making symbols. It is essential for memory retrieval – and making a theory of mind. This means being able to recognise other people have minds just like ours. It's essential for empathy and social awareness (Yeshurun, Nguyen, & Hasson, 2021).

The default mode network puts a narrative to the sensations which begin dreams (Domhoff, 2011; Domhoff and Fox, 2015). We tell ourselves stories all the time, and we free-associate much of the time (daydream). So when analysts ask for free association to amplify dreams, we're asking people to use the same part of the mind which made the dreams. This is why Freud's technique works (Castellet y Ballarà, Spadazzi, & Spagnolo, R. 2023; Zellner, 2013).

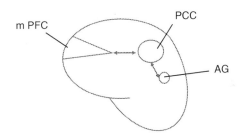

*Figure 5.5* The default mode network

| The Default Mode Network | STORYTELLING | |
|---|---|---|
| | Medial prefrontal cortex (mPFC) | re-organises and consolidates memory |
| | Posterior cingulate cortex (PCC) | where memory and emotion meet |
| | Angular gyrus (AG) | adds words to images, makes symbols, empathy |

### 5.2.5 *What happens if the default mode network doesn't develop or is damaged?*

The three networks are hardly even sketched out when we're born. In normal circumstances, they grow through childhood. This is why we are so emotionally vulnerable when we're small – we don't have 'the emotional suspension system' which they provide. And we don't have experience, memory, or a sense of time either. We can only be in the present moment. Until we're about 5 years old, if it feels bad now, it *was always* bad and *will always be* bad. This is the downside of 'present-moment awareness.' Gradually, as the default mode network develops, we acquire empathy with ourselves and with others.

But in some developmental problems, the default mode network does not grow properly. There are many different reasons. One neurodiverse group are called 'autistic spectrum disorder' – ranging in severity from disorders which make independent life impossible to those that create social awkwardness. Another group includes attention deficit disorders (ADHD) and the dyslexias. Each of these can occur separately or together. They share a tendency to get 'locked on' to an idea or an emotion. It's not yet certain if obsessive-compulsive disorder (OCD) is part of 'the spectrum,' but it does look as if the default mode network has got 'stuck.' It goes on repeating anxiety-making stories as if it is driven by the amygdala (fear) rather than being able to drive itself (Gonçalves, Soares, Carvalho, et al. 2017).

The default mode network creates and evolves our theory of mind so we can understand others by imagining their mental states, recognising and accepting that their beliefs, desires, intentions, emotions, and thoughts may be different from our own.

This is essential for relating, and, whilst it may be less developed in some autistic states, sometimes it is far, far more sensitive. So relating becomes acutely painful. Neurodiverse people may not understand why 'normal' people don't get things which are obvious to them – and vice versa. Neither are right or wrong; they're different.

---

**Box 5.2    Problems in the default mode network**

- ADHD
- Autistic states
- Obsession
- Bipolar disorder

Psychoanalysts speak about 'autistic' states in neurotic adults (complexes), where part of the mind is walled off and/or fails to mature (Fordham, 1976, pp. 77–96, and see 'Alan,' pp. 188–256). The symptoms may be similar to (neurological) autism, but the cause is severe emotional stress (Tustin, 1981, pp. 3–13, and pp. 67–77). Such complexes can sometimes open up with patient-intensive work [7.3].

The three network model is a present-day best guess at how our minds work. They have a crucial role in the formation and subsequent use of dreams. This will be out of date eventually, but it is nearer to 'how it is' than the models made by Freud and Jung, who didn't have the technology – though, as you'll see in the next chapter, they made very good guesses.

## KEY CONCEPTS

- Sleep, dreams, and consciousness arise from the interplay between conscious and unconscious minds
- They are put together by the three networks which bridge between the cortex and the limbic system

### The three networks

- The salience network          Risk assessment
- The executive network        Focussed attention
- The default mode network   Storytelling

## FURTHER READING

Robb, A. (2018) *Why we dream*, London: Picador.
Walker, M. (2017) *Why we sleep*, London: Penguin.

## REFERENCES

Castellet y Ballarà, F., Spadazzi, C., & Spagnolo, R. (2023) 'A neuropsychodynamic view of dreaming,' *Neuropsychoanalysis*, 25 (1): 17–26.

Davey, C.G., Pujol, J., Harrison, B. J. (2016) 'Mapping the self in the brain's default mode network' *Neuroimage*, 132: 390–397.

Domhoff, G. W. (2011) 'The neural substrate for dreaming: is it a subsystem of the default network?' *Conscious Cogn*. Dec: 20 (4): 1163–74. doi: 10.1016/j.concog.2011.03.001. Epub 2011 Mar 29. PMID: 21450492.

Domhoff, G. W., Fox, K.C.R. (2015) 'Dreaming and the default network: A review, synthesis, and counterintuitive research proposal' *Consciousness Cogn.* 33: 342–353.

Fordham, M. (1976) *The self and autism*, London: Library of Analytical Psychology vol. 3, Heinemann.

Gonçalves, Ó., Soares, J., Carvalho, S. et al. (2017) 'Patterns of Default Mode Network Deactivation in Obsessive Compulsive Disorder.' *Sci Rep* **7**: 44468. https://doi.org/10.1038/srep44468

Karahanoğlu, F. I., Van De Ville, D. (2017) 'Dynamics of large-scale fMRI networks: Deconstruct brain activity to build better models of brain function' *Current Opinion in Biomedical Engineering*, 3: 28–36.

Littlehales, N. (2016) *Sleep*, London: Penguin.

McGilchrist, I. (2009) *The master and his emissary*, London: Yale University Press.

Selemon, L., Zecevic, N. (2015) 'Schizophrenia: a tale of two critical periods for prefrontal cortical development' *Transl. Psychiatry* **5**: e623. https://doi.org/10.1038/tp.2015.115

Springer, S.P., Deutsch, G. (2001: fifth edition) *Left brain, right brain; perspectives from cognitive neuroscience*, London: W.H. Freeman and Co.

Solms, M. (2016) *The neuropsychology of dreams*, London: Routledge

Tustin, F. (1981) *Autistic states in children*, London: Routledge, and Kegan Paul.

Van Sant, G. (1991), *My own private Idaho*, Los Angeles: New Line Cinema (a division of Warner Brothers).

Yeshurun, Y., Nguyen, M. & Hasson, U. (2021) 'The default mode network: where the idiosyncratic self meets the shared social world.' *Nat Rev Neurosci* 22: 181–192. https://doi.org/10.1038/s41583-020-00420-w

Zellner, M. (2013) 'Dreaming and the Default Mode Network: Some Psychoanalytic Notes.' *Contemp. Psychoanal.*, 49(2):226–232.

# DEPTH PSYCHOLOGY AND DREAMING

## 6.1 WHAT IS DEPTH PSYCHOLOGY?

Freud said, "Dreams are the royal road to knowledge of the unconscious mind." Psychoanalysis is founded on the view that unconscious conflicts are responsible for many mental disorders. Therefore analysts are interested in dreams, and patients often oblige by reporting them. Analysis helps people discover how to interpret dreams themselves. It's not a new art. It's been practised for tens of thousands of years by shamans, priests, fortune tellers, and other go-betweens between people and the spirit world. In the West, a gradual separation of the spiritual and the scientific began during the seventeenth century. Interest in dreams, mysticism, and divination ended up in the category 'occult,' not a proper concern of 'true scientists.' This matters in the story about what analysis brings to dreams because Western culture made a split between 'true science' (materialist) and 'mysticism' (spiritual).

Q: Do you think they are separable? How would you explain your view to someone with the opposite view?

Analysis means to study a thing by examining its parts: first observe, then reflect. The word is now used as a name for the 'talking cure' (it's the listening cure, really). There are two main approaches – psychoanalysis, which follows Freud, and analytical psychology, which follows Jung. Neither discovered the unconscious. That's like saying, 'Columbus discovered America,' which was inhabited at least 25,000 years earlier. Both men 'self-analysed.' They remembered their

DOI: 10.4324/9781003319696-6

dreams and explored their meanings. Freud wrote about this in *The Interpretation of Dreams* (1900) and Jung in *The Red Book* (between 1913 and 1930, published in 2009). By twenty-first-century standards, neither had any analysis – they couldn't, because there were no analysts. But both shared dreams with one another on an ocean voyage to the USA. Jung felt that Freud held back. It wasn't a success.

Stories disagree about their conflicted relationship, beginning with idealisation and ending in bitterness. There are tales of 'irreconcilable theoretical differences about Freud's sexual theory' or about personality clashes: according to Jung's biographer, Deirde Bair, 'Freud was a prima donna, Jung was arrogant' (Bair, 2003, pp. 201–254). Also, Jung fell in love with his young Russian patient, Sabina Speilrein, and had supervision from Freud, who told him this was a bad idea. She later became one of the first female psychoanalysts and a pioneer of child analysis.

A natural tendency to follow, and then venerate 'the great leader' can cause unquestioning acceptance of them as folk heroes for their respective tribes. This gets in the way of understanding what they and their disciples created. Depth psychology is the common ground for analytic theory. The pioneers gave us tools rather than 'scientific truths' – basic ideas about how minds work and how people relate. Here I'll consider their theories, the assumptions behind them, and their respective cultural contexts.

As discussed in Chapter 8 [see 8.4], dream states happen both whilst awake and asleep. We create our sense perceptions from expectations (Barrett, 2021). We do not – probably cannot – see things as they 'really' are.

Practice creates expectations and skills. For example, in professional tennis, the ball moves so fast that hitting it would be impossible if the players didn't already have their racquets ready – before the ball is served. Amateur players can't predict so well. This same is true for a professional musician's finger memory. Awake, we move rapidly between conscious attending and unconscious reflection – using our default mode network [5.5.4]. During sleep, this helps build dreams – which may be unexpected and bizarre. Awake, we tend to interpret events along the lines of what we expect. For example, if your tribe believes that *they* (no matter who) are 'the enemy,' then *they* are the enemy, like fans of a rival sports team, regardless of annoying things like facts. This is called prejudice.

A continual interplay between material and spiritual truths shapes religions, cultures, and politics. It also shapes dreams and what we do or refuse to do with them. Were consciousness a surfboard and the unconscious an ocean, no surfer would ever imagine they could control the ocean. Why should anyone wish to? Surfers read the wave, tide, current, and wind, and they ride the board for fun. Analysis is not about controlling the unconscious; it is about listening to it and about experimentation. And it is not about 'helping people' – a common misconception – it's about giving people space and time in which to learn to help themselves.

To give you a sense of what dreams bring to analysis and analysis to dreams, I need to sketch what happens. Two people meet in the same consulting room for 50 minutes between one and five times per week for a fee. They continue as long as they wish – often for years. As with learning any skill, there is always more to learn. The process does not 'end'; patients go on by themselves after they stop seeing their analysts. Analysis brings back a sense of wonder. The result is usually that life becomes more playful, and we may rediscover 'beginner's mind,' a concept from Zen Buddhism. A beginner sees with curiosity, clarity, and wonder – whereas 'the master' might go, 'Ho hum, I've seen this so many times' (this attitude is a common cause of traffic accidents). We have space in which to become more childlike and less childish. I joked with my analyst as we stopped meeting, 'The change between before and after analysis is about a tenth of a second,' enough time to reflect rather than react. When driving, a tenth of a second can make the difference between living and dying.

Like therapy and counselling, the space is confidential and ethically boundaried. Unlike them, there is no agenda, nothing to achieve. No success. No failure. No goal. This is different from Western achievement-oriented culture. Both the patient and the analyst observe strange effects at boundaries – whether we are punctual or unpunctual; how we attach and separate; our body language, feelings and thoughts, appearance, and behaviour; the stories we tell and the secrets we keep. Both people look for stuck patterns in relating. 'Healing' is a natural by-product of this free-floating attention. It happens by seeing how old patterns replay in the analytic relationship. This is called transference [7.2]. In analysis, transference is a regular subject of our dreams.

## 6.2 ORIGINS

Depth psychology did not spring fully formed from Freud's head. Other pioneers include physicians Jean-Martin Charcot (1825–1993) and Pierre Janet (1859–1947) in France, and the psychologist and philosopher William James (1842–1910) in America. Henri Ellenberger describes their contributions in his book *The Discovery of the Unconscious* (1970, pp. 331–417). Eugen Bleuler (1857–1939), coined the term 'depth psychology,' and directed the Burghölzli, now called the Psychiatric University Hospital of Zurich. He and Jung, his assistant director, were the first to map differences between schizophrenia (then called dementia praecox) and bipolar affective disorder (then called manic depression). It made them world famous. In these severe mental illnesses, it is difficult or impossible for sufferers to distinguish between what is probably real and what probably is not.

Many philosophers have wondered about what was real and what a dream might be [5.7]. It's a moral question because if life's a dream – an illusion – are we responsible for our actions or not?

Pedro Calderón de la Barca (1600–1681), the Spanish playwright, wrote about this conundrum in his play *Life's a Dream* in 1638 (2006). A king, afraid that his son will become a murdering monster, imprisons him. The first time the lad is let out, he kills. Back in jail, the jailer says – 'It was all a dream. You were here all the time!' 'What do I do now?' asks the puzzled young prince. 'How do I know what's real or what isn't?' The jailer says, 'Act as if it is all real!' So, are we responsible *in* our dreams? Are we responsible *for* them? Can dreams answer moral questions? What are they *for?* In his 1914 book 'On Dreams,' the French philosopher Henri Bergson (1859–1941) suggested they have five main functions [Box 6.1].

---

**Box 6.1   Five functions of dreams by Henri Bergson**

- Vigilance – making up stories from sense perceptions during sleep
  - And so they are 'guardians of sleep'
- Hold and contain day residues
- Link to deep memory
- Predict
  - Rehearse for the next day, make long-term plans, and, sometimes, see into the future
- Socially engage – link us to the collective

Contemporary neuroscience shows his ideas are largely correct. Jung borrowed them all; Freud borrowed the first three. It isn't yet possible to 'prove' theories in depth psychology with neuroscience – though, amongst others, the South African psychoanalyst and neuroscientist Mark Solms has begun (2021, pp. 215–48) [5.3.1]. To move forward, we have to go back, so let's look at what 'the old masters' said. If you find yourself strongly agreeing or disagreeing, be curious about what feeling has appeared and where it came from. Their ideas are challenging.

## 6.3 FREUD AND PSYCHOANALYSIS

Sigmund Freud's (1856–1939) theories contain profound insights into the unconscious. He was a gifted neurologist. His animal research aided the discovery of how neurons and neural networks work. Educated in Vienna, the capital of the Austro-Hungarian Empire, he was a small, introverted man with a wicked sense of humour – and Jewish in an institutionally antisemitic empire. All his life, he struggled with racism, eventually fleeing to London in 1938 to escape Nazi persecution. Survival required cultural and political cunning.

He was highly defensive of his ideas and cultivated loyal followers. He imagined Jung would be his 'crown prince' – it seemed to him useful to have a world-famous Gentile colleague.

Like any nineteenth-century neurologist, Freud treated a condition then called 'hysteria.' It has other names now, including functional neurological disorder. Real symptoms (weakness, paralysis, loss of sensation) cause genuine suffering and distress, but the symptom patterns do not fit biomedical models of what an illness 'ought' to be. 'Hysteros' is Greek for uterus. The diagnosis is given far more commonly to women than men. To this day, women are diagnosed with mental illness far more than men. All Western doctors in the nineteenth century were men: it was a patriarchal world, and it still is. Then, as now, many doctors regard illnesses as either physical or mental. But most are both: a combination of the physical and psychological.

Freud found if he asked his patients with hysteria to lie on a couch and relax, gently pressed on their foreheads (a way to begin a hypnotic trance), and then asked them to say the first things which came to mind (free-associate), powerful stories of trauma emerged: childhood neglect, abuse (physical, mental, sexual); unfulfilled love; and

---

### Box 6.2   Primary and secondary process thinking

- **Primary process**: makes a mental image to satisfy a desire for something or someone. If you want to have sex but don't have a partner, you might visualise one in a dream.
- **Secondary process**: works with the image, reflects on it, and uses it: 'day-to-day' mental activity.

---

unbearable loss. Free association bypassed conscious defences against recalling disturbing, traumatic, and socially unacceptable experiences. His (mostly young, female) patients also brought dreams. When they did, he used the same technique – 'Say whatever comes into your mind.' Through this, he recognised two different kinds of thinking [Box 6.2].

Freud suggested that dreams have two linked functions, the first being to express repressed wishes (often from childhood, often sexual) in an acceptable form. The other is to guard sleep. His view was that our minds have a censor, like the Austrian Empire. The censor hides unacceptable wishes, subtly changing them into symbols. He supposed there were 'standard symbols' – as in 'a thing is a phallic symbol (a penis) if it's longer than it's wide,' whilst any container is a womb. But, for many people, this is reducing symbols (open meaning systems) to signs (closed meaning systems) – and it is a difference between Freud and Jung. Freud is credited with having said, 'A cigar is sometimes just a cigar.' And Jung, 'The penis? It's just a phallic symbol.'

Repressed wishes come from drives – basic desires, seeking fulfilment. Freud envisioned the unconscious as having layers, structures, and a hierarchy which might mirror the imperial and imperious culture of his formative years. The id – the often unconscious peasant within us – is our drives and instincts. The ego (Latin for 'I') is the nobleman who is in command, whilst the superego is 'judge and jury,' which approximates to the conscience. This is sometimes called Freud's 'hydraulic theory,' as it is about pressure, or his 'economic theory,' as it is about the supply and demand of emotional energy (which he called libido).

Dreams have a *manifest content*: the image (a cigar) and a *latent content* (an erect penis). The latent content is 'the true meaning' which your analyst can point out. His work *The Interpretation of Dreams* (1900) outlines the method – he looked at the foundations of dreams using his own. Dreams are built on 'day residues,' fragments of waking life. They draw on bodily sensations, particularly childhood experiences, which have created long-standing patterns of problematic relating. If your parents abuse you, how do you ever learn to trust? Whom can you trust? Can you even trust yourself?

Such problems reappear between patient and analyst in *transference* – patients transfer earlier experiences and expectations onto the analyst [Figures 7.1 and 7.2]. This happens by projection. A simple example: if you were badly bitten by a dog when a child, then you may project (imagine, expect) all dogs will bite. Dogs sense your fear and then may growl, confirming your view. If you were terrified by your parents, you may imagine all authority figures are terrifying and become either overcompliant or rebellious – or both at the same time.

Analysts may also project their own inner conflicts onto their patients in *countertransference*. Patterns of projection shape dreams. Our dream-making minds use four main tricks to bypass the censor [Box 6.3]:

---

**Box 6.3   How to 'get past the censor'**

- Condensation
  - A symbol means lots of things at the same time
  - (Cigar = penis = father = analyst)
- Displacement
  - Forbidden thoughts or feelings about one person are transferred to another
  - (I can't hate my father = analyst; instead, I dream of an angry bull)
- Clarifying
  - The symbols arrange themselves into stories
  - (The old bull is chased by a dog)
- Revision
  - Internal editing
  - (Father had brown hair, so it's a brown bull)

---

We see these tricks in many dreams. Try finding them in one of your own. It's a pattern recognition task. You may find that certain patterns repeat. What are they? Be curious; use 'free-floating attention.' You don't need to 'do' anything with what you find. Notice

---

**Box 6.4  Common criticisms**

- Emphasis on infantile wishes rather than other causes
- Anecdotal evidence is not scientific: based on 'stories' not hypothesis testing
- Minimises the meaning of the manifest content
- Dreams don't always protect sleep (nightmares wake us up)
- Formulaic interpretations ('It's your Oedipus complex'; 'it's your mother')
- Dreams can be the opposite of censored – if they're intensely erotic
- The theory is neither testable nor falsifiable

---

how hard it is not to be drawn into making judgements – or to have preconceptions. Being surprised and accepting what dreams say takes a 'beginner's mind.' Freud had this and, in the original German, his writings are very funny. He knew how dreams talk in puns, slips of the tongue, and plays on words, like the dream about the 'cagey bee' – KGB [2.9]. Freud's insights had a culture-changing impact, provoking both fierce loyalty and deep scepticism [Box 6.4]: on moralistic grounds (dreams can't 'all be about sex') and on scientific grounds.

Q:  Which of these criticisms seem important to you? Do you mind if something isn't 'scientific?' Would you mind if it were not 'artistic?'

Science has no monopoly on reality testing, nor do religion or politics. Dreams question any 'imposed truths.' Freud asked fine questions and encouraged his followers to ask finer ones. He introduced free association as a means of exploring dreams. He showed how dreams reflect on past experiences and reshape memory [Chapter 4]. For him, dreams are wish fulfilments. They take unconscious thoughts, feelings, and desires and transform them into less threatening forms, reducing conscious anxiety. Doing this when we're awake is called fantasy thinking – for example, when we imagine triumphing over people we dislike. Anxiety management is a necessary, but not sufficient, explanation of why we dream.

## 6.4 JUNG AND ANALYTICAL PSYCHOLOGY

Carl Jung (1875–1961) was Swiss, a doctor, an experimental psychologist, and a psychiatrist. He was six feet six inches tall, a noisy extravert (with a strong introverted side), a giant with a huge laugh. He invented the terms introvert and extravert. His father was a Lutheran minister who lost his faith. His mother, who suffered from depression, was interested in spiritualism and the occult. Jung's pioneering use of the word association test, an early psychological tool, brought him international fame. In it, the subject is given a list of stimulus words; the experimenter measures the time it takes to free-associate to this word and monitors physiological changes (like heart rate and blood pressure). The longer the time delay, the more likely it is that the stimulus word is associated with a complex – a hidden feeling or idea. This is how lie detectors work.

When Jung was in his 30s and Freud in his 50s, they wrote, met, talked all night, and became friends. Both accepted the unconscious is real – Jung had shown this with the word association test. But he could neither agree with Freud's ideas about sexual repression nor that psychoanalysis was 'a theory of everything.' Jung wasn't worried about what Freud called 'the black mud of occultism' (spiritualism) and wrote his MD thesis about his cousin Helene Preiswerk, a trance medium. He saw dreams as multifunctional, giving access to the spirit world (the paranormal) and the future. They argued, and shortly after Jung told Freud that he had fallen in love with his patient, Sabina Speilrein, they split.

Jung's model of the mind, like Freud's, has layers: consciousness, the personal unconscious, and the collective unconscious. There is no equivalent to 'the id' or 'the superego.' The unconscious makes dreams – writes the scripts; hires the actors, backstage crew, and director; and is the audience. Jung maintained that dreams compensate for the conscious attitude. If you believe you're worth nothing, you'll dream of being royalty – and vice versa – another purpose of dreams is to restore psychological balance. The deepest dreams use archetypal images drawn from the collective unconscious [Box 3.1] to personify drives and desires. There is no censor.

Dreams recreate the past and can describe the future – and they can get both wrong. Like Bergson, Jung thought dreams occurred in a 'time-free' space, neither past nor future, both past and future.

Freud saw dreams as neurotic – he was a neurologist treating neurotic people. Neurosis is a state of anxiety caused by repressed past trauma. Jung saw dreams as healthy: he was a psychiatrist treating psychotic people. Psychosis means 'completely out of touch with reality.'

An old name for schizophrenia was oneirophrenia – 'dream minded.' In a way, we all become psychotic every night because our reality testing (ego function) is suspended. And in many dreams, *they* (the monsters, the real and unknown enemies) are out to get the dreamer: this is paranoia. The word comes from the Greek 'para,' *beside*, and 'noios,' *self*. So, in dreams, we can try out being paranoid in a safe place. When we awake, if we recall the dream, we can consider if these fears have a basis in reality. Are 'they' really out to get us?

Jung's research into alchemy provided symbols for psychological processes. Searching for gold, or the philosopher's stone, is a metaphor for individuation – a lifelong process of becoming ourselves. In *The Red Book* (2009, p. 229), there's an argument between 'the Spirit of the Times' – time-bound, materialist, scientific – and 'the Spirit of the Depths' – time-free, soul-based, spiritual. Jung explores boundaries between two ways of experiencing time and understanding the world. It's pluralistic, holding and valuing two opposed views at the same time. Being able to hold opposites in one's mind is also called ambivalence. It is a sign of mental health.

Jung introduced two techniques: amplification and active imagination. In the first, take any symbol in your dream and connect it to myths, legends, and fairytales; to your culture, art, dance, theatre, literature, music, film; or to the political, religious, and spiritual. We might talk about St George and the dragon if you dream of a dragon. Using active imagination, you could *be* the dragon, the princess, or the knight [10.5]. Freud and Jung were pioneers who found language to talk about unconscious processes. Their two languages *almost* translate into the other.

Q:  Which do you prefer? What shapes your choice?

As a Jungian analyst, I'm biased – but I could not have practised analysis without the insights of Freud and his successors – particularly those from British object relations theory. There isn't space to tell you about them all. I've chosen those I know best, use every day, and whose ideas about dreams I find helpful.

## 6.5 FREUD'S SUCCESSORS – OBJECT RELATIONS THEORY

From psychoanalysis came object relations theory. A problem with the name is our immediate reaction is to object to the word 'object.' It's a grammatical term. When speaking about ourselves, we are 'the subject,' and everyone else is 'the object.' In pool and snooker, the white ball is 'the subject ball,' and the ball it is aimed at is 'the object ball.' An internal object is an internal symbol. Mother is both a real person out there – an external object – and a mental image 'in here' – an internal object.

We begin making internal objects before we are born – the rhythm of mum's heart, the touch of the uterus. The next objects we meet are her body, her smell, and her breasts. At first, we see a breast as a thing to meet our needs rather than a part of mother. Gradually, we discover mother is a whole person. Newborn infants can tell their mothers by the smell of their milk within hours. It takes days till a newborn's eyes can focus on her face – and months to discover her feelings are not the same as their feelings. Object relations theory is developmental. It says these earliest experiences shape personality and self.

Melanie Klein (1892–1960) came to London from Berlin via Budapest and Vienna. She analysed young children, suggesting pre-verbal anxiety (about attachment and separation from mother) caused splitting. There is a 'good breast' (mother who meets my needs) and a 'bad breast' (mother who doesn't). An infant doesn't know this is one and the same mother. Along with denial and projective identification, splitting is one of the three primitive defences of the self. Denial is – 'what climate change? There isn't any!' – when there obviously is. Projective identification is unconsciously putting our bad feelings into another – who then acts it out for us. We unconsciously wind someone up, then they attack us, and then we blame them.

Infants and small children cannot do 'both/and' thinking (ambivalence). Things are *either* all good *or* all bad. Klein called this developmental stage the 'paranoid/schizoid position.' It is the basis of conspiracy theories: whatever is wrong, it has to be *their* fault. Some people don't grow out of this and remain paranoid victims all their lives. Mother not doing what we want is felt as an envious attack. She's deliberately spoilt our day. And so we attack her back. But envy also creates an awareness of twoness – without which we can't separate. So, maternal failure is essential. Sadly, in Western society, the value of failure is often forgotten. By about 18 months of age, we realise that mother can be *both* good *and* bad, and so can we. This is the 'depressive' position. We learn how subjects (me) and objects (anyone else) are *both* good *and* bad at the same time – ambivalence.

Klein said a function of dreams is to 'work through the ego's envious attacks on the self.' In our dreams, simply put, we explore how we screw up. And just as an infant has to separate from its mother, so our ego has to separate from self. Why? Because self (used here to mean all our potential) is far too big for everyday use. It would be like using a supercomputer to make a shopping list. Ego focuses on the 'here and now,' using dreams to explore possibilities.

One of Klein's colleagues, the Scots analyst Ronald Fairbairn (1889–1964), said that we are born object seeking (needing others). When the object disappoints, as it always will, we discover shame and then guilt. Accordingly, if Mum isn't perfect, then it *must be because* I'm bad (primary shame). And, if Mum isn't perfect, she's out of my control, then it *must be my fault*. If I'm guilty, then I'm responsible. If I'm responsible, then I *must be* in control. This is called 'Fairbairn's moral defence' – a move from feeling completely bad and out of control (shamed) to feeling a bit bad and guilty but in control. This wish for control regularly appears in dreams; perhaps this is what happens in lucid dreams when the dreamer appears to be able to 'take control' [8.6]. Fairbairn argues that dreams help us work through urges to have omnipotent (all-powerful) control and learn how to deal with shame and guilt.

Dreams of shame (going naked in public, doing an exam when we can't remember anything) and guilt (we failed to save Princess Diana) are common. As children, we often experience such feelings and try hard (and lie if necessary) to avoid them. Donald Winnicott (1986–1971), a London paediatrician and psychoanalyst, pointed out, 'There is no such thing as a baby.' Why? Because there's always a mum or mother figure. If not, the baby dies. No one needs 'a perfect mum,' who will expect 'a perfect child.' Both need to be 'good enough' – real rather than ideal. This gives us space to learn how to reality test (grow an ego). We play; we can 'be alone in the presence of the mother.'

Winnicott invented 'the squiggle game.' Rather than interview little children, he gave them a pencil and paper. The child made a squiggle; Winnicott added to it. They played together. He valued their reality, and when mother values our inner reality, we learn to trust our self. We're 'good enough' too. If we can't play freely enough, we make a 'false self.' We habitually lie to ourselves and others. Sometimes people do this so much they can no longer tell the difference between truth and lies. Some politicians have this problem. Winnicott saw dreams as the unconscious at play, and dreams need to be played with rather than formally interpreted. Drawing a dream is like playing the squiggle game – it's not making art, it's playing.

Born in India, Wilfred Bion (1897–1979) went to boarding school in the United Kingdom, was a genius at maths, and a heroic young tank commander in World War One. A doctor, psychiatrist, and psychoanalyst, he 'invented' group analysis to treat post-traumatic stress disorder in soldiers during the Second World War. The lads were stuck, going over the same horrific battle memories, unable to move on. As they shared experiences, they stopped feeling alone and trapped.

His insight was to recognise 'alpha elements' (fully formed thoughts) are made from 'beta elements' (pre-thoughts). Pre-thoughts condense into thoughts – and the 'three network model' now gives a neuroanatomical basis for his ideas [5.5.1.] So, when, in analysis, there is a strong negative transference (the patient hates the analyst *as if* they were a hated parent); the patient's beta elements are being projected onto *and* into the analyst. It can be painful for the analyst when they meet their target, sometimes creating strong physical sensations.

In a dream, the feelings (rage/anger/frustration) are beta elements, and 'the evil dragon' is the alpha element they become. Pre-thoughts arise in the sensory, visual, and auditory cortex and then are assembled by the three networks into a story. Bion also introduced the concept of negative capability, which he called 'O' (this means "being with not-knowing"). It is an ability not to jump to conclusions. To wait before deciding someone or something is good or bad rather than shooting first and asking questions afterwards. He called this 'the suspension of memory and desire,' which is close to the Buddhist idea of present-moment awareness: there is only here, now. In a dream, present-moment awareness is what 'no-time' feels like. Ages seem to pass, but on waking, only minutes of 'real time' have gone by. Dreaming is like being in two places at once and not anywhere at all. We're writing the film, starring in it, and watching it all at the same time.

## 6.6 JUNG'S SUCCESSORS

Those who came after Jung went off in different directions. In London, they grew closer to psychoanalysis and adopted a developmental approach. In Zurich, they went into the archetypal and the transpersonal (beyond personal).

Marie Louse von Franz (1915–1998) first met Jung when she was 18. She was a gifted classics scholar. With a special interest in myths, fairytales, and alchemical texts, her research developed the idea of the objective psyche (the collective unconscious) as a source for dream symbols in any culture at any time. She explored active imagination, a form of conscious dreaming [10.5]. She wrote over 30 books, including *Dreams* (1991), and late in life, she made the film *The Way of the Dream* (1987) – (available on YouTube) – summarising her life's work. In 1948, she was involved in the founding of the C. G. Jung Institute in Zurich, where the American writer and analyst James Hillman (1926–2011) became director of studies.

Hillman's archetypal psychology moves away from 'ego and Self' towards the idea of *psyche* (soul) as the prime mover in our lives. Each person is born with a unique path before them, a soul's journey. Dreams are an essential part of soul making, showing us segments of our Self, like a kaleidoscope. We are inside the Self's dream rather than the dream being inside us. Similarly, misfortune, illness, and emotional distress are part of the soul's journey, a poetic metaphor we live out and live through. I find this questionable. It easily slides into 'it's all your karma' (in an ungrounded way) and seems to deny the bitter reality of suffering and mental illness. (I'm a psychiatrist and biased.)

Hillman encourages people to 'stick with the image' in any dream – amplify it, but don't interpret. If you do, then you lose touch with what the image could tell you. His book *The Soul's Code: In Search of Character and Calling* (1997) amplifies and expands his ideas. This is the 'transcendent' end of the Jungian family.

London analyst Michael Fordham (1905–1995) stands at the other pole, the developmental end. As a child psychiatrist, he agreed dreams are part of the individuation process. An infant's self gradually 'unpacks' (unzips) and opens (de-integrates) to take in the world, and then closes (re-integrates) to digest experiences and join them together. Dreams are essential for both processes (Fordham 1985, pp. 50–64). This is the 'immanent' end of the family. Immanence means being with the here and now.

His colleague Rosemary Gordon (1918–2012) introduced the metaphor of the bridge – dreams are an archetypal connection linking the conscious to the unconscious. They are made of symbols which join the inner and outer worlds (Gordon, 1993, pp. 69–85). Andrew Samuels (1949–), from London, suggests there is a political aspect to dreaming, as it is through political action that we become linked to the collective consciousness (1993). The inner and outer worlds mutually and continually interact. The one can't have meaning without the other.

## 6.7 HOW DO WE USE THESE IDEAS?

What happens when a patient brings a dream? A common misconception is that you consult your analyst, tell them a dream, and they give you an interpretation. This explains the dream and how it links past to present through the transference – and links you to others around you. A disadvantage of this is the analyst either gets idealised, denigrated, or turned into 'a wise old guru.' It takes away the chance for you to make your own interpretation.

An analyst will often ask what you felt in the dream, about the dream, before and after the dream. So, we link it to an unfolding feeling process – the context – before we discuss the content. And we link it to the feelings in the space between us – what is this dream doing in this session, here and now? Has it waited a week to get here? Is it fresh from the night before? Then most of us will explore it using free associations and link it to the preceding sequence of dreams.

For example, early in analysis, I had a sequence of dreams about South Africa – a country I have never visited. As a little child, my parents regularly had South African refugees stay with us – members of anti-apartheid groups fleeing political persecution. So, the dreams linked an early experience of envy. These strangers got more attention than me! This linked to splitting (black and white), paranoid ideas (they used my bed), and denial – I couldn't say I resented them. And this reflected how I felt about my parents and my analyst. They 'knew best,' which meant I didn't know anything. Dreams brought this to consciousness, and this helped heal a split.

## 6.8 SUMMARY

The two sides of depth psychology are like different toolkits – we can choose which one is the best for the job. We can go back to early experiences in dreams, out to the political world, or deeper into the collective unconscious. It depends on what feels right for the dreamer.

Q: How do you feel about these ideas? This matters as much as what you think about them. How would you 'prove' the truth of either theory [see Chapter 2 for a clue]

Depth psychology offers a holistic way to look at dreams. They are an ecosystem rather than a riddle to be solved. The 'riddle' notion comes from a serial model of information processing, whereas dreams use parallel processing. There isn't 'a centre of consciousness' to which information is presented and which then makes an 'executive' decision – a feudal model. Our mind is not like a court, with courtiers and a king – it's a disorderly democratic parliament, with multiple voices all shouting at once, an anarchy rather than a dictatorship. Why is it like this? Because dictatorships, like dictators, adapt so poorly to change. Self isn't a dictator: it's an anarchy. Dreams are anarchic.

## KEY POINTS

• Dreams are symbolic communications from the unconscious.
• Free association, active imagination, and guided imagery explore possible meanings the symbols may have.

## FURTHER READING

Ellenberger, H. (1970) *The discovery of the unconscious*, New York: Basic Books.
Freud, S. (trans., Strachey J.) 1900–1954, *The interpretation of dreams*, London: George Allen & Unwin.

## REFERENCES

Bair, D. (2003) *Jung, a biography*, Boston, and London: Little, Brown & Co.
Bergson, H. (1914–2023) *Dreams*, Chicago: Lushena Books.
Calderón de la Barca, P. (trans. Racz, G.) (2006) *Life's a dream*, London: Penguin Classics.
Barrett, L.F. (2021) *Seven and a half lessons about the brain*, London: Picador.
Fordham, M. (1985) *Explorations into the self*, London: Academic Press.
Gordon, R. (1993) *Bridges: Metaphor for psychic processes*, London: Karnac.
Jung, C.G. (2009) *The red book*, London, Norton.

Hillman, J. (1997) *The soul's code: In search of character and calling*, London: Bantam books.

Samuels, A. (1993) *The political psyche*, London: Routledge.

Solms, M. (2021) *The neuropsychology of dreams*, London: The Psychology Press.

Von Franz, M.-L. (1991) *Dreams*, Boston USA: Shambhala.

## FOR FURTHER INTEREST

For a detailed criticism of Freud's theories, see Binswanger, R., Wittmann, L., (2019) 'Reconsidering Freud's dream theory,' *Int. J. Dream Research 12*(1), 103–111.

# DREAMS AND THERAPY

## 7.1 CREATIVELY LISTENING TO DREAMS

We don't learn much about how to care for our mental health at school or college, yet one in four people in the Western world will have a problem with this during their lives. It could be after a stressful event, as part of a mental illness, or both. Often, people seeking help don't know where to start or recognise when they've found what they need or what a therapeutic relationship may bring. These things are not an everyday part of our culture. A common idea, especially for those in analysis, is that dreams matter. But as they usually vanish within minutes of waking, only a small percentage could ever be discussed with anyone, including ourselves. This chapter looks at what may happen if a dream makes it into therapy to help you listen creatively to your dreams yourself. It is a free, traditional, and natural way to care for your mental health.

In Chapter 1, I discuss dreams as a bridge between conscious and unconscious. Analytical psychologists call this 'the Ego–Self axis' (Edinger, 1962). Other therapists have different names: in psycho-synthesis [7.4.3], it's called 'the Will' – the part of the mind which makes choices. But therapists' descriptions of the mind are quite like medieval alchemy. We don't know; we're making 'best guesses.' Neuroscience does not map accurately onto analytic or therapeutic concepts – maybe it never can. Maybe it wouldn't help. Mapping a car engine doesn't teach you how to drive a car. It does help you not to imagine a car will do things it can't.

Rather than see the different theoretical models therapists use as competing with neuroscience or each other, see them as different

DOI: 10.4324/9781003319696-7

toolboxes useful for different tasks. I can't discuss them all, so I'll write about those I use clinically. But first, a brief explanation about the three modes of 'listening professions': counselling, therapy, and analysis: as this often causes confusion.

It is not true that one mode is better than another. 'Better' depends on what's appropriate and what's available. When life is hard, we may need to retell our story. In a safe setting, we make a 'director's cut.' It's no longer 'his-story,' 'her-story,' or 'their-story' – living out our family myth of being 'the troubled kid' (or whatever). It becomes 'my story.' Now, dreams retell our stories several times each night, linking past to present and to possible futures. This natural process is a foundation for conscious change. Does change depend on consciously remembering dreams [10.2]? No. Change happens anyway. It probably happens more easily if we consciously reflect on unconscious processes, but this has never been 'scientifically' proven.

Q:   What experiment could you design to show this?

Counsellors, therapists, and analysts aim to 'be with' the dream and the dreamer – together finding meanings related to the dreamer and their context. It's never 'mighty therapist gives humble patient' a change-making interpretation; after which, like a silent movie heroine tied to the railroad track, 'with one bound, they are free.' It's like learning to play music. It depends on what you want to play and in what style. We need space and time to learn to understand ourselves by ourselves. In all these different approaches, therapists model how to creatively listen so their patients can do the same. And this is how to be with dreams by creatively listening to them.

Therapists have purposes, intentions, motivations, and plans. The differences between the three modes relate to the size of the field and the size of the goal: to space, time, and expectations. Having done all three, counselling is by far the hardest. It's a sprint. Therapy is a marathon. Analysis is a trek in the mountains – the only goal is to be there.

Counsellors have a short time to assess a problem and find solutions together with their clients. A student with exam anxiety (and an exam tomorrow) needs a different approach than a student with an exam next week, next month, or next year. Counsellors ask questions and make suggestions (analysts try not to.) Time is often limited by economics: who pays? Is it a family member, an institution (work, school, or university), a health-care provider, or an insurer?

Usually, dreams hardly appear: there isn't space or time. When they do, they may give a 'one-stop' answer. I was talking to a friend's son, 'Will,' a fit young man in trackie bottoms and a tank top. He'd come home straight from the gym. Will worried he wasn't studying well, had his 'A levels' (final school exams) starting next week, and told me this dream:

### The bodybuilder's tutu dream

*I'm in the gym doing serious bench presses. I realise I'm only wearing a pink tutu.*

We both laughed. Will grinned, then grew serious and said, 'So, maybe I need to be more in touch with my feminine side, huh?' I answered, 'Well, maybe studying isn't about bench pressing the books. Could you be less serious? What if learning is like dancing? Do you like dancing?' He loved dancing. And he told me later that he'd passed all his exams, much to his surprise. Once he'd relaxed and saw studying as a dance rather than a competition, it was easy. He solved an immediate problem by giving his dream time to expand.

An old joke says, 'Therapy is what happens when there are two people in a room, and both get help.' Therapy happens once or twice a week for a few years. The theories derive from, and add to, analytic approaches. There is usually a 'request' – a 'something' which needs to be done. Therapists explore a problem's origin, looking for repeating patterns of unhappy relations as they reappear in the client's relationship with them. This is called transference, discussed in the next section. It shapes dreams in therapy – and anywhere else. Clients are helped to find their own answers or to accept that there aren't any, and the problem has to be lived with – as in bereavement.

Analysis happens three, four, or five times a week for years and years. There is time enough for dreams. It is about being, not doing. Presenting problems usually resolve anyway. I began analysis scared of dogs because I was bitten by a collie as a small child. I had long blond hair; he mistook me for a sheep. I had nightmares about dogs for years. After analysis, I was playing with my brother's collie and then I remembered I'd been afraid long ago. At some point, I'd completely forgotten.

Should you be looking for help, ask your friends or your family doctor, or check out the websites of counselling, therapy, or analytic groups. Be sure whoever you see is properly qualified and professionally registered. And trust your feelings. The emotional match between the two people is far more important than the 'theory.'

## 7.2 TRANSFERENCE AND COUNTERTRANSFERENCE

In Chapter 6 [6.1] I introduce the concept of transference and its companion, countertransference. Freud and Jung developed their techniques around them. They are foundational to how listening professions work – and to understanding what is going on in dreams. Therapies work because people project (unconsciously imagine) their inner world and past experiences onto the therapist and significant people in their here-and-now world. We use this predictive projection with anyone and everyone. In dreams, we are projecting onto our inner world. This uses the default mode network [5.3.1, 5.5.4].

We project our inner cinema onto the outer world and see what we expect rather than what is there – and we take our outer world inside when we dream (as day residue). Suppose when we were children, Mum/Dad often screamed at us and were violent and/or neglectful in an unpredictably unpredictable way. We never knew when we were safe. We lack inner security and can't recognise it even when we have it. We recreate this situation with friends, partners, employers, and our therapist – as in 'the footballer and the monster' dream [7.4.1]. Psychoanalyst David Malan (1979, pp. 66–67, pp. 92–94) describes transference using two triangles – the triangle of person and the triangle of conflict [Figures 7.1 and 7.2].

The triangle of person links relationships from the past (back then) to the present (out there) and to the experience with the therapist (in here). A therapist I supervise had a client who dreamed they were trapped:

#### The zombie apocalypse dream

*The Living Dead slowly stumble everywhere, dribbling blood. They want to devour me. I shelter with an old woman who sells milk and cookies, but I can't afford them.*

The patient claimed they couldn't afford therapy either and kept not paying but had a high-paying job. With help, they linked the dream to repeated childhood experiences of never being able to feed their

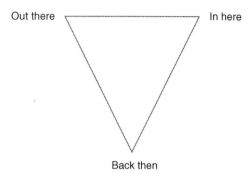

Out there — In here

Back then

*Figure 7.1* The triangle of person

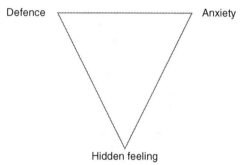

Defence — Anxiety

Hidden feeling

*Figure 7.2* The triangle of conflict

mum's devouring need for power and control, feeling controlled by girlfriends, and now by the 'greedy analyst' – another 'Zombie Mum' – (he was a man, but transferences don't trouble too much about gender.)

For this client, the anxiety that developed from the belief that the therapist would reject them (they were sure everyone else did) led to a defence – withholding payment – satisfying an unconscious wish to hurt 'Zombie Mum.' The therapist has unconscious feelings stirred up too – wishing to reject this 'rejecting patient.' This is countertransference. Anyone who chooses to be a therapist has issues of their own which they may or may not have resolved. They might seek to hide their problems of being a victim by becoming a rescuer, as shown in psychologist Stephen Karpman's drama triangle. This is about who gets to have the dominant discourse – the power to name what's going on [Figure 7.3].

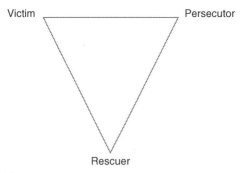

*Figure 7.3* Victim, persecutor, rescuer

This game needs three players. The idea of 'games' comes from the Canadian psychiatrist Eric Berne (1910–1970). His method is called transactional analysis. He suggests we have three main 'ego states' in our inner world: parent, adult, and child. There are transactions between these ego states in any relationship. If they match, it's fine. If I am a parent with my child, and they are a child with me – fine. Adolescence is turbulent as we move to and fro between child to adult, hoping our parents will change from parents to adults too – and meet us halfway. (Aged 50, on a cold day, my mum still made sure I put my coat on. We both laughed about it.)

But when I project my inner child's needs onto someone who imagines we are having an adult-to-adult relationship, it's not fine. In a typical version of this game – 'alcoholic' (Berne, 2016) – the drinker is the victim (child); their partner/employer/anyone in authority (parent) – is the persecutor; the barman (adult) is the rescuer. It's possible to play a 'solitaire' version using three sub-personalities.

In the *footballer and the monster dream* [7.4.] a child-self is the victim; the monster is the persecuting parent. There was no rescuing adult, so I got that role. The trick is to give it back to the dreamer. In the next dream, from an actor, try and work out who is who:

### The actor and the wolves dream

*I am in a beautiful garden. There I meet an old director, who says, 'Here are my friends.' A pack of wolves appear. I'm terrified. The director says, kindly, 'Be friends!' I realises the wolves want to be friends. They lick me. It feels good.*

The roles change. This is as common in dreams as in real life: for example, when politicians gain or lose power, they switch roles from rescuer ('Great Leader,' – *parent*) to persecutor ('tough on illegal immigrants' – *adult*) and then victim (of an 'evil witch hunt' – *child*). This pattern of politicians' behaviour was well established in Ancient Egypt, China, and India over 5,000 years ago. It's a negative aspect of the father archetype. When frightened, people want 'Big Daddy' to rescue them. They may not be too discerning in their choice. There are many contemporary examples.

And we do this in our inner world, too, when our psyche becomes dominated by a need to be 'Big Daddy' and have control. This never works – it's like King Canute trying to stop the tide coming in (Which he did to show up his flatterers.). Movement around the drama triangle illustrates what Jung called 'enantiodromia' (meaning to run around in a circle) – a concept he took from the Greek writer Heraclitus (fifth century BCE). Over time, everything turns into the opposite. And this role switching often happens in dreams, both as wish fulfilment and to compensate for our conscious attitude:

**The four analysts dream:**

*I'm in my second analyst's blue consulting room. My first analyst and two other analyst friends are there. I've told them a dream. My second analyst says, 'You interpret it, Kate.' Kate says, 'Oh, no! You do it, Peggy. He's your patient.' They argue amongst themselves till I say, 'Hey, it's my dream! Maybe I could interpret it?' – they cheer.*

I move from being a child to an adult. An aim of therapy is to know which of these three ego states we are in and whether it is appropriate. Said another way, the goal is to resolve the transferences.

## 7.3 HOW THERAPISTS WORK WITH DREAMS

Once we notice anything in our outer or inner worlds, there's a concern for its meaning – is it a threat, or is it safe? What happened last time? Which meaning will help me handle this with the least effort? Do I need to change? If we can't adapt, then we're trapped in a complex – a neural network walled off from the rest of our mind. When transference recreates a complex rather than what is actually happening, our therapist might become a 'Zombie Mum.' Some analysts call this an 'autistic barrier.' They do not mean the person has autism (a name for many learning difficulties which cause serious emotional problems) or is 'on the spectrum' (has a few autistic traits). They mean a part of the person has become so separated from the rest of their self that it has little ability to relate to others or itself – it lacks empathy (Tustin, 1981, pp. 21–33).

American psychologist Virginia Axline (1911–1988) described many years of work with a young boy, Dibs (1986), who was labelled autistic. Lost in his own world, he hardly spoke, rocked to and fro, didn't make eye contact, and couldn't play with others. Using toys and a sand tray, she gradually helped him communicate. Dibs' problem was not having a low IQ (it was 148, highly gifted) but being scared out of his wits by his parents' continual overwhelming emotional demands. He carried their Shadow. In the sand tray, he made images of his dreams and his fears, and then they could work together to build emotional defences – this is called child-centred play therapy. It is one of the most moving accounts of what working with the unconscious feels like.

From Chapter 5 [5.5.4], Dibs' default mode network, which 'does' empathy, had not connected together well enough to cope with his parent's demands. His problem, autistic encapsulation, is often seen in those who suffered extreme trauma, neglect, and/or abuse (including sexual abuse). Mindlessly cruel incidents replay endlessly, like a stuck DVD of a horror film, except it's real. They're trapped, screaming for help, but no sound comes. One patient brought a dream of being frozen in ice – unreachable. Dreams can and do cross this self-made protective barrier and reconnect the complex to the whole.

Sometimes the therapist has a dream on behalf of a patient. An analytic supervisee brought a dream they'd had about a young patient:

### The flower on top of the tower dream

*In a desert, standing in front of a huge, slender tower in front made from pink mud. I have to climb it. This takes hours. At the top is a beautiful narcissus being blown about by the wind. I have to take care of it, but I don't know how.*

The therapist was concerned by her patient's risky promiscuity. The young woman had suffered serious neglect as a child. In the dream, a phallic symbol (the tower) has a flower growing on top – a narcissus (about narcissism?) My supervisee expected their patient would get vaginal candida (a fungal infection – a 'flower') – she did. She guessed the patient would become pregnant (flower) – she did. She didn't tell the patient her dream. It would seem too much like magic. But it was a huge relief to the young woman when her therapist stayed calm and accepting as she told her these things. Here, the therapist's dream created space for her not to repeat being the actively disinterested parent.

## 7.4 HOW THERAPISTS THEORISE ABOUT DREAMS AND WORK WITH THEM

Therapists theorise about dreams in many ways. Sometimes these 'theoretical differences' are real; often, they are imaginary. It's the same as when political and religious groups divide and divide again into smaller and yet smaller groups, each claiming 'the truth' (the one true Holy Grail of theory) when it's really about squabbling personalities having power struggles. Therapists are human. We haven't avoided the curse of following 'the Great Leader' (starting with Freud and Jung) and acting out a 'drama triangle.'

Movements in our minds are called psycho-dynamics. Before depth psychology, spiritual traditions imagined an inner dialogue between the spirit world and ourselves. Any reputable shaman has special training and natural abilities to help them bridge the gap. They use rituals, shamanic theory, and an apprenticeship to do this safely. And so do therapists. All religious traditions, including Judaism, Christianity, and Islam, do the same. The monotheisms give helpful hints about how to tell if a dream is from 'God' or 'the Devil.' Priests, like shamans, function as therapists in their pastoral work.

A problem is 'mana transference' – mana is a Polynesian word for magic. Patients may assume a therapist has magical powers, like interpreting dreams (or a gift of healing). Or there may be an erotic transference – they are in love with the therapist. These have to be recognised and worked with. Sadly, both are highly seductive and can lead to abuses of power. To keep a relational balance means recognising countertransference rather than acting it out, having high ethical standards, and supervision, as well as developing three qualities: empathy, seeing the whole situation rather than only a part, and a transpersonal (spiritual) view.

This does not have to be a particular religious practice, more a deep recognition that everyone is of equal worth – one unit of humanity – and that our unconscious minds are profoundly interconnected. This is why I've chosen to look at the work of Carl Rogers (person-centred therapy), Fritz Perls (gestalt therapy), and Roberto Assagioli (psychosynthesis), whose theories and practices place these qualities centre stage. Their approaches are about the person, the dreamer

– not the theory. As Assagioli said, 'Theory is there to keep your mind busy whilst your heart does the work.'

### 7.4.1 *Person-centred therapy*

Carl Rogers (1902–1987), a famous American psychologist, grew up in an evangelical Christian family. Expected by his parents to become a minister, after a trip to China in his early 20s, he had deep religious doubts. He studied psychology and then worked with troubled children and adolescents. They taught him that the simple things matter far, far more than theory: building an accepting, warm, trusting relationship and giving them unconditional positive regard. Many had never had this before, so to receive it was life-changing. Rogers didn't 'do things to' them – most of his young patients had been 'done to' far too much – instead, he practised 'being with.'

Rogers was amongst the first therapists to write about 'field effects' – how the interactions of both people in therapy resonate around the network of relationships to which clients belong outside the therapist's room. This developed into an intersubjective approach – taken up by many others, including psychoanalysts. We can only ever see each other, and our dreams, through our own subjectivity (from our point of view). Attempting to be 'objective' or 'rigorously scientific' simply reduces people to things. This appears in dreams, for example, when the therapist is symbolised as a zombie.

Empathy is key for Rogers; today, we could say this is building a functioning default mode network. Dreams are a place of deep, healing empathy by our self towards our many selves (sub-personalities) and those around us. Dreams show us things our ego-based opinions do not want us to see: our greed, our hatred, and our delusions. This allows 'actualisation' – Rogers' name for wholeness – analytical psychologists call this individuation. There is an excellent account of how dreamwork is done in this tradition in Andrea Koch's book (2012).

It could look like this. A young, gifted, mixed-race professional footballer in analysis with me brought this recurring nightmare from childhood:

#### The footballer and the monster dream

*A huge evil monster is chasing me. Its claws are out. It gets closer and closer. I wake, soaked in sweat and terrified.*

'Fred' couldn't empathise with either himself as a boy or with the monster. He came to see me because his teammates were fed up with him getting red cards and sent off for starting fights. The third time the dream came back, he agreed to draw it. He sat on the floor with wax crayons, and I joined him. We both saw the boy's back was deeply scratched by the monster's claws. This reminded Fred of how 'Monster Dad' often belted him. He sobbed. Fred realised he 'beat himself up' all the time for never being good enough. And any referee turned into 'Monster Dad.' And he'd been doing the same with his teammates and with me.

There was no need for me to interpret; he'd done it himself. Fred was scared I would beat him up for being a 'bad patient' because I'm white – like his violent, alcoholic father. Then, we used 'two-chair work' to go further. 'Fred, imagine young Fred is on the other chair. What does he want? What does he need? Could you sit there and *be* him?' He cried lots. Some days later in another session, we tried talking to the monster and then *being* it. What did it want? What did it need? What could it give you? Among Fred's answers were 'strength' and 'being scary.' He realised he was 'a monster' to his opponents. He stopped getting red cards. He started scoring more goals. He was an adult, a 'striker,' rather than a struck child. He saw his teammates as mates rather than angry white fathers.

### 7.4.2 Gestalt therapy

With Fred, I added a technique (two-chair work) from gestalt therapy, evolved by Fritz Perls (1893–1970). Gestalt is a German word, meaning shape or form. It is about finding the whole of a thing, which is always bigger than the sum of its parts (see Perls, 1952, 1992). A dream is bigger than the individual symbols. It includes sensations, feelings, and intuitions. It seeks to include the whole inner world of the dreamer, like a hologram which gives a 3D image of an object.

A holographic picture is made using laser light. If the glass plate on which it is printed is broken, you still get the whole image by shining a laser through a tiny fragment. Jungian analyst Louis Zinkin (1987) described the mind as a hologram – any symbol is an image for the whole mind. The footballer and the monster dream is a shorthand for an abusive self-care system. 'If Dad beat me, then beating myself up *must be* how to father myself'; it's another variation of 'the Great Leader' complex. What was worse for Fred was recognising who was *not in the dream*. Mum wasn't there. She'd done nothing to stop his violent abuse – preferring he was beaten rather than her (he supposed). So, who is not there (and would complete the family gestalt) is as important as who is there.

Perls was a German psychiatrist who specialised in the treatment of soldiers with brain injuries and severe PTSD during and after the First World War. His analyst was Wilhelm Reich, an early student of Freud, who became controversial – partly because of his ideas about 'orgone energy' (an imagined human energy field). Perls emigrated to South Africa to escape Nazi persecution. He settled in the USA in 1946. With his wife Laura, they ran the first Gestalt Institute from their Manhattan apartment. He wasn't an easy person – he could be extremely confrontational and also extremely kind.

Their approach stresses personal responsibility. Rather than continuing to feel 'done to,' we could start to 'own the monster' – after all, we are the ones who are doing 'it' (whatever 'it' is) to ourselves right now. If we're stuck, we could imagine ourselves five years from now and let our future self tell us how we got there. We could imagine a closure. Any uncompleted life events look for closure – completion.

A common example is when someone we love has died, but we couldn't say goodbye. Dreaming about them is extremely common, as our unconscious continues the relationship. And using two-chair work, maybe talking to a photo of the dead person, can bring a healing change. Or sitting in the second chair and being them and saying what they would say. This does not help us 'get over' the loss, but it places it in context – as a funeral gives us a chance to see the network to which they belonged. This can be both a good and a bad thing – an ambivalent experience – ambivalence is mentally healthy.

Dreams naturally do this: 'the four analysts dream' [7.2] happened many years after everyone in it had died. It did bring closure. I still miss them, but I can interpret my own dreams if they need it. Often, they don't. Sometimes we experience 'premature closure' – if a close friend tells us to get lost or we choose to give up on something before we're ready. Again, dreams will try to complete the gestalt – open it up and suggest alternative solutions (fulfilling a wish, compensating for the conscious attitude). By engaging with the symbol, drawing it, or talking to it in a safe place, new insights arise.

There is a good caricature of this approach in the film *Analyse This* (director: Harold Ramis, 1999) when the therapist (Billy Crystal) tells his patient, a troubled Mafia boss (Robert De Niro), to get in touch with his buried anger and hit a cushion. The boss pulls his gun and 'hits the cushion' – his six shots demolish the sofa. The therapist is terrified, but the mobster is in tears and hugs him. 'I feel better now, Doc. I really, really do.'

### 7.4.3 Psychosynthesis

Roberto Assagioli (1888–1974) was Italian, and as a young psychiatrist, he worked at the Burghölzli Hospital in Zurich with Eugen Bleuler. He became a good friend of Jung. In those days, psychiatrists were called 'alienists' – because they worked with those alienated from themselves and others. At that time, there was much questioning of traditional Western Christian beliefs. As scientific materialism grew, so did the opposite – interest in 'the spirit world' – talking to the dead, having spirit guides. Freud was deeply sceptical – calling this 'the black mud of occultism.' Jung and his maternal family were deeply engaged with it. He wrote his doctoral thesis on his cousin Helene Preiswerk, a trance medium.

Theosophy, a curious mix of 'ancient wisdom' and ideas from Eastern religions, was invented by Helena Blavatsky, a Russian émigré. She imagined the 'spirit world' as hierarchical, with 'invisible masters' who guide earthlings. Annie Besant, a colleague of Blavatsky, was a friend of Roberto Assagioli's mother. He was into theosophy. Psychosynthesis describes itself as a 'transpersonal psychology' concerned with spiritual and psychological problems. It's not so much about healing mental distress as fulfilling human potential – the first 'humanistic' therapy. I trained in it, taught it, and enjoy it, but I question theosophy.

Assagioli had a developmental approach. He knew that unless childhood traumas are addressed, there can be no secure base for spiritual growth. Reality testing and strengthening the ego are basic. Psychosynthesis works with the transference – but not 'in' it. Sessions are usually longer (an hour and a half) than in analysis to allow time for active imagination [10.5]. Assagioli borrowed ideas from everyone. His idea of 'the seven types' of personality – will, love, active/practical, creative/artistic, scientific, devotional, and organisational – comes directly from theosophy, where 'the seven rays' correspond to the Vedic idea of the seven chakras.

Like Perls, Assagioli emphasised the importance of 'the Will' – (a technical term meaning personal responsibility; Assagioli, 1977). Will can be good, strong, and skilful. Goodwill includes being kind to yourself about what you can realistically do; strong will is keeping going; skilful will is planning and asking for help. The Will is the link between the 'I' (roughly equivalent to the ego) and the 'higher self,' not roughly equivalent to 'the self,' as it contains an as-yet-unborn spiritual potential. Some of Assagioli's ideas resemble those of James Hillman: the soul incarnates to go on a journey [6.6].

Psychosynthesis supposes dreams contain archetypal images and have a purpose – this is a 'teleological view' (Telos means 'goal' in Greek). Dreams may be amplified by free association, but – more usually – by using active imagination. Assagioli's most important concept is of a spiritual core deep within the mind – which gives meaning and purpose to life. And it talks to us in our dreams.

Perhaps the three approaches I've outlined are not 'different practices' – more like different ways to play music. Jazz, soul, rock, classical, and folk music all use the same notes. Maybe counselling is like learning a song – the 'Exam Anxiety Blues?' If that is all you need to do, that's fine. Therapy is learning to play your instrument better and to improvise. Analysis is like learning music; it has a beginning but no end. None are 'better' – it depends entirely on what you need.

## 7.5 PLAYING WITH DREAM SYMBOLS

'What does a therapist do with a dream?' has endless answers. Good examples of how to work with dreams are found in recent books by Leslie Ellis (2019) and Allan Frater (2021). The first thing is to give the dream space and time. Listen to it; notice what comes into your mind as you retell it – free-associate. You may wander far away from the dream symbols. Analytical psychologists talk about 'circumambulating' (walking around and around) dream symbols whilst staying close to the details. Be curious. If there's a dragon in a dream, what colour is it? Is it male or female, both or neither? How big is it? How do you feel about each other? What does it want? What does it need? What do you want or need from it (gestalt therapy questions)?

It may take years of the same symbol repeating for the meaning to emerge. My South African dreams at the start of analysis were a symbol for 'splitting' – the thinking part of me had separated from the feeling part. As this changed, the symbol gradually vanished. An analytic patient often dreamed of being stuck on a train, unable to get off. Their thinking tended to go along 'train lines.' As this changed, the dreams stopped. Dreams can have 'added value' when they are recorded and studied over time: the longer, the better. It is not about 'interpreting' – it is about 'being with.'

Q: I've shown you various therapists' theories in this chapter. Which do you prefer and why? Which might you use with one of your own dreams? Try it and see what happens.

## KEY CONCEPTS

**Dreams are easier to understand if you do the following:**

- Empathise with all the characters, including the monsters
- Look at the whole dream
- Look for symbols of wholeness
- Include a transpersonal (spiritual) possibility
  - This develops relationships

## FURTHER READING

Ellis, L. (2019) *A clinician's guide to dream therapy*, London: Routledge.
Frater, A. (2021) *Waking dreams: Imagination in psychotherapy & everyday life* London: Transpersonal Press. https://wildimagination.uk/book/

## REFERENCES

Assagioli, R. (1977) *The act of will*, London: Penguin.
Axline, V. (1986) *Dibs in search of self*, London: Ballantine Books.
Berne, E. (2016) *Games people play*, London: Penguin.
Edinger, E. (1962) 'The ego-self axis,' *Journal of Analytical Psychology*, 5: 3–18
Koch, A. (2012) *Dreams and the person centred approach: Cherishing client experiencing* Monmouth: PCCS books.
Malan, D. (1979) *Individual psychotherapy and the science of psychodynamics*, London: Butterworth.
Perls, F. (1952/1992) *Gestalt therapy verbatim*, Gouldsboro, Maine: Gestalt Journal Press.
Ramis, H. (dir.) (1999) *Analyse this*, Los Angeles: Warner Bros.
Tustin, F. (1981) *Autistic states in children*, London: Routledge, and Kegan Paul.
Zinkin, L. (1987) The hologram as a model for analytical psychology *Journal of Analytical Psychology*, 32:1: 1–12.

# DREAMS AND CREATIVITY

## 8.1 WHAT IS CREATIVITY?

This chapter is about how dreams inspire creative processes. Everyone is creative; it's not the special gift of 'creatives.' To explore this in more depth, I recommend record producer Rick Rubin's *The Creative Act* (2023). He emphasises any creative process needs a beginner's mind, being surprised, open, spontaneous, and not striving after results. Dreams naturally do all these things. Rubin says it's not what you do; it's who you are which matters. You need a toolkit, but you are the one who shapes what you make.

Dreams link toolkit concepts together in unexpected ways – with new interpretations and messages from our unconscious. Creativity is another word for playing, one of the most important things we ever do. When we play as children, we practice reality testing, try things out, learn, and learn by making mistakes. My son, aged eight, and his friends were using sticks as guns to fight off a zombie apocalypse in our back garden. His Mum said, 'What are you doing!?' He said, 'Mum! It's just pretend!' as his friends cleared the last zombies from the flowerbed. Mostly, we know when we're playing. Play involves risk. We could fall out of a tree, come off our bicycle, or get hurt playing sports. In dreams, our minds play with minimal physical risk – because we're asleep.

In this chapter, I look at how dreams bring new ideas and re-form old ones, using examples from different practices. Inspirations come from daydreams, nightmares, lucid dreams, and the play between 'the spiritual' and 'the material' called precognition. I'll not go into

DOI: 10.4324/9781003319696-8

whether the 'spiritual' is real or imaginary, but everyone has experiences of something 'bigger than ourselves.' It could be a piece of music, our first trip to a festival, or a sudden, unexpected friendship – a moment when we feel 'a part of life' rather than 'apart from life.' I'll say more about this in Chapter 10, linking play to the transcendent function – a bridge between conscious and unconscious – and between spiritual and materialist worldviews.

When I re-read something I wrote, I usually wonder, 'Where did that come from?' Most artists, performers, and sports people have this experience. Fred, the footballer in Chapter 7, was always amazed each time he scored a goal. Suppose self-expression isn't about 'you' (ego) – but is a gift which flows through you: perhaps from the Self, or the collective unconscious, or from 10,000 hours of practice. Perhaps from 'the spirits.' Many people report precognitive dreams. You may have had them. These are 'between' experiences, and some people are more open to them than others. Or maybe they are intuition – like this:

### The Leicester Square dream

*I am at Leicester Square underground in London, with a friend, an artist. As we're going up the escalator, I realise they've vanished. They're looking for the Circle Line.*

Awake, I realise my friend is 'going round in circles' with their art practice. The Circle Line doesn't go through Leicester Square, but it is the station to get off at for Soho, a home for artists, musicians, and actors. Being able to go round in circles, getting lost, is crucial to creativity. We discussed the problem and their frustration at 'not knowing.' We both realised that to create, as in play, we *have to* not know. If we know, where is the space to imagine? We need the basic skills of our practice, to know how to draw, or dance, or whatever. But to find new things means being with *not knowing*, also called *negative capability*. As my music teacher said when I was stuck with a new piece, 'Live dangerously!'

Curiously, the Circle Line isn't a circle. It begins and ends at Edgware Road – the terminus. Creativity needs an endpoint. We make something we're happy with, or we give up and do something else. But creativity, like dreaming, cannot be done to order. That's like shouting at a jazz musician, 'Go on then, improvise!' Creativity is planned chaos. Its opposite is being stuck in a complex – a repeating pattern of thoughts, feelings, and behaviours where time becomes a loop, a circle line.

I mentioned in Chapter 2 [2.6] the difference between 'real time' and 'dreaming time.' Consciousness tests reality using 'ego' time – 'Chronos time,' measured in seconds. There is also 'present moment' time – time in dreams – 'Kairos time,' which is unmeasurable. These ideas were developed by French philosopher Henri Bergson and taken up by Jung, whose idea of synchronicity as an 'acausal connecting principle' – actions outside time – was developed with physicist Wolfgang Pauli [8.3.5]. 'Kairos time' is a flow state; we are completely unaware of time because we're totally engaged [10.7].

## 8.2 CREATIVE DREAMS

In her book *The Committee of Sleep*, Prof Deirdre Barrett (2001) gives examples of how ideas grow in dreams. In her stories, the dreamers are often experts facing a seemingly insoluble problem, which they've worked on for months or years. A personal example: a friend, a surgeon, didn't know what to do to help a man with a serious spinal injury. One night, he dreamed of performing a new operation. He did, and it worked.

Expertise helps – you can't solve a problem like 'how do I speak Greek' unless your conscious mind is immersing itself in the language. You need skill, effort, and motivation. This is making an act of Will – using good, skilful, and strong Will [7.4.3]. Sometimes a dreamer hopes to solve a problem with the help of a dream, but often, one 'just happens' (at a timeless moment). You never need to shout at the unconscious. If you do, it disappears. Let's look at different examples of creativity and see how dreams influence the work.

### 8.2.1 Artists

The Spanish surrealist artist Salvador Dali (1904–1989) often worked with dreams. He used the 'penny in the hand' technique: sit comfortably in a chair with a penny in your hand, held over a tin bowl. When you nod off, the 'penny drops.' You wake and record whatever was in your reverie. His painting, *Dream: Caused by the Flight of a Bee (around a Pomegranate, Seconds before Waking Up)* – (1944, Museo Thyssen-Bornemisza, Madrid, Spain) – shows a bee buzzing around a pomegranate. It becomes a fish, then a tiger, then a rifle with a bayonet, aimed at Gaia, his naked, sleeping wife. Dali met Freud in the 1930s and was fascinated by his ideas about sexual symbolism. Here, the symbol is obvious.

Henri Fuseli (1741–1825), a Swiss painter, depicted *The Nightmare* in 1781 (Detroit Institute of Arts, Michigan). A sleeping woman in white slumps on a divan. On her chest sits an ugly, naked demon. In the background is a wild black horse – a real Night Mare – with wild, staring eyes. It is an erotic image, painted when Fuseli was infatuated with an unavailable woman and having sexual fantasies about her. His painting is a wish fulfilment which gets around 'the dream censor.' The horse was not there in the first sketches. Including the horse is the work referring to itself – it came from a nightmare. 'Self-referring' is common when a dream provides inspiration. It's as if the unconscious signs the work.

American Artist Jasper Johns (1930–) became famous for his paintings of flags. The first, called *Flag* (the Stars and Stripes – subtly changed) (1954), came directly from a dream. If you capture dream images by drawing, you don't have to interpret them. They could be an artwork.

Q: Could you try this yourself? You don't have to identify as an artist to do so.

### 8.2.2 Film and literature

Christopher Nolan, the Oscar-winning director of *Oppenheimer* (2023), in a recent *Times* interview, describes how he woke up at night after dreaming the ending of the film. He wrote it down, commenting, 'Fortunately I was able to read my handwriting in the morning.' He also dreamed the ending of *The Dark Knight Rises* (2012) the Batman film starring Christian Bale. In the book on Nolan's work by *Sunday Times* film critic Tom Shone (2024), gives further examples of how films and dreams work together: many smaller directorial problems were solved by dreams.

Malorie Blackman (1962–), recently Children's Laureate in the United Kingdom, is best known for her young adult fiction Noughts and Crosses (2001) series. In this imagined world, the social roles of black and white people are reversed. Black people, the Crosses, are rich; white people, the Noughts, are dirt poor.

Sephy, a black girl, and Callum, a white boy, fall in love. Malorie was stuck about how to end it. The unexpected ending came in a nightmare. (I won't tell you what it is, but it upset her so much she didn't want to write it.) J. K. Rowling (1965–) daydreamed the Harry Potter books (1997–2007) when stuck on a train between Manchester and London.

Samuel Taylor Coleridge's (1772–1834) poem 'Kubla Khan: A Vision in a Dream' (written 1797, published 1816) is a fantasy about an imaginary city, Xanadu. He wrote it on waking from an opium-induced dream after reading a book about a Chinese city. Scots writer Robert Louis Stevenson (1850–94) dreamed *Dr. Jekyll and Mr. Hyde* (1886). Respectable Dr Jekyll has his evil inner opposite, his Shadow, the murderous Mr Hyde. Jekyll changed into Hyde by drinking a potion. But transformations started to happen when he fell asleep. Stevenson wrote the story in less than a week.

### 8.2.3 Music

In *The Dreams Behind the Music*, C. S. Webb (2016) gives hundreds of examples from all genres of musicians whose songs and symphonies were found in dreams. Keith Richards (1943–), guitarist and song-writer with the Rolling Stones, slept with a cassette tape recorder by his bed in case he had a helpful dream. One morning, he woke and played the tape, sure he'd not recorded anything. He heard himself hum a riff and then sing, 'I can't get no…uuh…satisfaction…' He worked on it with Mick Jagger, creating the Stones' first number-one hit in the USA in 1965.

Amongst classical musicians, German Romantic composer Richard Wagner (1813–1883) dreamed the music and the lyrics for his opera *Tristan and Isolde* (dream, 1854; completed opera, 1859). Mozart and Beethoven 'downloaded' concerti from dreams. The shy Austrian Anton Bruckner (1824–1896) revised his eighth symphony frequently between 1884 and its first performance in 1890, rearranging the movements as a result of listening during sleep. The 'audience of sleep' gave feedback about what worked and what didn't. Dreams can fill a concert hall, a festival, or a jazz club, or give you a guitar tune. One of my patients, a young rock guitarist, regularly played the songs he'd dreamed in our sessions. The lyrics described what he was doing in his analysis with huge feelings.

### 8.2.4 *Dance*

A young contemporary dancer I saw for analysis sometimes danced what he wanted to show me, because it wouldn't go into words. One day, he was upset, as he didn't know how to perform a solo. He dreamed:

**The dancers' dream**

*I watch myself dancing naked and feel self-conscious.*

He explained that the self-consciousness was not about being naked. He'd performed naked before. He realised he was afraid of messing up the moves. So, early the morning after the dream, he danced his solo – naked – in an empty studio. It felt liberating. Then, in tights, he danced it for the rest of the company. His dream helped him recognise a hidden feeling – vulnerability – which he named and faced.

### 8.2.5 *Science*

August Kekule (1829–1896) was a German chemist who worked on molecular structures; famously, he discovered the benzene ring in which six carbon atoms form a circle. It's foundational to organic chemistry. He spent many years trying to work out the structure. One day he fell into a daydream beside an open fire. The flames seemed to join together, making a ring – reminding him of the Ouroboros, the snake which eats its own tail. In Ancient Egypt, this image represented the serpent Apep, who tried to eat the Sun god, Ra. It is also found in Norse mythology – the Midgard serpent, one of Loki's sons, circles the world. The daydream put together information Kekule had from different knowledge areas in a new pattern, which fitted the data together in a better way.

The Austrian Wolfgang Pauli (1900–58) won the Nobel Prize for physics in 1945 for 'the exclusion principle' – his insight that in any atom, electrons stay in distinct orbits around the nucleus. It's the quantum physics explanation of chemistry. In 1932, during a deep personal crisis, he asked Jung for help. Jung didn't analyse him himself, but they worked together on over 400 of Pauli's dreams and became lifelong friends. Pauli's dream of the world clock (1953, CW 12, para. 307–313), in which different clocks each drive the other, inspired his idea of electron orbitals. The two men collaborated about an 'acausal connecting principle,' calling it synchronicity (Main 1997, pp. 93–103).

Here is a personal example:

### The philosopher's stone dream

*I am in an alchemist's laboratory belonging to my first analyst. She hands me a philosopher's stone. It's iridescent, green, gold, and purple. There is an eye-like lens in the middle.*

After my session, I drove to work, by chance parking outside a shop selling glass. The object from my dream was in the window – a beautiful glass paperweight, which looked exactly like the philosopher's stone in the dream. I bought it. It sits beside me whilst I work.

Random events may be meaningfully connected. One event does not cause the other – as when we call a friend at the same time as they call us. Synchronicity is a consequence of 'the Jung-Pauli conjecture,' which is that a psycho-physical reality exists outside conventional 'space-time' from which both matter and spirit derive (Atmanspacher and Fuchs, 2014, pp. 1–7, pp. 181–201). It is one of several possible ways to solve a major problem in quantum physics: how to include gravity with the other fundamental forces. It could also reconcile the split between materialism and spirituality (Le Shan, 1974, pp. 3–79).

## 8.3 DAYDREAMING (PART TWO)

Sleep and waking seem subjectively different, but the boundary is fluid. The {*both/and / neither/nor*} idea helps here. We can be both awake and asleep, and neither awake nor asleep – daydreaming. Daydreams are the unconscious appearing in consciousness: lucid dreaming is the opposite. In Chapter 5, I described the three major networks in the mind which bridge between the cortex and the limbic system: the executive network, the salience network and the default mode network. The executive network specialises in 'command and control,' when we're 'on task.' But most of us spend around 50 per cent of our waking life in daydreams, using the default mode – the storyteller.

In Scots, daydreaming is called 'awa' in a dwam,' meaning a reverie or 'in a world of our own.' We all spend so much time doing this. What for? Well, no one can attend continuously. This is why passenger aircraft have a pilot and co-pilot. Our attention spans are quite limited and change as we age. Infants can't concentrate at all; they don't yet have an ego. Between five and twelve, the maximum attention span is about ten minutes; for young adults, it's about twenty. As we age, it gets less.

When I counselled students at the London School of Economics, a regular problem they had was being unable to study. The commonest cause was trying too hard, for far too long – rather than not trying. Taking a break every twenty minutes for a few minutes increases productivity and emotional well-being. To have 'uptime,' we need 'downtime.' This is when we create new ideas, find new links, remember what we've done, and integrate it. We need to daydream. We cannot learn anything new if we don't.

As we habituate to familiar events and surroundings, we attend less to what's going on outside. What's inside fills the screen. The first time we go to a new school, we attend to the route. The 500th time, we don't. In these moments of reverie, we imagine possible futures. These may be good or bad: pleasing success or humiliating failure. We can, of course, imagine both at the same time. And we get bored.

Every child says, 'I'm bored.' Maybe we're waiting for something, like a bus, or enduring some awful lesson we are not interested in. Time slows. It may seem to go backwards. We watch the clock. We're using the salience network, but not finding anything which sticks out. We're not even telling ourselves inner stories (using the default mode network to daydream). Short amounts of boredom are part of any creative process. It's like letting a car engine idle, warming up before driving off. We can't be creative, it seems, without periods of being uncreative. Can creativity come out of fear? Sometimes.

## 8.4 NIGHTMARES

All children have nightmares; about 30 per cent have them frequently. In adults, the frequency drops, but about 10 per cent have them often enough to cause insomnia. At least 80 per cent of those with post-traumatic stress disorder (PTSD) have vivid nightmares – after an acute trauma almost everyone has dreams of re-living the terror, trying to process something too big for our feelings. There are folk myths about nightmares, but they're not caused by eating pickles and cheese last thing at night.

A nightmare is like living in a horror film; *they* are after us. We can't escape. We're anxious, scared, terrified, panicked. Many cultures explain nightmares as attacks by evil spirits, demons, or vengeful ancestors. Both Freud and Jung agreed they relate to overwhelming stress in daily life. The more stress, the more nightmares. We're trying and failing to resolve a daytime fear.

When we're under three years old, the outside world is enormous. People and things quickly become unpredictable and overwhelming. Huge feelings of shame, guilt, and rage can flood us. We have meltdowns. The frontal lobes have just begun connecting. Our reality testing function (ego) is still growing. The three networks are not well-formed till around puberty nor 'fully connected' till the early twenties. We don't have a fully functioning emotional suspension system. Part of the problem for people with autistic spectrum disorders is their default mode network is not quite able to manage their social needs. They can't tell themselves stories to insulate themselves from overwhelming feelings. My young rock guitarist patient had this problem. Fortunately, music gave him a cushion. He'd play guitar to keep himself sane.

Young children can't tell *Chronos* time (clock time) and live in *Kairos* time – the here and now – a state Zen masters hope to reach after a lifetime of meditation practice. Being in Kairos time is fine if everything is fine – and a total nightmare when it isn't – if your carers are absent or unpredictably unpredictable and violent. So, we work on the terror at night. We may become afraid to go to bed or be left alone in the dark. We wake, unreassurable, usually in the second half of the night, from REM sleep. Waking from a nightmare is part of its function. If we didn't, we'd not remember them.

The unconscious lets us practise dealing with terror in a safe place. It needs a kind grown-up to explain to their child that it's a dream, to listen and to comfort. Compassion for the dreamer is the cure, not an analytic interpretation – though sometimes this is needed.

If it is, then sand play is a good way to do this, as described in *Dibs: In Search of Self.* (Axline 1986) [7.6.9]). Dibs had terrifying nightmares. He was scared out of his wits by his parents' emotionally cut-off behaviour – which led to his unconscious creating a psychological complex like a nuclear bunker.

How can such dreams ever be creative? I've given an example already – the ending of Noughts and Crosses. But it is a demand for kind parental attention which is their most creative function. They are a request for empathy. As adults, we may not have 'good enough' inner parents to do this – so we use friends, partners, therapists, analysts. When patients bring nightmares to sessions with me, this is a special gift from their unconscious. I'm trusted enough to be used as a 'good object,' and they are learning to trust themselves by being vulnerable.

> **Box 8.1   A dream is lucid if**
>
> - You know you're dreaming in a dream
> - You can concentrate
> - Your memory works
> - You can make decisions
> - You can change the dream

## 8.5 LUCID DREAMING

In lucid dreams [Box 8.1], you know you are dreaming in the dream, and then you can change it. Lucid comes from the Latin word *lux*, meaning light, clear, transparent, and easily understood. Our daytime ego is awake and co-creating a lucid dream. If the unconscious is an ocean, consciousness an island, and dreams happen on the beach, then a lucid dream is like building a sandcastle.

A Dutch psychiatrist, Willem Van Eeden (1860–1932), invented the name early in the twentieth century. Such dreams have long been known from shamanic practices, religious, and spiritual beliefs. They occur during REM sleep and resemble 'false waking' – you imagine you're eating breakfast, and then you wake up. Lucid dreams are rare. I remember one from childhood – trapped in a burning room, scared, and then choosing to put my hand into the flames and saying, 'Stop!' They stopped. I have never had one since. My daughter had nightmares as a child and was able to do the same and tell the monsters to go away. She still can. Few have this gift; most don't, and if we do, we seem to grow out of it.

Recognising you are dreaming probably happens in the dorsolateral prefrontal cortex (dlPFC) – the back of the prefrontal cortex. This brain area is normally turned down in REM sleep. It's where choices about working memory occur. There is a delicate balance between recognising you're dreaming and staying 'conscious enough' to move the dream about.

This involves the amygdala – the brain's 'panic button' – balancing fear against curiosity. A lucid dream turns down the volume from the amygdala.

Each of these abilities is an ego function. You consciously direct aspects of 'your inner movie.' This skill is practiced in Tibetan dream yoga, and their lucid dreaming techniques lead to and are supported by visualisations of spirit beings in mediation practise (Knauft, in

Mageo and Sheriff, 2021, pp. 204–226). In 1980, Professor Stephen LaBerge at Stanford University, California, asked lucid dreamers to count out ten seconds whilst dreaming and signal the start and the end of the count with a blink. His team discovered time perception in lucid dreams is about the same as during waking life. (In normal dreams, time can flow at many different rates or not flow at all.) Many studies used his 'blink technique' to let the dreamer communicate with the researcher.

The range of control is highly variable – the unconscious still designs the set, but how we interact with the characters is easier to change. We can talk to them. However, we usually get ambiguous answers. We cannot change 'the genre' of a lucid dream – from slasher horror movie to rom-com – but we may alter the outcome. Fred, the footballer [7.4:1] had lucid dreams about talking back to the monster after we'd talked to it in a session. I didn't show him how to lucid dream; he did it spontaneously. *Exploring the World of Lucid Dreaming* by La Berge and Rheingold (1990) is full of hints and tips. If you want to learn, here are some things you could try [Box 8.2]:

---

### Box 8.2   Tips for lucid dreaming

- Prepare – keep a dream journal. What are the common signs you're dreaming? A change in the light? A particular sensation? A feeling?
- Compare – do you see these signs whilst awake? Notice when you daydream. Is it like 'night' dreaming?
- Target – set a goal, maybe learn to fly, deal with monsters, be invisible.
- Monitor – record what happens!

---

A Polish colleague, Professor Krysz Rutkowsky, at the Jagiellonian University, Krakow, worked with patients suffering severe PTSD. They could not dream about what had happened and kept having 'flashbacks.' Using active imagination and social dreaming groups, gradually they began to dream about the trauma. Their unconscious could process feelings which had been too big. Slowly, their PTSD resolved. But this was not an exercise in learning to lucid dream. It was an exercise in active imagination [10.5].

Can we learn to lucid dream? If we did, what would we use it for? One answer is to deal with nightmares: talk to the monster, find out what it needs. Another might be to actively use dreams to solve problems. But as dreams are a spontaneous portrayal from the unconscious of things which matter to us, I wonder why try and control them? We have so many demands to achieve and control when awake; why spoil sleep by turning it into a task-oriented space in which we have to 'achieve?'

Our unconscious is 'there for us' – it *is* us. Trusting our creative unconscious means any dream shows us something it feels we need to know. Consciously, we can never know what this is. For me, the idea of 'controlling' a dream is like going into a wood at night looking for badgers with a bright searchlight and a megaphone, loudly shouting, 'Come out, badgers!'

Lucid dreaming may simply be a brief period of wakefulness. When we dream, we wake for a few seconds to 'process' the dream through consciousness, then fall asleep. I've watched dreamers do this in a sleep lab. Some suggest 'early morning waking' in depressive illness happens because we wake to remember a dream but can't and then can't get back to sleep. Or lucid dreaming could be an example of dissociation during sleep. Dissociation is part of a psychological defence called splitting – when we blame another person for something which is our fault, '*they* made me do it!' We can use the same defences in dreams – perhaps that's what happens when we talk back to the monster.

Are there risks to lucid dreaming? If you are new to it, you may not understand what's happening and feel overwhelmed. A bigger risk is that if you try it and it doesn't work, then you get angry with yourself. But this is like getting angry with the sea because the tide came in and washed your sandcastle away. It is a scale problem. The ego is small, and the unconscious is limitless. Trying to 'control' the unconscious can't ever work.

## 8.6 PARANORMAL DREAMS

Have you had a dream which told you the future – a precognitive dream? If you have, you know they are unforgettable. My mum dreamed about her school Latin exam the night before. She revised these topics when she woke. Her dream was correct. She passed when she thought she'd fail. When I'd a Latin exam, I tried doing the same – it didn't work. Every student has the opposite dream – sitting an exam but knowing nothing, or it's the wrong exam, or their pen explodes – anxiety dreams. We have the anxiety in the dream, so hopefully we won't have so much when we're doing the exam. Dreams help us manage anxiety – like this:

### The Taj Mahal dream

*I meet my first analyst at the Taj Mahal. I was anxious about the Christmas break, and then I knew she was going to India. She'd not told me.*

In the session, I was just about to tell her when she said, 'Yes, I'm going to India. It's OK. You don't need to tell me you dreamed about it.' We were both highly intuitive; this happened quite often. Any two people who know each other deeply may find they can predict what the other might say or do. It's not magic or telepathy; it's listening to the unconscious. A problem with intuition is it always *feels* right. Half the time it is, half the time it isn't – and you don't always know which half is which.

Some dreams tell the future. One of the most famous precognitive dreams was by the 16th US president, Abraham Lincoln (1809–1865). He dreamed he saw a long coffin in the White House Oval Office and asked the honour guard who was inside. He said, 'Sir, it's the President of the United States.' Lincoln was assassinated the next day. We know the story because the president told Mrs Lincoln his dream. Another example: In 1946, Sir Victor Goddard, an Air Marshal in the Royal Air Force, was piloting a plane to Tokyo. His life was saved because the night before, a fellow officer dreamed Victor would die in a plane crash the next day. The plane iced up, as in the dream, and he crash-landed it on a pebbly beach. No one was killed. He'd been pre-warned. The story became a film *The Night My Number Came Up* (Norman and Sherriff, 1955). He had many other paranormal experiences (Goddard, 1975). For him, there was no split between 'the spiritual' and 'the material.'

There are many stories of people who decided not to sail on the Titanic, or take a plane, or stand *over there* in a battle and so survived (Johnson, 1953, pp. 148–175). A psychiatrist, Dr John Barker, became fascinated by such dreams after the tragedy in Aberfan, a Welsh mining village (October 1966). A waterlogged coal tip slid, smothering the village primary school and killing 144 people, mostly children. There were numerous after-the-event reports of predictive dreams. Barker started the Premonitions Bureau with the *Evening Standard* newspaper. The idea was to give forewarning of disasters by collecting 'disaster' dreams (Knight, 2022). This could never work.

Q: Because? See how many reasons you can think of.

However, collective dreams do occur. Jung had one in July 1914 when he dreamed Europe was covered in blood, which broke in waves against the Swiss mountains. He thought he was going crazy. The First World War began a month later. How such dreams happen is unknown. A traditional explanation is that 'the spirits talk to us.' Amongst those who share dreams, like indigenous people of the Great Plains in America, dreams might say where the buffalo would be; they'd set out hunting, and there they were. An analytical psychologist's explanation might be as the unconscious is time-free, it can guess about what happens next; it's an intuition (only right some of the time!) For those who wish to read more about *the Reality of the Paranormal*, Professor Arthur Ellison's book is a good introduction (1988).

NEXTUP [4.10] is a theory about dreams by Zadra and Stickgold, sleep researchers and Professors at Montreal and Harvard (2021, pp. 108–129). They suggest dreams arrange weak associations into 'near predictions.' For example, if you get bullied, then you dream about it. The dream will use symbols from all your experiences to suggest possible answers – maybe you shame those responsible, or take up martial arts, join a gang of evil bikers or buy an A-Bomb on eBay. Dream suggestions don't have to be practical; they are ways to reconfigure the problem (like Kekule and the benzene ring). It's 'blue sky thinking.' As we dream for about 50,000 hours in a 70-year life, statistically, sometimes, there will be highly accurate predictions. So, it could be coincidental. Or it could be synchronicity.

Q: What do you think? What do you feel?

And what about 'visits' from the ancestors? Many of us have dreams where the dead talk to us. I had one about going to the pub with my (late) friend Nigel to discuss this chapter. Recently, a family friend, Asha, died of breast cancer. A few weeks later, my wife, Carola, dreamed she was walking on Hampstead Heath with her. Carola said, 'But you died!' Asha laughed and said, 'The doctors got it wrong, as usual.' Maybe you've had a dream like this? It could be the spirit of the dead person visiting. It could be they are alive in your mind as a 'good internal object' – or both. Explanations and interpretations are probably far less important than the feelings they open up.

This is why a 'dream dictionary' can't work – each time we get a symbol, the feelings will be different. Dreams try to bring closure (complete a gestalt) and suggest new ways to learn from an old relationship. Common examples are dreams about childhood: we continue relationships with friends whom we may not have seen since. People no longer there for us in the outer world continue as symbols in the inner world.

Q:  Who does this for you?

My friend Nigel and I studied medicine and psychology together. He helped me with this chapter. He died about ten years ago. In a way, this made our conversation easier.

## 8.7 CONCLUSION

Where does creativity come from? It is a strange effect at the boundary between conscious and unconscious. Are some people 'better' at handling this boundary than others? Probably, just as some are better at sports, or feelings, or doing maths. We dream within our skill set – doctors dream of their patients, musicians dream about music, dancers dream about dancing. Sadly, sometimes creativity becomes an overvalued idea – a thing only 'creatives' do. This false belief relates to a dominant Western discourse that we 'must always work hard,' as seen in the curious American habit of taking only two weeks' holiday a year. Play isn't work, and our unconscious needs to play, sometimes seriously – all the time, which is why we daydream so much.

You may suppose you can't be creative unless you *work hard* to remember your dreams. No. Your mind always processes all the dreams you have, including ones you forget – the large majority. Creativity involves 'effortless non-effort' – going with the flow. Setting goals, aims, objectives, targets, schedules, achievements is the best way *not* to be creative. Creativity is not a competition. It's not necessary to mine your dreams for meaning.

## KEY CONCEPTS

- Dreams open us to creative solutions to problems.
- First, recall and record as soon as possible.
- Second, reflect and play with the dream for as long as it takes.
- Third, be patient!

## FURTHER READING

Barrett, D. (2001) *The committee of sleep*, London: Oneiroi Press.

Knight, S. (2022) *The premonitions bureau*, London: Faber and Faber.

La Berge, S. & Rheingold, H. (1990) *Exploring the world of lucid dreaming*, New York: Ballantine.

Rubin, R. (2023) *The creative act*, London: Penguin.

## REFERENCES

Atmanspacher, H. & Fuchs, C.A. (eds) (2014) *The Jung – Pauli conjecture*, Exeter: Impact Academic.

Axline, V. (1986) *Dibs: In search of self*, London: Penguin Modern classics.

Blackman, M. (2001) *Noughts and crosses*, London: Penguin.

Ellison, A. (1988) *The reality of the paranormal*, London: Harrap.

Goddard, V. (1975) *Flight towards reality* London: Turnstone.

Johnson, R. (1953) *The imprisoned Splendour*, London: Hodder and Stoughton.

Jung, C.G. (1953) *Psychology and alchemy*, London: Routledge and Kegan Paul.

Knauft, B.M. (2021) Life is but a dream: culture and science in the study of Tibetan dream yoga and lucid dreaming, in Mageo, J., & Sheriff, R.E., *New directions in the anthropology of social dreaming* London: Routledge.

Le Shan, L. (1974) *The medium, the mystic and the physicist*, London: Turnstone Books.

Main, R. (ed), (1997) *Jung on synchronicity and the paranormal*, London: Routledge.

Nolan, C. (2023). *Oppenheimer*, Universal City, CA, USA: Universal Pictures.

Nolan, C. (2012). *The dark knight rises*, Burbank, CA., USA: Warner Brothers.

Norman, L., Sherriff, R.C. (1955) *The night my number came up*, London: Ealing studios.

Shone, T. (2024). *The Nolan variations*, London: Faber and Faber.

Webb, C.S. (2016). *The Dreams Behind the Music* https://dreamsbehindthemusic.com/

Zadra, A. & Stickgold, R. (2021). *When brains dream*, New York: W.W. Norton.

# SOCIAL AND CULTURAL DREAMING

*by Carola Mathers*

## 9.1 INTRODUCTION

This chapter, in contrast to individual dream neuroscientific and psychological theories, considers cultural and social theories of dreaming. I will include social dreaming as a practice with examples. All over the world, and in the distant past, dreaming has been and is thought of as fundamentally relational, a social experience with effects in waking life. Recent anthropological research shows that only contemporary Western culture views dreams as exclusively intrapsychic phenomena or as having no meaning, personal, social, or cultural. In the West, we have an egocentric rather than a sociocentric orientation; thus, we tend to view dreams as belonging to the dreamer alone. When we share dreams with family or friends or when we study our dreams, this is for our individual understanding rather than a collective endeavour bringing us closer to our community.

Cultural anthropologists regard dreams as cultural artefacts, which they, as researchers, explore together with the peoples they study, thus extending their understanding of those peoples (3.3). Psychotherapists and psychoanalysts regard dreams as having individual importance: talking with the client, they arrive at meaning together. Both groups of professionals bring their knowledge of the subject to the conversation, enlarging the understanding of the dream and of the dreamer/dreaming society. There is of course an overlap: Jung, a psychologist, said dreams have a social function, and anthropologists consider dreams can help individual dreamers

DOI: 10.4324/9781003319696-9

become aware of and digest unconscious responses to events in their social world. Unfortunately, the two disciplines do not communicate their findings with each other.

Q: Why do you think this might be?

It is a well-known joke that when in therapy, clients' dreams match their therapists' expectations. For example, people who see a Freudian therapist will have Freudian dreams. This has some truth in it, for anthropologists have shown that what people dream depends on what they believe or what they understand dreams to be.

Mageo, a cultural dream anthropologist, asserts that dreams regulate and advance cultural change. They can reveal the dark sides of our culture which we may be reluctant to acknowledge, and when shared, they provide a way of thinking together about collective problems and possible ways to change them (as happens in a social dreaming matrix; see p. 137). 'Discontents drive dreamers to work on collective problems of meaning and inspire similar resistances and cultural innovations in others' dreams' (Mageo 2021, p. 8)

Dream symbols and events are otherworldly; at the same time, they are rooted in our everyday existence. They may help us live with ambiguity by offering different, even opposing, perspectives on our world. When dreams are shared with others, each person is changed: a new perspective on current issues becomes available through sharing. Their dreams are also changed, so there is a cycle of dreaming, sharing dreams, and cultural change.

Both cultural anthropologists and social dreaming matrix researchers come to the same conclusions about dream sharing. Dream sharing, in its different forms, formal and informal, is a creative, social act which furthers the participants' creativity. The activity of dream sharing and social dreaming changes the dreamer and encourages further dreaming. It is also fun!

> Culture is both a creative expression of dreaming and a generative force in the formation of dreams.
>
> (Bulkeley, 2021, pp. 114–115)

> Dreams become new generators of culture, not just reflective mirrors of it.
>
> (Ibid., p. 121)

The act of sharing dreams in these different contexts is a generative cycle which can lead to individual and social fulfilment and well-being, based as it is on communication, relationship, and trust. These are gifts our world sorely needs at this time of geopolitical and ecological struggle.

## 9.2 DREAM SHARING

Anthropologists describe a culture which focuses on dreams as being socially meaningful, a 'collective dream culture': one in which dreams are regularly shared. In such cultures, dreams are both personally and collectively significant. In Iceland for example, dreams are freely shared and feature in daily conversations. They are experienced as bearing messages for others in the dreamer's social network, as well as for the dreamer: Icelanders see dreams as inherently social. Dream encounters with the dead or with beings such as 'elves' are taken seriously: children may be named after such dream visitors.

For Aboriginal Australians, dreaming, as an activity involving a personal body/mind/emotion while sleeping, is a way of reinforcing their relationship with the land, with the ancestors, with each other, and with non-human beings. Shared dreams form an important part of their social and cultural activities. Craig San Roque, a Jungian analyst working in relationship with Aboriginal peoples in Australia, kindly shared with me some experience from his association with Anangu people in the Western desert of Australia. A feature is 'The morning news' (Aalpiri/Alpiri in local languages). People wake up from their campfires:

> As people wake from sleep they may recount a dream or incident in the night or an idea that comes to them... (these) begin to be shared and gathered into information, a message, or a plan for the working day... (this) is an intuitive, spontaneous, feeling-full communication in process (which depends on a basic trust in each other).
>
> Alpiri is a gathering of wits on the threshold of sleeping and waking. It may set the direction of the day's work.

It should be noted that this dreaming is not the same as Dreaming or The Dreaming – a term used in English to describe complex indigenous Australian stories as part of group cultural activity sometimes referred to as Song Lines. These are shared cultural dream stories located in landforms (features of the terrain), as well as in mythological stories. Individual dreams may well reinforce relations with a relevant 'Dreaming Story.' Overall, the experience in the 'morning news' (Alpiri morning events) reinforces the value such people find in personal dreams and group sharing, as well as the value of The Dreaming stories (San Roque, personal communication, 2023). The Senoi in Malaysia similarly share dreams in the morning, giving meaning to the day's activities (3.3.1).

In Egyptian Muslim culture, dreaming is a social experience. Dreamers may have collective dreams and 'meet' in their dreams. When sharing dreams, a dreamer may complete another's dream narrative without having been told the dream in advance. Their understanding of this is that they were in the same dream together. Dreams of the dead are seen as real visitations so that while asleep and dreaming, the dreamer may converse with the dead person. Thus, the dream allows the dreamer access to a spiritual world. Similarly, the dream may offer spiritual guidance when the Prophet appears in someone's dream. Sometimes the imam may need to be consulted. For example, the culture recognises that a dream of God could instead be a visitation from Satan, and in this case, guidance is requested (Mittermaier, 2021, pp. 188–189). Working with dreams in this way, Egyptian Muslims may deepen their spiritual understanding during both waking and sleeping hours: dreams thus serve a collective religious purpose, bringing them closer to their community and to God.

Dream-sharing groups exist in Western cultures where, as we have seen, dreams are viewed as individual experiences with or without meaning. Such groups are not (yet) part of mainstream cultural practice and may be formed spontaneously: families or social groups interested in sharing their dreams, or more formally, such as in a social dreaming matrix, a dream webinar, or as part of research, such as the Dream Mapping Project described by Bulkeley. He is an anthropologist with an interest in the creativity of dreams; in particular, he regards dreams as play. 'Dreaming (is) a kind of imaginative play in sleep,' a 'form of spontaneous imaginative creativity' (2021 p. 118). Bulkeley is influenced by the English psychoanalyst D. W. Winnicott, who described the comfort objects infants use, such as a blanket, as a transitional phenomenon:

There is a direct development from transitional phenomena to playing, and from playing to shared playing, and from this to cultural
experiences.

(Ibid., p. 121)

In 2016, Bulkeley gathered together a group of artists who were
immigrants, in response to harsh policies in the United States and
elsewhere towards immigrants. Care was taken to provide a safe and
structured space. He hoped by exploring their dreams together, each
participant could be empowered to 'create alternative versions of
identity, selfhood and community' (ibid., p. 125).

In their dream-sharing workshops, enacting the dreams flowed
naturally from the dream telling and led to performances for small,
invited audiences. The participants experienced this way of working
with dreams as profoundly helpful in relation to their outer world
encounters. Bulkeley felt this showed how dream sharing can lead to
new forms of creativity and well-being in participants.

## 9.3 SOCIAL DREAMING

'Social dreaming' is an intermediate between the cultural anthropology of dreams and the research into dreams as individually meaningful.
Gordon Lawrence, a leading practitioner and developer of this particular dream-sharing method, describes social dreaming as 'a tool of
cultural enquiry (which) seems to illuminate the current problems of
existence' (Lawrence, in Clare and Zarbafi, 2009). Gordon Lawrence
and Paddy Daniel devised 'social dreaming' at the Tavistock Clinic,
London, in 1982; she (Paddy) suggested the term 'matrix' [Box 9.1].

---

### Box 9.1   What is a dream 'matrix'?

- The word 'matrix' comes from the Latin for 'pregnant woman,'
  later 'womb.' The root 'mat' means 'mother.'
- A matrix is a womb within which something can grow and
  develop and is safely contained.
- Within the dream matrix, participants are free to tell their dreams:
  when dreams are 'offered' to the matrix, they no longer belong to
  the individual dreamer.

---

---

**Box 9.2   Social dreaming**

- The starting point is always the Dream and not the dreamer
- The creative act of telling the dream leads to further creativity
- Immersing ourselves in the other's dream tells us something known but hitherto unthinkable

---

Since then, they and their colleagues have trained social dreaming group facilitators, known as 'hosts.'

'Social dreaming is a method that focuses on dreaming with a view to understanding not the 'inner world' of dreamers but the social and institutional reality in which they live' (Neri, 2003, p. 15). The 'primary task' of the social dreaming matrix is to transform the thinking of the dreams of the matrix by means of free association so as to make links and find connections among the dreams in order to be available for new thinking and new knowledge.

In a social dreaming matrix [Box 9.2], individuals come together to tell their dreams; they may or may not know each other. The specific instruction is that this is not a group process, nor is it a venue for exploring each other's dreams for their meaning to the individual. In this way, participants may begin to move from an egocentric perspective to a social perspective, thinking about the 'other' – that is, the social-cultural world we live in. This can be strange for those in a Western culture who are used to thinking about our dreams as belonging to, and meaning something particular for, ourselves. A social dreaming matrix is not an analytic, interpretative approach to dreams.

Dreams offered to the matrix evoke other dreams quite spontaneously, as if the dreams are associating to each other. Participants may add associations to the dreams, something the dream reminds them of, maybe a memory, an image, a song, or an emotion. Interestingly, what happens in the matrix is that the dreams relate to each other in subject matter and/or feeling content. A social dreaming matrix runs for a specific time duration. Participants do not address each other directly, nor do they refer to 'so-and-so's' dream. This is so that group processes, such as competitiveness, anxiety about revealing one's dream, or feeling one's dream is not important, are kept to a minimum. After each dream matrix, there is an opportunity to reflect on the dream and make hypotheses about what the images, feelings, intuitions, and sensations arising from the dreams may tell the participants and reach new knowledge. This is called a Dream Reflection Dialogue. It usually happens that some meaning is found which helps individuals understand and/or relate to their present social circumstances or those of the society/culture they are living in.

The facilitator of the matrix is called a 'host,' this reflects the idea that we are there to receive the dreams; they are our valued guests. The host prepares the room, begins and ends the matrix, and makes sure the task is kept to.

Immersing ourselves in the other's dream tells us something known but hitherto unthinkable. The matrix usually lasts an hour, and the Dream Reflection Dialogue lasts 30 minutes. A matrix may be as small as five people or as large as several hundred.

Interestingly, anthropologists and social dreamers reach similar conclusions based on their respective experiences. Anthropologists assert from their research that dreams comment on current social issues and situations, particularly revealing the undersides of culture, the tricky situations dreamers find themselves in: things that often go unspoken in waking life. The collective situation gives rise to the dreams. Anthropologists and social dreamers notice recurring themes in the dreams, which refer to and elucidate the collective situation [Box 9.3].

In Chapter 2, we learned that time is both linear and not linear. Unconsciously, we have access to nonlinear time; dreams may emerge from this part of our psyches and lead us to experience the dream as having unusual wisdom. Social dreaming is widely used in organisational development and management consultancy, usually when problems arise in organisations [Box 9.4]. Dream matrices may take place on a regular basis with the same group of people, out of individual interest, as part of a research enquiry, or out of a particular need.

---

**Box 9.3   Dreams may point to 'solutions' by trying to understand the inside and outside world**

- Identify significant areas of difficulty, personal and political
- Show missing elements of the self and social world
- Provide tools to help us think and act personally and publicly

---

### Box 9.4    Applications of social dreaming

- Used in organisations facing difficulties to uncover and deal with problems
- As a way of mediation between conflicting parties
- To give voice to groups in difficulty

---

Participating in a dream matrix is an enlivening and moving experience. There is great satisfaction and power in being together with other people in a way which is open, respectful, and non-judgemental. It is a curiously intense relational experience despite (or because of) the lack of our usual social constraints. Whether we know any of the others in the matrix or not makes no difference to this quality of relatedness. The contact is through working together with the dreams.

On the other hand, it can be unnerving to be in a space with other people without being able to use our normal social defences. The hour is full of uncertainty; we don't know what will happen, what we will feel, think, or experience. Many emotions may follow each other, often contradictory. There may be difficult feelings and thoughts – unwanted knowledge. And yet, it can be intensely healing: in our twenty-first-century world, many of us live online, using social media, smartphones, and text messaging, rushing from one activity to another, constantly feeling we don't have enough time, and focussed on what we ought to achieve. Social dreaming gives us an opportunity to stop and reflect in a quiet space without any pressure or striving to achieve something. We are given permission to be who we are rather than who we think we should be to please an ideal version of ourselves or how we think other people want us to be. We do not have to 'do' anything. 'by not trying to get anywhere we arrive somewhere new' (Clare and Zarbafi: 2009, p. 195).

The creativity and freedom of social dreaming have led it to be banned in many totalitarian societies. These societies recognise the power of shared thinking and of thinking new thoughts. Most importantly, social dreaming and the insights and discoveries that ensue cannot be controlled: this makes the practice dangerous to authoritarian societies.

Q:   Can you think of situations where you might want to participate in social dreaming?

In May 2022, I hosted a dream matrix as part of an online venture to support Ukrainians during the attacks on their country by Russia. What the Ukrainian participants valued most was being heard, being listened to, without commentaries. They knew we didn't have any 'answers'; in any case, that's not what they needed. They needed a space to tell their dreams, which also gave them permission to express their feelings of fear, anxiety, despair, and even hope.

New thinking arriving in a social dreaming matrix may be unwelcome: we may not want to know consciously what the dreams have brought forth from the unconscious. I have noticed a reluctance to participate in a matrix, and this may be one reason. Another may be that it is a leap into the unknown; we have no idea where the matrix will take us. In *Dreaming the Future* (Chapter 3 in Experiences in Social Dreaming, op cit), Clare describes a social dreaming matrix held for a year in London (2000–2001). In this matrix the dreams appeared to warn of future catastrophes. One example, nearly a year before the attack on the Twin Towers in New York, is a dream of a high-rise building being attacked; a man outside the building was in a flying contraption, unafraid of death, and those watching could not understand what was happening, there was a sense of helplessness. Clare writes, 'In retrospect this (dream) gives a chilling sense of what was to come on 11 September 2011' (ibid., p. 42).

## 9.4 EXAMPLES OF SOCIAL DREAMING

I was a part of a group in difficulty some years ago when we were devising a new training in Jungian Analysis. Other groups criticised us and tried to stop us. Our group felt attacked and undermined: members started dreaming about the situation spontaneously and we emailed our dreams to each other. These dreams kept us going by showing us our project was both viable and valuable. We agreed that but for this unexpected dream matrix, we would have given up our task. The first dream gave us the hope to continue:

> *I dreamed about our meeting with poison and vitriol about the new training. At the entrance, I had left a little black pouch the size of the palm of my hand with a baby inside. Though I dropped the pouch on a zebra crossing just before going into the meeting, and though it was run over by a car, when I checked inside, the baby was alright. The pouch had become three gold coins, and still the baby was alive inside these coins.*

The 'baby training' did indeed grow, and in the first intake, there were three trainees (paper given to the IAAP conference, Montreal, 2010).

I would now like to discuss a social dreaming matrix which was conducted by email during the COVID-19 pandemic, 2020–2021. The participants were socially and spiritually activist Jungian analysts. We are an international online discussion Google group affiliated with the International Association of Jungian Analysts (IAAP). Our group began several years before the pandemic started, after our first Analysis and Activism conference in London in 2014.

In the early weeks of the lockdowns, which we all experienced at various times, living as we did in different countries, the discussion group became a source of support for many of us, tied as we were to our home environments. Quite spontaneously, we started writing our dreams to each other. The first dream (14.3. 2020) was remarkable:

In the words of the dreamer:

> *The scene happens in the middle of a thick forest. No light is coming through the healthy-looking huge pine trees which are standing closely by one another and through their intense dark green colour almost form something like a protecting 'wall.' At this place there is a very tall pavilion made from glass, transparent, high like about up to the second floor of a building and cylinder shaped. I am standing inside this glass house. There is an entrance, but without a door that could be closed.*
>
> *I feel secure.*
>
> *Now, an owl, a huge owl walks by, standing upright, in the middle of the forest, from the left side, coming slowly, fiercely, not possible to be overlooked, extremely present, self-conscious, autonomous, conscious of her power, not scary, not mean, not evil (at least I wasn't scared in the dream), like an important proud queen, knowing that she IS – and it's unavoidable: 'I am now here and walking by', matter of fact and reality. This is how it is queen, Corona.*

The dreamer's associations:

The owl helps me in a very amazing way. It represents the virus, the illness, also my attitude or my wish to develop this attitude within this tricky situation. It reminds me of Dante, beginning of Divina Commedia:

Nel mezzo del cammin
Mi ritrovai per una selva oscura
Ché la diritta via era smarrita

Midway upon the journey of our life
I found myself within a forest dark
For the straightforward pathway had been lost.
                    (Dreamer's translation)

The selva oscura is the dark wood in which Dante finds himself at
the beginning of 'Hell,' the first book of the Divine Comedy. He has
strayed from the right road and is lost in the dark wood, trying to
escape by climbing a mountain, but is stopped by three wild beasts: a
leopard, a lion, and a she-wolf. The shade of Virgil stands in his way
as he runs from the beasts. Virgil says he will guide Dante through
Hell by another route.

We were in the dark woods of this unknown virus, which was
killing so many of us. There was huge anxiety, and we were isolated from each other. Like Dante, we could see no way out; at the
moment of despair, something came to our aid from the heavens:
this dream. Dante was sent Virgil as a guide through the intercession
of three women: the Virgin Mary, St Lucy, and Beatrice. Many of
us were very moved and somehow comforted by this dream, which
showed us the presence of the coronavirus, just as it is: not evil,
though powerful and important. For many people, COVID-19 has
been a disaster and deathly event, a 'hell,' but for others, it opened
opportunities – for wildlife, too, which appeared unexpectedly:
birdsong in London, dolphins in Venice's canals. An understanding developed of the roots of the pandemic as connected to human
intervention in wild areas of land and trade in live animals. Just
as the wild beasts represented Dante's sins, our sins were those of
destroying wild habitats and failing to respect our non-human fellow beings.

A spontaneous email dream matrix then started: we posted our
dreams thick and fast: 27 dreams in March. There was a pressure to
let our unconscious knowledge emerge and communicate with each
other. I began collecting the dreams. We shared a sense of awe at the
creativity, wisdom, and knowledge in the dreams, as well as tumul-
tuous emotions – fear, exhilaration, sadness, loss, and hope. The
dreams spanned over the course of a year, from March 2020 to April
2021. After this time, the pressure to share dreams diminished, and
now we rarely post dreams. We noticed the vast majority of dreams
were shared by women, and we wondered about this – were the men
not dreaming, or did they feel it was inappropriate to share their
dreams? Did they feel excluded, or did they fear intruding into this

arena which seemed to be feminine? Some writers on social dreaming suggest the first dream of the matrix contains all the dreams. The association to Dante's 'Hell' gives the three holy women as framing our guidance through the months of 2020, so maybe it was the women's dreams that contained our troubled situation.

It is difficult, if not impossible, to communicate the feeling, atmosphere, and flow of a dream matrix in words. Simply recording the dreams can lead to a feeling of flatness or distance. I will give some of the images in this matrix which occurred most frequently, with some illustrative dreams. Dreams have been edited for the sake of clarity.

## 9.5 DREAMS

I've grouped the images and dreams into their subject matter. Most frequent, at least initially, were dreams of the natural world. Animals, birds, reptiles, insects, trees, forests, fruits of the earth, landscapes, the sea, and fresh waters. These were present all through the year, lessening in the last few months as political concerns took over. Nature appeared as both beneficial and fruitful (a panther and her cubs, a fire ritual in the forest, crocodiles with creation myths) and threatening (a stormy sea possibly invading the house, dead or dying vegetables, and injured or tortured animals). Some dreams nourished and gave hope, others felt dangerous, though these elements were simply being true to their nature.

> An old and twisted tree, ancient and huge. A black panther and her two babies were curled up in a nest in the tree. They came towards me and were not at all displaced by my presence.

The dreamer saw the panther as a power animal, and all the animals and insects representing our instincts trying to adjust to the fears and uncertainties of the pandemic.

There were a number of crocodile dreams:

> I dreamed I was on the shore with my daughter, who was young. We were looking at the cartilaginous skeleton which had been washed up, of a sea creature. We suddenly noticed a full-size crocodile on the shingle close to us, just by the skeleton. It snapped its jaws and seemed to come after us. On waking I had a sense that we were safe.
>
> I saw a large crocodile walking through empty suburban streets. A pair of legs were protruding from the mouth of the crocodile, but I felt safe

*because the streets were empty, and concerned about the person being*
*swallowed by the crocodile, and their family.*

Australian members of our group told us there were many creation myths about crocodiles. There was a story by an Elder about a husband and wife being caught up in their fishing nets; the nets made markings on their skin similar to crocodile skin. The people thought they were dead, but they hadn't died; they had become crocodiles. The crocodiles had come to us in our dreams as reminders of death and rebirth. One member noted our need for watchfulness: the crocodile's eyes move independently of each other, so he/she can see different objects at the same time.

Snakes featured often:

*I had walked a long way: through dark forests, deserts, swamps. I had cuts and*
*bruises from the journey. I arrived at a large boulder and discovered a ladder*
*embedded in the side of a large rock. On climbing to the top, I saw a large*
*snake sleeping in the sunshine. It opened its eyes, observed me, and went back*
*to sleep. After admiring the view, I sat down, placing my hand onto a painted*
*hand left by a neolithic ancestor.*

A second group included dreams of people in the natural or built world facing aloneness, hostility, threat, scarcity, and being unable to travel by air. These reflected our conscious anxieties. Dreams of danger, being pursued by hostile men:

*I was being pursued through the woods by terrorists. They were so close I*
*could hear their voices.... I was scared, and I could feel my heart beating in*
*my chest, running as fast as I could. Suddenly the security forces appeared*
*and surrounded the terrorists. I looked at them as they stood disarmed and*
*unmasked and realised I had met them all before.*

Curiously, there were few dreams overtly about the virus, but there were dreams of separation from, and loss of, children. There were also the opposite kinds of dreams, perhaps to give encouragement: Celebrations, redecorations, fire rituals, churches, and worship. Co-operation:

*I'm in a large open space in a forested area with people at a safe distance*
*from each other. There is a rather beautiful pattern to this. From several piles*
*of wood, each person chooses small pieces of wood and larger logs and takes*
*them to a large bonfire somewhere out of sight and places them on the fire.*

*As one person returns, the next person chooses their wood and takes it to the fire. Nothing is said.*

Mythical themes were present:

*I was returning to Australia because I had found the fur seal coat of a selkie and had returned it to her so she could go back to her people. Later in the dream, I was travelling along a path and found a large wooden sign saying, 'aboriginal water hole, follow this path.' I followed the path through the bushland and discovered the waterhole...it never ran empty because it was continually fed by a river running deep inside the earth. I cupped my hands and drank the clear water. I looked up to see a man and woman, elders for the local people who seemed pleased that I had followed the signs to the waterhole. They were smiling and said something about platypus dreaming.*

The dreamer associated selkies, mythological creatures, seals who can transform into women and are part of Nordic lore. Platypus is a special mammal which lays eggs and yet feeds its young on milk, is at home in the water, and breathes air. Perhaps we were being encouraged to develop more flexibility in living?

And environmental concerns:

*There was a pathway through an Amazon jungle through people's disregard for the environment and a need to find a place to dump rubbish. I attempted to clean it up because I knew the Amazon are the lungs of the world, but I heard someone sniggering and sneering. I had no hope of cleaning it up, but I persevered. Other people saw me working and joined me, so we continued to clean up together. I stopped, straightened up, and looked, and I saw we were not only having an impact on the mess, but it was being sorted, and the pathway through the jungle was now simply part of the environment.*

As the year progressed, we dreamed less of separation and loss, and more of political themes.

We dreamed of US president Trump and 'trumped up' charges. The problem of racism:

*A Black American woman sitting on a chair by a city street selling individual cigars. With each cigar, she tells a story. A different story with each cigar. I wonder if they are ancestral stories. Each time a story is told society is altered. This is subversion; this is medicine. I see a signpost with two street names for the same street. The street has two names.*

This was dreamed before the suffocating of George Floyd by police in America, which gave rise to worldwide protests. The road with two names reminded me of the renaming in Washington, DC, to Black Lives Matter Plaza the month after the dream.

Another prescient dream, six months before the attack on the Capitol in Washington:

> I return to a classroom/studio (as if in a university) to retrieve work I had left there. Papers are all over the floor. Instead of getting my things, I see a paper that seems to be shredding itself. I pick it up: it is the US Constitution. Paper ants are pulling it apart. The ants are everywhere on the floor, and they all have a piece of paper they are carrying. I put the constitution back on the floor and want to leave. I don't want the ants all over me.

Other world concerns such as refugees:

> I was supposed to give a talk at a conference about the lives of Palestinian children in Israel. On my way, I kept being rerouted because of construction. I found myself in a place of ever narrower streets. I couldn't turn my car round. I was getting further and further away from the venue and very anxious as it was extremely near my time to speak. I was in a warren of tiny dwellings, newly constructed and with thin walls. Not many people about. Somehow, I was then above the place looking down and saw it as like a refugee camp but permanent dwellings, not tents. Two separate camps like big rectangular blocks seen from above. I never got back to the conference.
> I woke up disturbed.

In the last few months, some of the anxiety dreams recurred, such as storms threatening our home. Concerns about politics and the wider world resurfaced as many of us were moving back into public spaces. Our last recorded dream was a warning of civil unrest following the January attacks on the Capitol in Washington, DC.

> I was in a small official-looking room. President Jeb Bartlett (from the TV series 'The West Wing') was there. He gave me a pair of worn but sturdy wool pants and a black belt: I was to be his aide-de-camp in the field, though my rank was that of a private. He handed me a hat, one that Union privates in the Civil War wore. His senior officers were whispering that there was a spy in the camp. Should I warn Bartlett, or was it not my place, considering my low rank? I was aware we were entering a Civil War.

---

### Box 9.5  Results of pandemic social dream matrix

- Reflecting and giving meaning to our feelings of horror and dread
- Supporting us in our isolation and fear of infection and death
- Acknowledging our separation from loved ones
- Giving voice to the loss of our way of life
- Showing us the beauty of the non-human world and our need for it
- Giving us symbols which nourished our spirits
- Giving us hope for repair and reconstruction
- Giving voice to our concerns for the future

---

What was the value for the participants of this dream matrix, which had to be conducted by email rather than video calls, as we were in different time zones [Box 9.5]? It was exciting to receive the emails containing new dreams; they were fascinating and led to reflections on what they could tell us. Some were prescient; some gave us feelings of recognition and support. Some gave hope for the future; some echoed our concerns for the environment or for democracy. As dreamers, we felt connected though mostly we did not know each other. That the dream matrix met a need was evident in how the dreams tailed off and stopped when the need was no longer present.

## 9.6 CONCLUSIONS

Both cultural anthropologists and social dreaming matrix researchers come to the same conclusions about dream sharing. Dream sharing, in its different forms, formal and informal, is a creative, social act which furthers the participants' creativity. The activity of dream sharing, and social dreaming changes the dreamer, and encourages further dreaming. It is also fun!

'Culture is both a creative expression of dreaming and a generative force in the formation of dreams' (Bulkeley, 2021, p. 114-5) 'dreams become new generators of culture, not just reflective mirrors of it.' (ibid., p. 121)

The act of sharing dreams in these different contexts is a generative cycle which can lead to individual and social fulfilment and wellbeing, based as it is on communication, relationship, and trust. These are gifts our world sorely needs at this time of geopolitical and ecological struggle.

## KEY CONCEPTS

- Sharing dreams is a universal human activity.
- In many non-Western cultures, sharing dreams is a social activity carrying meaning for the community as a whole and may direct communal action.
- A social dreaming matrix is a form of dream sharing in the West which finds meaning in the social and communal activity of dream sharing.

## FURTHER READING

Mageo, J & Sheriff, R. E. (ed.) (2021) *New directions in the anthropology of dreaming*, London: Routledge.

Lawrence, W.G. (2005) *An introduction to social dreaming*, London: Karnac.

Lawrence, W.G. (ed.) (2003) *Experiences in social dreaming*, London: Karnac.

Clare, J. & Zarbafi, A. (2009) *Social dreaming in the 21st century*, London: Routledge.

## REFERENCES

Bulkeley, K. (2021) 'Dream sharing, play, and cultural creativity' in *New Directions in the Anthropology of Dreaming*, ed. Mageo, J & Sheriff, R. E., London: Routledge.

Clare, J. (2003) 'Dreaming the Future' in *Experiences in Social Dreaming*, Ed. W. Gordon Lawrence. London: Karnac. pp. 41–42.

Lawrence, W. G. (2009) Foreword, *Social dreaming in the 21st Century*, Clare, J & Zarbafi, A. London: Routledge.

Mageo, J. (2021). 'Defining new directions in the anthropology of dreaming' in *New Directions in the Anthropology of Dreaming*, ed. Mageo, J & Sheriff, Robin E., London: Routledge.

Mittermaier, A. (2021) Godly dreams: Muslim encounters with the divine, in *New directions in the anthropology of dreaming*, ed. Mageo, J & Sheriff, Robin E., London: Routledge.

Neri, C. (2003) 'Social Dreaming: Report on the workshops held in Mauriburg, Raissa and Clarice Town' in *Experiences in social dreaming*, Ed. W. Gordon Lawrence. London: Karnac. p. 8.

San Roque, C. (2023) Personal communication.

# 10

# PLAY AND THE TRANSCENDENT FUNCTION

## 10.1 INTRODUCTION

Leonardo Da Vinci (1452–1519) said, 'Life is a firmament of mistakes.' No matter how hard we try to get things right, something goes wrong. We may feel anxious and out of control. We may give up. Perfection and control belong to a dominant Western discourse (cultural illusion) which imagines either of these are possible, necessary, or wise. Many religious practices, particularly monotheisms, share Da Vinci's view – in Islamic cultures, carpet makers always make sure there is a deliberate mistake because only God is perfect. Dreams try to balance out a conscious perfectionist attitude or help us give it up. This is part of their reality testing function. We need to play around, make mistakes, and mess up, or we'll learn nothing and create nothing.

The climate change disaster stems from humans trying to 'control,' nature. As a complex emergent system, nature is more than able to control itself. Wars are always about 'control.' Dreams, symbolic communications, are *beyond* control. Our minds are complex emergent systems [3.2] which continually change and evolve. Each night we remake our relationship to our self, to each other, and to our social, political and spiritual worlds. Dreams offer a firmament of possibilities as we retell our stories to ourselves.

In this chapter, I'll look at ways to remember and then play with dreams, and two dream-like experiences – flow states and meditative states. Both show the transcendent function in action. This is a name for a bridge between conscious and unconscious, between a materialist and a spiritual perspective, between the inner and outer worlds.

DOI: 10.4324/9781003319696-10

It's a concept Jung introduced to depth psychology but didn't invent. It's central to spiritual traditions. Dreams are not just about 'me!,' but make strong unconscious links to our society, through the collective unconscious, described in Chapter 9.

Playing with dreams is more user-friendly than 'working' with them. Work implies effort, goals, achievements, rewards – winners and losers. As if something has to be done to a dream to squeeze meaning out, like juice from a lemon. Do we have to work to make an interpretation, to 'reveal the deep hidden meaning?' Our unconscious is on our side. Who else's side could it be on? We can trust it because it *is* us. We don't have to turn messages from our unconscious into problems to solve, because they are solutions. Some therapists are reluctant to 'work with dreams' as they imagine a range of special skills are required (Ellis 2019). The most important skill is patient listening.

## 10.2 REMEMBERING DREAMS

We can't play with a dream if we can't remember it, and the first thing to do is to wish to. This is not simply about making a rational choice; there needs to be an accompanying deep feeling. If it is just a passing fancy, then nothing will happen except disappointment. Between 2 and 5 per cent of people never remember dreams (unless they're woken from REM sleep in a sleep lab). Over 80 per cent of dreams never reach consciousness, yet they evolve empathy and memory perfectly well. As dreams are a natural, nightly gift from the unconscious, we can't command them to appear. We can be receptive and ready to be surprised. Often, after participating in a social dreaming matrix, or a series of them [Chapter 9], those taking part say, 'I haven't remembered any dreams since childhood, but now…'

So, if you wish to recall dreams, it helps to have companions in a formal or informal dream-sharing group. This needs clear, ethical boundaries to avoid drifting into becoming a 'therapy group.' The focus is on the dream, not on the dreamer. Social dreaming lets dreams help us build links to our community. As we do so, the community builds links to us – it's a positive feedback loop. If you wish to recall dreams, then the creative use of the Will [7.4.3] supports the process.

Psychosynthesis suggests the Will has three parts. Good Will means making it easy for yourself; be forgiving when it doesn't work; don't turn it into yet another thing to achieve. A strong Will means keep going. We'd not expect to master the guitar in one self-taught lesson. Skilful Will means 'plan and then remember to carry out the plan.' And revise it when it doesn't work. Notice the benefits of the practice. Encourage yourself.

Good sleep hygiene is important: if you don't sleep, you won't dream. Have a simple, sustainable routine. Don't use your mobile or laptop in bed. Use cues like a hand-written sign, 'What did I dream?' Have a dream notebook ready and a pencil. I've lost many dreams by having one but not the other. Record a dream as soon as you can. Find a symbol which suggests a title – 'the bowler hat with sleeves dream.' You could draw it, maybe like a comic book strip cartoon. Pictures give different results to words.

I once dreamed I met a wise dwarf beside an underground stream. It was awe-inspiring. It wore glasses as big as its head. When I drew the dwarf, I realised the glasses were the same as my analyst's glasses. She was quite small. My awe of her could be worked with once we'd named it. And we could both see the joke in the dream. Looking for jokes makes recall easier. So does focussing on the feelings a dream contains. They are a clue to the meaning.

Find a regular time to review what you record. The more you practise, the easier it becomes. If nothing happens, stop for a couple of weeks, or you'll discourage yourself. Once you have several dreams, look for themes and patterns. Be curious rather than judgemental. You are listening to yourself, and there is no 'right way' to do this.

## 10.3 PLAYING WITH DREAMS

Play suspends aspects of reality testing; we don't switch our ego off; we tune it in to a play world (a magic kingdom) in which a stick can be a gun, a sword, or a wand. Play isn't 'for' anything. There are no goals. We string actions and stories together for the fun of it. 'Dreamwork' is a technical term in psychoanalysis, meaning the work done by the unconscious to create a dream. Work suggests effort and reward – perhaps it might be 'a deeper sense of self,' as if 'becoming your self' were a task rather than a gift.

For children, work is something grown-ups do; play is what we do. Counsellors, therapists, and analysts often talk about 'the Inner Child,' meaning both what happened to us as children and seeing the world like a child again, with awe and wonder. Even though an analyst listens to thousands of dreams, each is new and surprising. There are no 'standard symbols' or interpretations. It's always an improvisation, like jazz music. And, of course, classical music is interpreted differently each time it's played.

James Hillman's archetypal version of analytical psychology says the best thing to do with a dream is engage with it. Play in the dream stream. We learn to reality test through play (Winnicott, 1974, pp. 3, 15, 153). Playfulness is one of the seven core emotions – the others are seeking, rage, fear, lust, care, grief – all these emotions shape dreams (Panksepp, 2012, pp. 1–46, 63–80).

Play is recreation ... re-creation. It's both fun and deeply serious at the same time. A complex is a closed system, so it's almost impossible to play with it or within it – it can only be serious. Some people approach politics and religion in this way, as if they were arrangements of rules which we *must* take seriously – or we'll be damned, or sent to the death camp, or whatever. Dreams are never bound by the rules and regulations of a complex, a politics, or a religion. They can be *about* it, but they are not *part of* it. They are often keys to the door of a complex.

> *Dreams are invariably seeking to express something that the ego does not know and does not understand.*
>
> (Jung, CW 17, para. 187)

Here are some playful ideas. Be curious about how a dream feels: during and afterwards when you wake. Look for what isn't there when it might be expected. Tell the dream's story backwards. Or start in the middle and go through it till you get back to where you began. Dreams can be read in any direction. You can play at being any of the people or objects in the dream and tell the story from their point of view. If there's a dragon, a hero, and a princess – draw them, or make a model, or find images online, or research myths and fairytales about this trio. Write a poem or a story. Act it. Dance it. Compose a song or piece of music.

Analytic patients I've learnt from wrote rock songs, plays, detective novels, poetry, made art, acted, or danced. Fred, the footballer, used his dream moves to score goals. They applied their dreams to their existing creative processes.

Dreams arise from life and relate to it and to the dreamer's cultural context. So, interpreting out of context can never work. It is possible to 'free-associate' by yourself, saying or writing the first thing that comes into your head, but usually, as soon as the associations become troubling (confusing, violent, sexual, or too confronting), we stop. Then it feels like we've failed. An analyst is like a personal trainer in the gym – they encourage you to keep going, but they don't lift the weights for you.

As shown in Chapter 9, you don't have to interpret anyone else's dreams in a group. It is best not to. Sherlock Holmes said, 'Never theorise without data.' In an informal group, you may not have any information about the other participants, so 'interpretation' is an intrusion into their personal space. Dream interpretation has a place, but learning from a dream comes about through play far better than trying to work out a meaning from analytic first principles. That kind of interpretation can easily turn into an intellectual defence – by both the patient and the analyst. Jung commented on the hazards of interpreting:

> *Enlightening as interpretation on the subjective level may be ..., it may be entirely worthless when a vitally important relationship is the content and cause of the conflict. Here the dream figure must be related to the real object.*
> (CW 8: para 515)

You can treat a dream as 'a play' or a film – written, produced, directed, and starring the dreamer – who is all of the cast and the film crew, director, and producer. Use the same techniques as any art critic – not just 'what does this mean,' but 'what genre is this? Is it well told? Is it aesthetically pleasing? What feeling is it illustrating …?' and so on. Whilst writing this, I had a 'blockbuster action movie' dream. A gang of Scots bandits were having a shoot-out with the cops. The cops won by spraying them with 'the black mud of occultism.' As I'm going to talk about the transcendent function next, this may be an appropriate image.

## 10.4 THE TRANSCENDENT FUNCTION

Transcendent is Latin for *to go beyond*. In maths, it describes non-algebraic numbers like $\pi$ or $e$. In biological science, it is a way to talk about living beings as complex emergent systems which go beyond their immediate environment because they are always part of an ecosystem. In Greek philosophy, transcendental properties include being, truth, beauty, and goodness: concepts which can't be reduced to anything else. In later Western philosophy, it is a name for explorations about how it is possible to know anything, explored by

Hume, Kant, and Bergson [5.6]. It's a meditation technique based on ancient Hindu practices, where silent inner repetitions of a mantra increase self-awareness, reduce anxiety, and allow different states of consciousness to appear. In religions, it talks about those aspects of God (and/or the spirit world) outside human understanding.

In analytical psychology, the transcendent function is a bridge – a third space – linking the conscious and unconscious. It's 'between' – {*both/and / neither/nor*} – both conscious and unconscious, neither conscious nor unconscious. Dreams can have a transcendent function, but not all of them do. Jung first wrote about it in 1916, though his essay 'The Transcendent Function' was not published till 1957 (CW 8: Para 131–193). He describes a dialogue where both conscious and unconscious are like 'two adult human beings with equal rights': neither is in charge. Freud imagined the unconscious contained 'bad stuff,' which had to be kept there during sleep by a dream censor. Jung imagined the unconscious as an inner world where dreams compensate for and often disagree with the conscious. Both are true, each are true, neither are true, nor not true.

The transcendent function balances conflicting interests and demands and speaks in symbols. A *symbol* = *sign* + {*x*}, where {*x*} is an unknowable rather than an unknown [2.3]. No dream can be distilled to find the essence of its meaning. There are no magic formulas. Sometimes Jungian analysts try to do this by talking about the archetypal images in a dream but then start mistaking these concepts for *things* – as in, 'the Anima wants this,' 'the Hero is doing that,' and this is the same problem of turning a concept into a thing as Freud's 'standard symbols' only using fancier language, which is why free association, an open system, helps. We stumble over things we've tried to hide from our ego. Play does this too. It lets us go beyond the known and the safe.

The transcendent function suggests new ways to learn from mistakes and how to make bigger and better ones.

> It is a natural process – a manifestation of the energy which springs from the tension of opposites, and it consists in a series of fantasy-occurrences which appear spontaneously in dreams and visions.
>
> (Jung, CW7 para. 121)

However, Jung had several views about the transcendent function, and changed his mind over his lifetime. He said sometimes dreams 'didn't have enough emotional tension for the function to operate,' and sometimes they did (Miller, 2004, pp. 72–75). I think this shows that the transcendent function is not a way of *doing*. Nor is it the opposite – a way of being 'done to' by a Spirit in the Sky. It's about *being*. A good question to ask of any dream is, 'What happens if I *be with* this?' Sometimes '*being with*' is the only thing to do. It is going beyond any need for perfection or control, moving away from 'knowing the facts' towards being wise ("being with not-knowing"); recognising and accepting that many things are forever outside of our control, as do members of Alcoholics and Narcotics Anonymous.

Ex-addicts in recovery trust a 'Higher Power' to help them. If you understand this Higher Power as a spiritual being, fine. If not, not. A Higher Power can mean the collective wisdom of a group – the others in recovery; it certainly means loving acceptance by those who have 'been there too.' Many religious and spiritual groups share this idea of collective wisdom – but not all. It depends on whether those involved can stand back (transcend) the power needs of their ego. Is the group spirituality mature or not? This applies to political groups. We need discernment to discover what these social groups truly are rather than what their marketing says they are, which is equally true in the psyche: the marketing department of any complex will always try to persuade you that living without it is impossible. A function of dreaming is to develop discriminating wisdom and ask better questions.

Q: What would the results of this look like?

---

### Box 10.1   Developing wisdom

- Experience goodness
- Judicious
- Empathy and humour
- Knowledge comes from direct experience rather than 'belief'
- Discernment
- Finding your own meaning
- Sense of belonging
- Intuition

---

These eight factors are drawn from *the Tao of Wisdom* (Rosen and Crouse, in Young-Eisendrath and Miller, 2000, pp. 120–129). To develop these qualities, it helps to look for them in dreams and imagine them in action.

## 10.5 ACTIVE IMAGINATION

Marie-Louise von Franz described dreams as a letter from the self (1997, p. 72), and in *Alchemical Active Imagination*, she describes how this technique has been used since ancient times as a way of projecting unconscious content onto and into the physical world. The listening therapies use active imagination, drawing on work by the French psychotherapist Robert Desoille (1890–1966), who specialised in 'waking dreams.' He'd invite his patients to lie down comfortably, close their eyes, relax, and 'go inside' – imagining a setting in which they see themselves solving a problem and then come back to the room and work out how to apply what they found. In psychosynthesis, an exercise might be, '… imagine you are in a beautiful meadow where you meet a wise *being* …' In one training group, I misheard the instructions and met a wise *bean*. This worked too. The therapist may make suggestions. You might write the images down or draw them. You can use the same technique with dreams. Relax, close your eyes, go into the dream – perhaps 'dream it on' and imagine what happened next, or rewrite it as if it were a film; then this is like shooting the same scene in different ways.

Do you wonder, 'What would happen if you shot the dragon, or gave it a cake, or filmed the scene from its point of view?' Turn it into 'the Disney cartoon version,' the 'slasher horror,' or even 'the rom-com' – you and the dragon are on a date? There is no need to be reverent about any dream or its images. There is no rule saying you must take it seriously – the more serious it is, the more useful humour is. And this is true for mindfulness and meditation. A good way to spoil any meditative practice is to take it too seriously and strive after a result. After all, 'enlightenment' means 'to lighten up' – to discover life does not have to be one struggle after another.

## 10.6 MINDFULNESS AND MEDITATION

It may not be immediately obvious what this is doing in a book on dreams. We don't dream when we meditate, do we? Well, as discussed in Chapter 5, the three network model shows how dreams balance the body, feelings, and mind. Mindfulness and meditation use exactly the same balancing act – whilst awake (until the meditator falls asleep, which often happens). These practices alter consciousness over time and with patient repetition. There are thousands of feelings and reasons why anyone chooses to meditate, and at least ten thousand ways to do it. A few people try to learn it on their own. But you need a teacher and a group to practise with. I don't think it is safe to miss out on personal instruction or learn how to meditate from a YouTube clip – nor it wise to learn to fly an aeroplane this way. The problem isn't taking off; it's landing. Mindfulness and meditation work, powerfully. Grounding again afterwards is the hardest part.

Mindfulness recently became an addition to therapy (Shapiro and Izett, n.d., pp. 161–175, in Hick and Bien, 2008). It was developed by Jon Kabat Zinn (1990/2013), a student of Zen and professor of medicine in Cambridge (Massachusetts). Some see it as 'Buddhism without beliefs.' The mindfulness-based stress reduction technique is used worldwide, emphasising the connections between emotional and physical well-being. However, as with any medical treatment, 'a third of patients get better, a third stay the same, and a third get worse.' The skill is guessing which group any patient will end up in. And, of course, anxious people get anxious about mindfulness, depressed people get frustrated, and obsessional people obsess.

Like many treatments, mindfulness works best for those who are not ill – 'the worried well.' The technique is a 'mental calisthenic' – an exercise which uses one strength against another. We use the executive mode against the default mode – and vice versa – with the salience mode as the balance point for the seesaw. And this is the same in meditation.

They work like this. We find a comfortable position for the body, relax into it, and focus on a 'meditation object,' usually the breath, sometimes a word or phrase, or a mental image. This does not mean breathing in a special way (though that can be done). It means noticing breath going in and coming out, arising, and passing away. As we're no longer doing any other task, the executive network goes 'on hold.' As soon as it does, the default mode network does what it does, which is tell us a story – any story – the same as when we dream. Often, the stories are anxious ruminations or wishes (as in dreams); sometimes they are quite random. Then the salience network goes, 'Hey guys! What about the breath?' And the executive network goes, 'Oh, yes! The breath' and turns the default mode network down. This lasts a few minutes, and then it repeats. Hundreds of times – thousands of times. Eventually, we are able to observe this without judging ourselves.

In some meditation practices, the meditator adds active imagination – in Tibetan Buddhism, this might be visualising a protective deity, and this can be attempted during sleep (Knauft, 2021, pp. 2–4, p. 226). Dreaming and meditation start to merge. To do this safely, you need to be a Tibetan monk or nun because community support is essential to avoid losing the ability to reality test and becoming psychotic.

Slowly, gradually, meditators give up imagining there is a 'right way' to do meditation. We realise it isn't about 'controlling the mind' or even 'purifying the mind'; it is what it is. We can't help but tell ourselves stories; that's what the default mode network does. They are only stories. We might get caught up in an unresolved emotion. We can't help this either. We learn to go, 'Oh, there I go again, telling a story. I don't have to get drawn in,' or 'I'm worrying about something someone said sixty years ago.' The story and the emotion may stop, change, or get louder. But the ability to observe (to see what is salient, use the salience network) increases. When we learn to watch dreams, this strengthens the same skill.

We can never disconnect the default mode network, but we don't have to believe it. What we do, by coming back to the meditation object, is to develop *present-moment awareness*. 'I am here, now.' This is a skill any analyst uses in any session: 'We are here now. Nothing needs to be done. There is nowhere to go.' With dreams, this is why it's best not to 'work' on them. Be *with* them. This is quite different.

A version of mediation is found in many religious traditions. It's part of the contemplative movement in the monotheisms: the spiritual exercises of St Ignatius Loyola in Catholicism, or the 'waiting on God' in a Friends' Meeting (Quakers), the inward practices in Sufism, the many mystical aspects of Judaism. It's a key practice in Hindu and Buddhist traditions and in shamanic practices, where it is often combined with active imagination.

Mindfulness and meditation do not 'raise consciousness'; they balance the three networks. This may (sometimes) allow consciousness to become clearer. The 'storyteller' (default mode network) keeps putting a word in. We can't do meditation 'right' and achieve an ever-tranquil mind, except for maybe a few monks, nuns, and wandering Indian holy men. They are professional meditators.

Doing an activity which is bound to fail is the point of doing it. It's a paradox. We can let go of a need to 'be in control' once we know we can't be. This is the same for dreams. In meditation and dreaming, our ego is temporarily suspended. It can have a holiday. Both are examples of what analysts call 'being with not knowing' – we can't know; we can only be in the moment. Here is another example.

## 10.7 FLOW STATES

An 'ego holiday' also happens in flow states. This is the complete absorption in a task, in which we lose track of time and the world outside. It could be doing anything we deeply love: painting a picture for an artist, writing for a writer, skiing for a skier, playing football for a footballer – we are 'in the zone,' concentrating so much we forget we're concentrating. It was named by the Hungarian psychologist Mihály Csíkszentmihályi (in English, his name is Michael St Michael) in 1970. As a youth, he'd heard Jung talk about UFOs, explaining they were a projection from the unconscious mind, as people have an inner need to find explanations outside of themselves. Inspired, he became a psychologist, wondering what happened in 'flow' (Csikszentmihályi, 1988, pp. 15–35; Box 10.2). His findings are summarised here:

---

**Box 10.2  Characteristics of a flow state**

- Intense present-moment awareness
- Actions flow seamlessly
- No self-consciousness
- Keen sense of control
- Lose all sense of external time
- Feels rewarding in itself

---

Action and consciousness melt together. It is a form of 'hyper-focus,' like what happens if you play a computer game non-stop, forgetting to eat or sleep. Then, it is a kind of autistic encapsulation – getting lost in a fantasy world, perhaps for protection against emotional pressures from within or without. In a creative flow, the three networks are fully cooperating. Indian classical musicians, jazz artists, and rock drummers can be in this state when they are 'in the groove.' They can play all night.

Q:  What other activities become flow states? Have you been in one yourself?

## 10.8 DREAMS, POLITICAL AND SPIRITUAL PRACTICE

Transcendence is play: play is transcendent. Through the book, I've played with a tension between materialism and spirituality, as if they were separate. This is a dominant Western discourse. What if it's wrong? Suppose we try the same conjunction used by dream symbols. We are material {both/and / neither/nor} spiritual beings. This gives a huge number of possibilities: it's another way of using the Jung-Pauli conjecture [8.3.5], of exploring a level of reality in which both are true – a transcendent reality, which we glimpse in mindfulness, meditation, flow states, and, particularly, dreams. So, dreams may be 'a portal to the source' and 'a gateway to the self' – but most are not.

Q: When dreams have a direct religious and/or political content, could or should this be taken literally and be a basis for action?

A spiritually seeking friend having a hard time grumbled, 'But I've been working so hard on myself,' which to me sounded like a surfer saying, 'But I've been working hard on the ocean.' There's a problem of scale. If self means 'the totality of my being' (like the iceberg picture in Chapter 2), then it's self which works on our ego, our reality testing function. 'Personal growth'– or 'spiritual development' (these terms get used as if they are interchangeable) – is not an ego-directed task. It is not about power or control.

The problem is a fantasy that control of the unconscious is possible, necessary, or wise. This illusion generalises to the religious and political world. There has never been an example of any religion/political system in which 'one-size-fits-all' works – attempts to do this drift into authoritarianism and empowering a 'Great Leader.' Dreams – whether wish fulfilments or compensations for the conscious attitude, or both – work against 'grand narratives' and 'theories of everything' simply because they use a language which can't be pinned down: symbolic language.

Here is a suggestion about how this works based on the work of the Californian analytical psychologist and Kabbalah scholar Stephen Joseph (1996). Kabbalah is part of the Jewish mystery tradition. After I heard him give this paper, I spent years wondering about it. I'm still not sure if I understand it. But it applies to how we are with any dream. He suggests there are four ways we can experience the Spirit (God) or the meaning of a dream [Box 10.3]:

---

**Box 10.3    Presence and absence, luminous and non-luminous**

|  | Presence | Absence |
| --- | --- | --- |
| **Luminous** | Angel | Loss |
| **Non-luminous** | Tranquillity | Meditative calm |

---

God is construed as existing before, during, and after time; being everywhere in space (omnipresent); and able to do anything (omnipotent). We can't imagine this. We sometimes have moments when we have a 'numinous' (spiritual) experience. These can be luminous, light, and bright or non-luminous, dark, and shadowy. We can experience them as a presence – a 'something' or an absence – a 'nothing.'

When we recall a dream, it is, at first, a luminous presence – we may carry the feelings in it around all day (or our whole lives). As it fades, it becomes a luminous absence – we know we dreamed but aren't sure what, and we may search for the lost dream. Or it may be that we wake with a new feeling: perhaps optimism instead of despair. The dream itself is invisible (non-luminous), but its presence remains. Or we wake with no dreams and no new feelings. Adults almost always dream for at least two hours a night, so we will have dreamed. But we neither remember nor miss the dream. It's non-luminously absent.

When playing with dreams, have this in mind: if there are four possibilities and an equal chance of each, then only one in four dreams will be 'luminously present,' another quarter we know we've missed, and half are 'non-luminous.' If it's difficult to remember dreams, this isn't because you're 'not doing it properly'; it's because this is their nature. If you suppose, as some do, dreams are communications from the spirit world, or maybe from God, no one expects an angel to appear when we 'command' them – (that's hubris) – it's the same with dreams. An old-fashioned Christian term is 'grace' – meaning they are a gift from God.

Dreams are certainly a gift from our unconscious. And, as self is beyond the personal (it's transpersonal), then 'growth' isn't achieved by jumping up and down and shouting 'grow, grow, grow!' or trying to shovel meaning into a dream. Self emerges patiently – like any other complex emergent system. This is especially true if/when dreams seem to suggest religious or political actions – developed wisdom is needed to consider 'what happens if?'

## 10.9 CONCLUSIONS

Some people imagine the mind can be explained, perhaps by analytical theories, or religious/political ideas (like the Marxist notion of 'the power of the class struggle' or the Christian one of 'salvation'), or by neuroscience; 'if only we had a good enough map, we'd know what a mind was.' This is like supposing we could explain the universe if only we had a big enough telescope. Structure does relate to function, but overemphasising structure is like seeing a car as a collection of parts rather than as a vehicle. Put simply, the brain is 'the parts,' and 'the mind' chooses the direction you want to drive and what you'll do at your destination: it is the navigator.

It is not necessary to 'make meaning' from any dream. It's an option. Meaning making will happen anyway as the three networks balance each other. And, truly, they are not 'the mind.' This includes the whole of the body and extends deeply into the social, political, and spiritual world we live in. We can find what a dream's meaning and purpose is only by referring to and engaging in the real out-there world. This is what dreams are for.

## KEY CONCEPTS FROM THE BOOK

**Dreams are involved in**

- empathy;
- connection to culture, society, and the world;
- memory and future memory;
- reality testing, using the counterfactual;
- creativity; and
- transcendent experience.

## FURTHER READING

Ellis, L. (2019) *A clinician's guide to dream therapy*, London: Routledge.

Panksepp, J. (2012) *The archaeology of mind*, New York: Norton.

## REFERENCES

Csikszentmihályi, M. (1988).'*The flow experience and its significance for human psychology.' Optimal experience: psychological studies of flow in consciousness.* Cambridge, UK: Cambridge University Press.

Joseph, S. M. (1996) 'Presence and absence through the mirror of transference: a model of the transcendent function', *Journal of Analytical Psychology* 42:1, 139–156/?2, 3.

Jung, C. G. (1953–1977) *Except where indicated, references are by volume and paragraph number to the collected works of C. G.* Jung, 20 vol. (ed. Herbert Read, Michael Fordham & Gerhard Adler; trans. R. F. C. Hull). London: Routledge, Princeton: Princeton University Press.

Hick, S. F., & Bien, T. (2008) *Mindfulness and the therapeutic relationship*, London: The Guilford Press.

Kabat-Zinn, J. (1990/2013) *Full catastrophe living: Using the wisdom of your body and mind to face stress, pain, and illness* London: Random House.

Knauft, B.M. (2021) Life is but a dream: culture and science in the study of Tibetan dream yoga and lucid dreaming, in Mageo, J., & Sheriff, R.E. (eds.), *New directions in the anthropology of social dreaming*, London: Routledge.

Miller, J. C. (2004) *The transcendent function*, Albany, NY: The State University of New York Press.

Rosen, D. H., & Crouse, E. M., in Young-Eisendrath, P., & Miller, M. (eds) (2000) *The psychology of mature spirituality*, London: Routledge.

Shapiro, S. L., & Izett, C. D. (2008) Meditation a universal tool for cultivating empathy. In Hick, S.F. and Bien, T., (eds) *Mindfulness and the therapeutic relationship.* pp. 3–18, New York: The Guildford Press.

Winnicott, D. (1974) *Playing and reality*, London: Pelican.

Von Franz, M. (1997) *Alchemical active imagination*, London: Shambhala.

# GLOSSARY

*This is a guide to technical terms in the book. Some words have more than one meaning, depending on who is using the word and what for. You may have to make up your own mind about their meaning. Neuroanatomy terms are in a separate glossary.*

**Archetype**   an inborn, genetic capacity for a range of physical and psychological behaviours; for example, 'parenting' is an archetypal pattern similar in all mammals. In analytical psychology, it is the first form of a thing or idea, which succeeding forms imitate.

**Boundary**   the edge between two things: the edge of a cricket or baseball pitch is the boundary. The edge between one person and another, and one nation and another.

**Category error**   (philosophy) to put a thing or idea in one category when it belongs in another: if when watching a team game we are told it depends on 'team spirit,' and then we ask, 'Which player is "team spirit?"'

**Collective unconscious**   (analytical psychology) archetypal patterns unconsciously shared by all people, at all times, in all cultures. This holds and contains the personal unconscious. Jung thought this explained why mythologies and religions take similar patterns everywhere.

**Complex**   a pattern of thoughts, feelings, and behaviours often originating from traumas in early life in which a 'triggering event' will produce an inevitable, overwhelming, and irresistible response. For example, if bitten by a dog as an infant, then all dogs trigger anxiety.

**Container/contained** (psychoanalysis) an idea introduced by Wilfred Bion. The mother, 'mothering functions,' and her container (her partner, family, and culture) contain an infant's developing body, feelings, and mind (the contained). In dreams, the container is the image or story; the contained is the symbol and the feeling within.

**Conscious** (from Latin, *con* – with, *sciere* – to know) knowing, alert, awake. Awareness of a sensation, feeling, thought, or intuition.

**Cybernetics** (from Greek, *kubernetikos* – a steersman, a pilot) the study of communication and control in a system, whether a machine or a living system (an ecology). A simple example is central heating: a thermostat controls a heat source, and there is a feedback loop between it and the boiler. A complex example might be a forest where the demands of different species compete.

**Discourse** a system of thought by which we create our world or by which a world is created. There are power issues involved in discourses: who gets to name what is important, as seen in any political or religious statement about what is 'true.'

**Dreamwork** *(psychoanalysis)* a technical term meaning the work done by the unconscious to create a dream.

**Ego** (Latin for *'I.'*) It mediates between the primitive demands of the id (cf) and superego (cf), is concerned with reality testing, and has perceptive, defensive, and decision-making functions. This uses 'if–then' thinking: if I do {x}, then I predict {y}.'

**Epistemology** (Greek, *episteme* – knowledge, logos – *knowledge about*) philosophical questions about how we know what we know. If I say, 'It's true,' and you say, 'It's false,' how do we discover who is correct?

**Flow state** (Latin, *fluos*, to flow) able to perform an action so well that it looks effortless, as when a native speaker talks in their own language or when a skilled musician improvises.

**Fluent form** a system in which each part continually changes, yet the appearance stays the same – like a waterfall, or a candle flame.

**Fractal** (Latin, *fractus*, broken) a mathematical process which produces a figure with self-similarity: if you zoom in or out on it, it looks similar. Shorelines, clouds, trees, and galaxies – all natural objects have fractal boundaries, as do consciousness and unconsciousness. We feel as though there is a boundary, but it's hard to say where it is.

**Free association**   saying (writing or drawing) whatever appears in consciousness, often in response to a dream, without censoring it. Allowing new images and connections to emerge, unforced, from the unconscious.

**Hallucination**   a conscious perception without an external stimulus; we see, hear, taste, smell, or touch something which is not there.

**Homoeostasis**   maintaining a desired condition – like room temperature. In a living being, keeping the internal world physically and chemically at the best conditions for survival and growth.

**Liminal**   (Latin, *limen* – a doorway, a threshold) beginning, in between, neither inside nor outside. A liminal person lives on the edges of society – a tramp.

**Logical operator**   a set of instructions, like those used in computer programming. For example, {either/or}, {if/then}, {neither/nor}. Ego uses them to reality test.

**Metaphor**   (Greek: *meta* – across, and *phorein* – to carry) a figure of speech, where one thing is described as like another: 'as strong as an ox.'

**Myth**   a folk story with a cultural purpose. For example, an 'origin myth' explains how a people came to be (In America, the myth of 'the Pilgrim Fathers' founding the nation. In Western cultures, the myth of Santa Claus.) A 'religious myth' explains a spiritual truth: 'an Angel dictated the scriptures to…'

**Narrative**   a story. A fiction or non-fiction created to entertain or inform.

**Ontology**   (Greek, *ontos* – being, logos, knowledge about) the philosophy of being, how we categorise things and ideas – their properties and relationships. Apples and cherries are in the category 'red fruit,' 'capitalism and communism' are in the category 'political system.' But to say communists are 'reds' and so they belong to the category 'red fruit' is an ontological error.

**Persona**   (Greek, *persona* – the mask worn by an actor in Ancient Greek theatre) the face or faces we show to other people and the outside world.

**Personality disorders**   in psychiatry, a pattern of behaviour characterised by rigid thoughts and actions. They result in a person having a reduced emotional range. Two common disorders are:

**Borderline personality disorder**   extreme black-and-white thinking (uses 'either/or,' as in 'I'm right, and you're wrong!') with an unstable self-image and emotions.

**Narcissistic personality disorder**  overinflated sense of self-importance, brittle, aggressive if challenged. Often can't tell the difference between the truth and lies.

**Self**  a person as the subject of their own consciousness; it includes our self-image (who we imagine we are) and how we imagine others see us; it exists in relation to others and contains our potential. It includes the body, feelings, mental formations, and consciousness; most of the self is unconscious, unknown, and unknowable.

**Semiotics**  the study of signs and symbols to explore the process of creating and validating meaning. It is like 'an aesthetics of meaning': aesthetics helps us decide if an artwork is beautiful or not, well-made or not, truthful or not.

**Sign**  a word, object, or gesture which gives specific information: a red light means stop; 'EXIT' means exit. It does not change over time. A closed system.

**Sub-personalities**  different characters and personalities which are part of us and often come from a complex like 'a wounded inner child' or 'critic.'

**Symbol**  (Greek: *sym* – together, and *bolos* – to throw, hence 'to put together') a word, object, or gesture representing a concept or idea: an open system whose meaning emerges across time. In maths, {x} is often used as a symbol for an unknown, which can be found. When a cross symbolises Christianity or an eight-spoked wheel Buddhism, then the image suggests deep ideas which can't be put into words.

**Teleology**  (Greek: *telos* – end, *logos* – explanation) to explain things in terms of their purpose – 'the purpose of a knife is to cut,' or 'the purpose of a life is to...?'

**Transcendent**  (Latin – *transcendere*, to exceed) in maths, a transcendent function is a value which cannot be expressed in algebra – a logarithm or an exponential. In philosophy, properties of being, such as truth, beauty, and goodness. In analytical psychology, a bridge between the inner and outer world where the spiritual meets the material.

**Transference**  literally moving a thing from one place to another: in analysis, when a patient moves an emotion from a previous relationship (a parent) onto another person (a partner or their analyst). A countertransference is the same movement of emotion in an analyst towards a patient. Both always occur together.

**Unconscious**  (same Latin root as conscious, the prefix '*un*' – not) not aware, alert, or awake.

# NEUROANATOMY GLOSSARY

This short glossary gives more detail about the anatomical areas which are discussed in the book. You can find out more in the references at the end.

## INTRODUCTION

An adult human brain weighs about 1.5 to 2 kg. From the outside, it looks like a walnut. It's made of neurons; the cells which support and nourish them, called glial cells; and blood vessels. There are spaces inside, called ventricles, filled with cerebrospinal fluid (cushioning against knocks on the head and for cleaning and nourishing). A brain is the consistency of thick yoghurt. It's hard to know where one part ends and another begins.

The study of neuroanatomy probably began in ancient Egypt. Since then, doctors have recognised traumatic injuries to certain parts of the brain and that certain illnesses cause loss of function. Until the twentieth century, neuroanatomy was mostly descriptive. This century has seen a huge increase in the understanding of function using fMRI scans [5.5.1]. When part of the brain is working, it uses more oxygen, so it's now possible to map out what's working and when.

In the 1950s, neuroanatomist Paul D. MacLean described the brain as having three different layers ('the triune brain'): At the base is the 'reptilian' brain – clusters of neurons called 'basal ganglia' in the medulla and pons responsible for instincts and body maintenance: heart rate, respiratory rate, waking and sleeping, maintaining temperature, and awareness of pain. At the back is the cerebellum, which is responsible for balance.

Above them sits the limbic system –'the old mammalian brain' – the cingulate, amygdala, hypothalamus, and hippocampus. They are responsible for feeling and emotion.

Above this is the cortex, 'the new mammal brain,' divided into two halves – the right and left hemisphere – and four lobes.

Behind the forehead is the frontal lobe; it is responsible for thinking. Above the ears is the parietal lobe, which is responsible for sensation and movement. Behind and below the ears is the temporal lobe; it is responsible for hearing and speech. At the back of the head, the occipital lobe is responsible for vision.

This is a huge oversimplification, as no part of the brain ever operates independently. All perceptions are multi-modal – we use all of them all the time because we search for perceptions rather than passively noticing what's going on. It is true that certain areas are responsible for certain functions. Today, the key concept is 'networks,' not 'areas.' These networks, working together, make a mind. The body, its maintenance, and our thoughts and feelings are inseparable.

Three key networks (salience, executive, and default mode) are described in Chapter 5. They are involved in vigilance, decision-making, and 'storytelling.' Understanding what they do, how they interact, and how problems in them contribute to a wide range of emotional distress and mental disorders is only beginning. They all have crucial roles in developing empathy, memory, and a sense of self. None of them are the 'self,' nor are they the 'ego.' And there are many, many other networks.

**Location** Anatomists use these terms to locate a structure's position:

> Inferior – below
> Superior – above
> Anterior – in front of something
> Posterior – behind something
> Medial – near to the middle
> Lateral – near to the side
> Dorsal – towards the back
> Ventral – towards the front

Most of the structures and functions of the brain have been deliberately left out in order to focus on those parts involved in sleep and dreaming. Beginning at the base of the brain and going upwards:

## The medulla and basal ganglia:

**Periaqueductal grey matter** A nucleus (set of neurons) around the canal between the third and fourth ventricles. Crucial in autonomic function, responses to threats, and maternal behaviour. Involved in initiating dreams.

**Reticular activating system** (*looks like an old-fashioned net handbag called a reticule*) Engaged in networks which control heart rate and modulate pain. Responsible for arousal and sleep. If these parts are damaged, the result is an irreversible coma.

## The limbic system:

**Amygdala** (*'the almond'*) There are two, one near the middle of each temporal lobe. They have key roles in memory processing and emotional response – including decision-making, and fear. This is why memory and emotion are so intricately connected, as we code both at the same time. It's like the mind's 'panic button.' The right side seems more concerned with sadness and distress, and the left with pleasure and joy – they always work together. Essential for memory consolidation and transfer from explicit to implicit memory.

**Cingulate cortex** Immediately under the cortex, like the lining of a cap, and above the corpus callosum (the bundle of nerve fibres connecting the right and left hemispheres). It has inputs from the thalamus (below it) and the rest of the cortex (above it). Essential for all aspects of information processing, memory, and learning. It links sensation to feeling to thought and is responsible for motivation. It's likely all major mental illnesses (depression, bipolar disorder, and schizophrenia) involve serious changes to its function.

**Anterior cingulate** (at the front) Attention, decision-making, solving difficult problems, impulse control, and emotion. Part of the executive network.

**Posterior cingulate** (at the back) The most active part of the brain, day and night. Sews thoughts and feelings together. Connects to everything else, especially the thalamus. A key part of the default mode network. One of the first parts affected by dementia.

**Hippocampus** (*'the sea horse'*) There are two, one on each side at the base of the cortex, in the medial part of the temporal lobe. They network closely with the amygdala. The hippocampus is essential for memory consolidation and moving short-term memory to long-term memory. In Alzheimer's disease, they are amongst the first parts damaged. They have a key role in spatial orientation and location recognition, and network with the cerebellum. Their exact functions are not yet fully understood.

**Hypothalamus** *('under the thalamus')* Links the nervous system to the endocrine (hormonal) system via the pituitary gland. Manages body temperature, hunger, and thirst; maternal attachment behaviours; sleep and circadian rhythm; and social behaviours, including sex and aggression. Crucial to directing the autonomic nervous system.

**Mammillary bodies** *(look like tiny breasts)* At the bottom of the hypothalamus. Connect to the amygdala and the thalamus. Essential for recollective memory – damage leads to several forms of amnesia.

**Thalamus** *(bridal chamber)* Above the medulla and pons (*'bridge'*) and just below the right and left hemispheres. Marries everything above (the cortex) to everything below (the limbic system and the midbrain). The thalamus also connects to all parts of the 'three networks' and is probably where we fine-tune levels of consciousness. Particularly alert for pain.

**Cerebellum** *(the little brain)* Looks like a cauliflower. It is located at the back of the head, just above the neck. Coordinates all movements, responsible for balance and muscle tone, but it doesn't initiate movement. Crucial role in body memory and in speech (which involves lots of muscles, as well as breathing – and in verbal memory); learning any physical activity depends on networks in the cerebellum. It seems deeply engaged in many cognitive processes, including working memory. When we dream, it helps create the visuospatial landscape (the dream's stage set); so, the set design happens before the story.

### The two cerebral hemispheres:

**Right hemisphere** Sensation and movement on the left of the body. Problem-solving, memory, vigilance, arousal, making 'gestalts' (seeing the whole from the parts, getting the big picture) – may be more 'artistic' and 'creative' – an idea popular in the 1990s. Always talking to the left hemisphere.

**Left hemisphere** Sensation and movement on the right of the body. More 'academic' – responsible for memory, language, and speech; it goes for the detail. Always talks to the right hemisphere.

## The lobes of the cortex:

**Frontal and prefrontal** The frontal cortex is better at learning by rules and patterns. It is responsible for concrete thinking, planning, and moral choices, as well as damping down emotion so we don't get flooded.

**Prefrontal cortex** Just before the frontal cortex: about a finger's breadth back from the end of the eyebrows. The prefrontal cortex does 'abstract thinking.' It is one of the most highly connected areas of the brain – so, it's involved with everything. Also known as the association area because this is where information gets put together from all the sensory inputs – where 'pre-thoughts' form.

**Medial prefrontal cortex** Involved in planning, decision-making, social behaviours, speech, and language. It is a key part of the default mode network, enabling us to narrate ourselves to ourselves (tell stories about who we are and what we're doing from moment to moment). Probably writes the scripts for dreams. It is responsible for choices about what to attend to and whether to attend at all.

**Dorso Lateral prefrontal cortex** Decision-making, planning, most cognitive processes, working memory, ethical and moral choices – along with the angular gyrus.

**Parietal lobes** Above and behind the ears. This is where we sense the body and initiate movements. Involved in spatial recognition, manipulating objects, and coordination.

**Parietal-temporal-occipital (PTO) junction** Where the parietal, temporal, and occipital lobes meet. Along with inputs from the cerebellum, this area is crucial in the formation of dreams. The sensations come first and then sound and pictures are added.

**Angular gyrus** At the lower rear part of both parietal lobes. Makes meaning when we read – by joining letters into words. Concerned with language, memory retrieval, attention, and theory of mind, as well as recognising and accepting that other people have minds just like our own. This is vital for developing empathy.

**Temporal lobe**   Behind and below the ears. It recognises sound and puts together sound and vision to make meaning; it allows their reconstructive imagination. Responsible for encoding long-term memory and networking with the hippocampus and amygdala.

**Occipital lobe**   At the back of the head. The visual cortex is responsible for sight. Different parts process 'what, where, and how'; detect movement; and predict what movement is likely to happen next (which is how we can catch things). During sleep, a different part from what we use when awake provides the visual images for dreams.

**Pineal gland**   (*'the pine cone'*) A small gland in the centre of the brain. In darkness, it makes melatonin, and it is involved in the wake/sleep cycle (circadian rhythm). It is involved in bone growth and in the changes at puberty.

## FURTHER READING

Afford, P. (2019) *Therapy in the age of neuroscience s* London: Routledge.
Gellatly, A., and Zarate, O. (1998) *Mind and brain for beginners*, Cambridge: Icon Books.

# SELECTED BIBLIOGRAPHY

If you wish to read further, here is a list of key texts:

Afford, P. (2019) *Therapy in the age of neuroscience: A guide for counsellors and therapists*, London: Routledge.

Barratt, L. F. (2021) *Seven and a half lessons about the brain*, London: Picador.

Domhoff, G. W. (2022) *The Neurocognitive theory of dreaming: The where, how, when, what, and why of dreams*, Cambridge, MA: MIT Press.

Ellenberger, H. (1970) *The discovery of the unconscious*, New York, Basic Books.

Ellis, L. (2019) *A clinician's guide to dream therapy*, London: Routledge.

Freud, S. (trans., Strachey J.) 1900/1954, *The interpretation of dreams*, London: George Allen & Unwin.

Jung, C. G. (1986) *Memories, Dreams, Reflections*, London: Fontana.

Littlehales, N. (2016) *Sleep*, London: Penguin.

McNamara, P. (2019) *The neuroscience of sleep and dreams*, Cambridge: Cambridge University Press.

Mageo, J., Sheriff, R. E. (2021) *New directions in the anthropology of dreaming*, London: Routledge.

Maitra, B., & Krause, I.-B. (2015) *Culture and madness*, London: Jessica Kingsley.

Robb, A. (2018) *Why we dream*, London: Picador.

Rubin, R. (2023) *The creative act*, London: Penguin.

Rycroft, C. (1996) *The innocence of dreams*, New York: Jason Aronson.

Solms, M. (2016) *The neuropsychology of dreams*, London: Routledge.

Vedfelt, O. (2017) *A guide to the world of dreams: An integrative approach to dreamwork*, London: Routledge.

Walker, M. (2017) *Why we sleep*, London: Penguin.

Zadra, A., Stickgold, R. (2021) *When Brains dream*, New York, W.W. Norton & Co.

# INDEX

Page numbers: **bold** refer to box, *italics* refer to figure

Aberfan tragedy (1966) 129
Aboriginal Australians: 'morning news' 135–136
abuse 62–63, 89, 91, 109
accidents 71, 87
active imagination 157, 159
actor and wolves dream 107–108
actors 7, 61, 93, 118
adenosine 70
adolescents and adolescence 69, 107
adults 107–108, 112
advertising 8–9
alcohol 76, 107, 112, 156
alpha rhythm 72
Alzheimer's disease 63, 172
ambivalence 94, 96; 'sign of mental health' 12
American 'dream' (wish) 44
amphetamines 70, 77
amygdala 58–59, 74, 82, 170, 174; brain's 'panic button' 126; glossary 171
*Analyse this* (film, 1999) 113–114
analysis 87, 97, 102–104, 115, 168; etymology (Greek) 3–4
analytical psychologists 24, 115, 130

analytical psychology 165, 168; follows Jung 85, 93–94; *see also* depth psychology
ancestors 36, 124, 130, 135
angels: etymology (Greek) 42
angular gyrus (AG) 81, *81*; function 81; glossary 173
answers 2–4, 7, 17, 104, 127, 130, 141
anterior cingulate cortex *79*; glossary 171
anterograde amnesia 63
anthropologists 133–135, 139
anthropology 39–42
anxiety 55, 63–64, 76, 92, 103, *106*, 106
anxiety dreams 47, 62, 128–129, 147
apophenia: etymology (Greek) 55
archetypes (Jung) 11, 24, 48–49, 93, 99, 108; etymology (Greek) 38; glossary 165
Aristotle 22–23
artists 137; creative dreams 119–120
Asclepius (son of Apollo) 36
Assagioli, R. 110–111, 114–115

Athens 22, 44
attachment anxiety 95
attention deficit hyperactivity
    disorder 70, 82
attention span 123–124
Augustine, Saint 27
Australia 135, 145–146
autism 82–83, 108–109, 125
Axline, V. 109; *Dibs* (1986) 125

Bair, D. 86
balance 68, 80, 170, 172
Barker, J. 129
Barrett, D.: *Committee of sleep* (2001)
    119
basal ganglia 169–171
Beethoven, L. van 121
beginner's mind (Zen concept) 87,
    92, 117
'being with' 156
benzene ring 122, 130
bereavement 104, 113
Bergson, H. 27, 93, 119, 155;
    *Dreams* (1914) 23, **88**
Berne, E. 107
Besant, A. 114
beta elements (Bion) 80
'between space' 13
biology 8, 154
Bion, W. 28, 80, 97, 166; 'alpha'
    versus 'beta' elements 97
bipolar affective disorder 76,
    88, 171
birds 57, 72, 143–144
black dream 73–74
Blackman, M.: *Noughts and crosses*
    (2001) 120–121, 125
Blavatsky, H. 114
Bleuler, E. 88, 114
blink technique (LaBerge) 127
blue dream 73
blue elephant dream 5–6, 10, 12

blue flowers dream 19, 28
body language 15, 35, 87
bodybuilder's tutu dream 104
boredom ('part of creative process')
    124
boundaries 12, 16, 18, 24, 37–38,
    40, 47, 87; conscious and
    unconscious 131; glossary 165;
    politics and religion 35
boundary problem 38, 42–43
brain xii, 163; hard to imagine
    'anything less like computer'
    9, 60; 'no evidence to support
    gendering' 73; terminology 170;
    three-level model 52–53, 169;
    weight 169
brain injuries 113
breast cancer 74, 130
Brewster, F.: *Race and unconscious*
    (2023) 48
bridal chamber *see* thalamus
bridges 15–33, 68, 99; conscious and
    unconscious 118, 150, 155; inner
    and outer worlds 150; materialism
    and spiritualism 150
Bruckner, A. 121
Buddhism 41–42, 87, 97, 125,
    158–159, 168
Bulkeley, K. 134, 136–137
bullying 49, 55, 130
Burghölzli Hospital (Zürich)
    88, 114
butterfly effect 43

C. G. Jung Institute (Zürich) 98
caffeine 70
Calabrese, J. D. xv, 39
Calderón de la Barca, P.: *Life's a
    dream* (1638) 88
cannabis 56, 76
category error 30–31; glossary 165
cats 57, 72

cerebellum 70, 80, 170, 172–173; 'crucial to body memories' 60; glossary 172

cerebral hemispheres: glossary 172–173

cerebrospinal fluid 74, 169

Chalmers, D. 23

change 17, 103

Charcot, J. M. 87–88

Chetwynd, T. 1

childhood trauma 18, 114

children 69, 107–108, 112, 145, 152

China 108, 111

Christianity 42, 159, 162–163, 168

Chronos time 27, 119, 125

chronotype 69–70

cingulate cortex 170–171

circadian rhythm 69–70, 174

circumambulating (analytical psychology) 115

Cirlot, J. E. 1

clarifying **91**

class struggle (Marxism) 163

climate change 39–40, 43, 95, 150

Cluedo (board game) 65

Coleridge, S. T.: 'Kubla Khan' (poem) 121

collective dreams 130, 135

collective unconscious **38**, 98, 100, 118, 151; glossary 165

complex emergent systems 16, **43**, 50, 150, 154, 163; religious dreams 43–44

complexes 18, 49, 55, 83, 153; glossary 165

concept: definition 24

condensation (Freud) 24, **91**

conscious: glossary 166; psychological map (iceberg model) 25

conscious mind xii–xiii, 21–22, **25**; like an island 126

consciousness 67–68, 158; 'closed system' 24; definition problem 21; philosophy 22–25; psychology 22

conspiracy theories 17, 96

contained 28, 32; glossary 166

container and contained 5, 28, 32, 90; glossary 166

context 1, 15, 19–20, 30, 36, 50, 99, 113

control 26, 41, 96, 150, 156, 159

corpus callosum 171

cortex 57, 60, 68, 78, 123, 170; folds like walnut 8; lobes (glossary) 173–174; outer layer of brain 8; right and left hemispheres 72–73

counselling 103, 115

counterfactuals 65, 68

countertransference 105–108, 110, 168; definition 91

COVID-19 pandemic 17, 142–148; social dream matrix **148**

creative dreams 119–123; artists 119–120; dance 122; film and literature 120–121; music 121; science 122–123

creativity 68, 117–131, 153; daydreaming 123–124; key concepts 131; lucid dreaming **126**, 126–128; nightmares 124–125; paranormal dreams 128–131; social dreaming **138**, 140

Crisp, A. 68

crocodiles 144–145

cross 17–18

Csikszentmihalyi, M. 160

cultural dreaming 133–149; key concepts 149

culture 7–8, 10, 23–24, 34–50, 165

curiosity 5, 31

cybernetics 16, 166

Da Vinci, L. 150
Dalí, S. 29; *Dream* (painting, 1944) 119–120
dance 153; creative dreams 122
dancer's dream 122
dancing 104, 131
Daniel, P. 137
Dante: *Divina Commedia* 142–144
daydreaming 65, 122; creativity 123–124; default mode network 80–83, *81*; executive network 79, 79–80, 83; salience network 78–79, *79*, 83; three network model 77–83
daydreams 7, 13
decision-making 171, 173
default mode network 7, 52, 54, 59, 61, 63–65, 74–75, 78, 80–83, *81*, 86, 105, 109, 111, 123, 125, 158–159, 170, 173; damage 82–83; daydreaming 124; failure to develop 82–83; posterior cingulate 'key part' 171; problems **82**
dementia 52, 63–64, 171
dementia praecox *see* schizophrenia
democracy 44–45
depression 56, 72, 75–76, 171; symptom (early morning waking) 68
depth psychology 85–100, 151; key points 100; origins 87–89; use of ideas 99; *see also* psychology
Descartes, R. 22; Cartesian dualism 22
Desoille, R. 157
developmental approach 95, 98, 114
developmental archetypes **38**
developmental problems 82
disaster dreams 129–130
discourse 9–10, 13, 35, 43, 46; glossary 166
displacement **91**

dissociation (psychological defence) 128
dogs 57, 72, 91, 104, 165
Domhoff, G. W. 40–41, 65
dorsolateral prefrontal cortex (dlPFC) 79, 80, 126; glossary 173
downtime 65, 124
dragon in supermarket dream 18–20, 46, 55, 64–65
dragons 10, 24–25, 30, 94, 97, 115, 153, 157
drawings 9, 97, 113, 120, 167
dream censor 120, 155
dream content 28
dream dictionary 131
dream ego 28
dream grammar 31–32
dream interpretation 154
dream language 3, 15–17
dream matrix **137**, 138–141
dream rebound 71, 76
dream reflection dialogue 139
dream sharing 134–137
dream symbols 115–116
dreaming: depth psychology 85–100; duration 69; empathy-learning function 34; function 156; happens in mind 7–9; storytelling 1–7
dreaming time 28–29, 119
dreams: added value (recording and study over time) 115; bridges 15–33; 'can be read in any direction' 153; 'change meaning over time' 6; creative listening 102–105; creativity 117–131; duration 6; ease of understanding (key concepts) 116; ego and self 26–27; 'essential to mental health' 71; 'five basic elements' 10; functions 1, **88**, 90, 96; 'happen on beach' 126; how unconscious

evolves memory 61–62;
importance 59; introduction
1–14; key concepts 14, 32, 50,
83; key concepts (overall) 163;
key questions 49; 'latent' versus
'manifest' content 90; linking
and not linking 11–14; making
of 74–76; 'meaning-making'
issue 163; memory-processing
(evidence) 64–65; most 'not
remembered' xii; natural function
62; natural philosophy 67–83;
'natural product of unconscious
mind' xiii; 'never have right
interpretation' 5; 'not fictionalised'
in this book xii; philosophical
questions 29–31; playing with
152–154; point to 'solutions' **139**;
political and spiritual practice
161–163; 'portals to source' of
wisdom 68; 'problem-solving
stories' 28; purpose 9–10, 163;
qualities (Vedfelt) **2**; reflections and
memories 52–66; remembering
151–152; 'sense-driven' 75; signs
and symbols 17–21, **19**; therapy
102–116; 'transcendent function'
xii; use storytelling techniques
10–11; why this dream now 11
*Dreams: portal to source* (Whitmont
and Pereira, 1989) 4, 10, 161
dreamwork (technical term) 2–3,
152, 166
drug dealer dream 39
*durée* (eternal present, Kairos) 27

ecstasy 59
Edelman, G. 8–9
effort after meaning 56
ego (Freud) 25–27, 67, 78, 80, 94,
96, 98, 115, 118, 123, 125–126,
153, 161, 167; etymology (Latin)
90; glossary 166

ego holiday 159–160
ego states (Berne) 107–108
ego-self axis 102
Egypt 46, 108, 122, 136, 169
electroencephalogram (EEG) 58,
71–73, 77
Ellenberger, H.: *Discovery of
unconscious* (1970) 88
Ellis, L. 115
Ellison, A.: *Reality of paranormal*
(1988) 130
emotional suspension system 63, 82,
125
emotions 54, 153, 168, 170–171;
interface with memory 81
empathy 1, 34–50, 54, 79, 81–82,
109–111, 125; angular gyrus 173;
etymology (Greek) 34
emptiness 13
enantiodromia (Jung) 108
Enkidu 46
envy 95, 99
*Epic of Gilgamesh* 43, 45–46
epilepsy 58, 72
epistemology 30–31, 166; definition
21
*Evening Standard* 129
exclusion principle (Pauli) 122
executive network 52, 57, 64, 78,
79, 79–80, 83, 123, 158, 170–171
experience 21, 23, 59, 135
experiences 4, 28, 80, 90–92, 95,
137, 150
*Exploring world of lucid dreaming*
(La Berge and Rheingold, 1990)
127
eyewitness 62

faces 34–35
Fairburn, R. 96
false memories 58, 61–64
fantasy 3, 6, 54, 62, 74, 92, 121,
155, 160–161

fathers 56, **91**, 93, 108, 112
fear 55, 59, 82, 124, 171
feedback loops 17, 20, 53, 151;
    culture and dreams 36; example 16
feelings 54–55, 58, 79, 95, 170;
    processing during sleep 68
field effects 111
films 154, 157; creative dreams 120
First Cultures 24, 36, 40
flash memory 57–58, 63
flow states 150, 160; characteristics
    **160**; glossary 166
flower on top of tower dream 109
Floyd, G. 147
fluent form: glossary 166
foetal dreams 6, 8, 11, 69
foetus: beginning of consciousness
    22; 'sleeps about 40 per cent of
    time' 69
footballer and monster dream 62,
    105, 107, 111–113, 118, 127, 153
Fordham, M. 98
forms (Plato) 22–23, 38
Fox, K. C. 65
fractal: glossary 166
Frater, A. 115
free association 4, 19–20, 81, 89–90,
    93, 99, 115, 138, 153, 155;
    glossary 167; weak associations
    64
free floating 87, 91
Freud, S. 6, 23–24, 46, 81, 83,
    85–87, 94, 105, 110, 113–114;
    borrowing from Bergson 89;
    contested by Grotstein 28;
    criticisms **92**; and Dalí 120;
    dream censor 155; 'dreams
    fulfil wishes' 62–63; 'economic
    theory' 90; 'hydraulic theory'
    90; *Interpretation of dreams* (1900)
    86, 90–91; nightmares 124–125;
    primary process thinking 73;
    psychoanalysis 89–92; 'standard

symbols' 155; successors 95–97;
    thinking (primary and secondary
    processes) **90**; writings 'very
    funny' 92
frontal cortex: glossary 173
frontal lobes 64, 68, 80, 125, 170
frontal lobotomy 75
frozen-in-ice dream 109
functional magnetic resonance
    imaging (fMRI) 65, 73, 169;
    workings 77–78
functional neurological disorder 89
fundamentalism 13, 16, 49
Fuseli, H.: *Nightmare* (painting,
    1781) 120

games 37, 107
gamma rhythm 72
George, Saint (and dragon) 94
gestalt 131, 172; etymology
    (German) 112
gestalt therapy (Perls) 110, 112–115
Gilgamesh's dream 46
Glasgow coma scale 21
glass ceiling 49
glial cells 169
glycogen 70
Goddard, V. 129
Gordon, R. 99
grand narratives 161
Great Leader 47–48, 57, 86, 108,
    110, 112, 161; *Epic of Gilgamesh*
    45–46
Greece 36, 48
Grotstein, J. 28
*Groundhog day* (film, 1993) 21
group analysis (Bion) 97
guilt 41, 96

hallucination 64, 71; definition 29;
    glossary 167
Hannibal 9–10, 47
Harry Potter books 10–12

Heraclitus 108
hertz (one brain wave per second) 72
higher self 115
Hillman, J. 115, 153; *Soul's code* (1997) 98
Hinduism 42, 155, 159
hippocampus 57, *58*, 58–59, *79*, 80, 170, 174; glossary 171–172; involvement in spatial awareness 61; 'severely affected' in Alzheimer's disease 63
Hitchcock, A. 32
Holmes, S. 154
hologram 112
homeostasis 16; glossary 167
humanistic therapy 114
Hume, D. 155; *Treatise of human nature* (1739–1740) 23
humour 89, **156**, 157
hunter-gatherers 36, 55
hyper-focus 160
hypothalamus 72, *79*, 170; glossary 172; 'helps build up memory' 78
hypothalamus damage 77
hysteria 89–90; etymology (Greek) 89

iceberg model *25*
Iceland 47; dreams 'inherently social' 135
id (Freud) 90, 93, 166
identity 11, 42–44; symbols 18
images of absence 12–13
imagination 115; active 157, 159
improvisation 80, 153
*Inception* (film, 2010) 29
India 97, 108, 129
individuation 94, 98, 111
infants 54, 63, 69, 95, 123
inferior parietal lobe (IPL) *71*, 71, *79*, 80
infinite regress (philosophy) 8, 23, 29
inner cinema 10–11, 105, 126
insomnia 65, 76, 124

instinct 57, 90, 144, 169
insula *79*, 80
International Association of Jungian Analysts (IAAP) 142
intersubjective approach 111
intuition 129–130
Iona 12–13, 19
Islam 42, 136, 150, 159

Jacobi, J. 25
James, W. 88
James Webb space telescope 77
Janet, P. 88
Japanese dreaming 41–42
jet lag 71
jigsaw analogy 11–13
Johns, J.: *Flag* (painting, 1954) 120
Johnson, B. 30
jokes 7–8, 31–32, 49, 87, 104, 134, 152
Joseph and Pharaoh 46–47
Joseph, S. 161
Judaism 42, 159
Jung, C. G. xiv, 24, 27, 38, 44, 83, 85, 88, 105, 110, 119, 122, 130, 151, 165; analytical psychology 93–94; approaching the unconscious 36; autobiography (1986) 53; borrowing from Bergson 89; 'conflicted relationship' with Freud 86; difference from Freud 90; dream interpretation (hazards) 154; dreams 'have social function' 133; engagement with occultism 114; good friend of Bleuler 114; model of mind 93; nightmares 124–125; *Red Book* (1913–1930, published 2009) 86, 94; research into alchemy 94; role of dreams 153; Spirit of Depth versus Spirit of Times 94; successors 98–99; 'Transcendent function' (essay)

155–156; UFOs 'projection from unconscious mind' 160
Jung-Pauli conjecture 123, 161
Jungian analysts' dreams 141–148

Kabbalah 161–162
Kairos time 27, 119, 125
Kant, I. 155; *Critique of pure reason* (1781) 23
Karpman, S.: drama triangle 106–107, *107*
Kawai, H. 41
Keats, J. 13
Kekule, A. 122, 130
KGB (cagey bee) dream 31–32, 65, 92
Klein, M. 94–95
Koch, A. 111
Korsakov's syndrome 63

LaBerge, S. 127
language: definition 15
law of evidence 62
Lawrence, G. 137
learning 1, 21, 55, 59–61, 65, 87, 104, 115, 154, 171–173
left hemisphere 72, 170–172; glossary 173
Leicester Square dream 118
Lewy body dementia 64
libido (Freud) 90
lies 4, 97, 168
limbic lobe 80
limbic system 68, 78, 123, 170; glossary 171–172
*limen* (Latin, 'threshold') 13, 167
Lincoln, A. 129
linking things together 5–6
listening 102–105; 'most important skill' 151
listening therapies 157; three modes (counselling, therapy, analysis) 103

literature: creative dreams 120–121
little brain *see* cerebellum
Littlehales, N. 76
logical operators 167; both-and 12, 14, 22, 31, 74, 123, 155, 161; either-or 12, 167; if-then 12, 167; neither-nor 12, 14, 22, 31, 74, 123, 155, 161, 167
*logos* (Greek etymology) 7
long-term memory 57–58, 174
Loyola, I. 159
lucid dreaming 123; creativity **126**, 126–128; 'like building a sandcastle' 126; risks 128; tips **127**

Mageo, J. 134
Malan, D. 105
mammals 2, 11, 69, 72, 146, 165
mammillary bodies *58*, 58, 63; glossary 172
*mana* transference 110
Marx, K. 44
materialism versus spirituality 17, 123, 129, 150, 161
mathematics 154, 166, 168
Mathers, C. xi, xv
Mathers, D. xi–xiii; 'analytical psychologist' 24; 'Jungian analyst' 4
medial prefrontal cortex (mPFC) 61, 74, *75*, 75, 80, *81*; function 81; glossary 173
meditation 24, 150, 155, 157–160
medulla 67, 70, 169–170, 172; glossary 171
melatonin 69–70, 174
memories 9, 52–66; 'usual paths' 55
memory xii, 1, 171, 173; 'concealed' versus 'revealed' 62–63; dreaming 'essential' 60–61; explanatory models 56–59; 'explicit' versus 'implicit' 56–57, 59–61, 171; 'feeling-based rather than thought-based' 52; key concepts

65–66; 'predicts possible futures'
('prospective function', Jung) 53,
56; 'reconstructive imagination'
60–61; role 52; spatial and sensory
component 59; stages **59**; turned
into 'mind' 52
memory circuits *58*
memory consolidation 59, 171–172
memory loss 58, 63–64
mental health 12, 26, 71, 94, 102
metaphor 32; glossary 167
Miller, M. E. xv
mind 163; basic function 53;
'disorderly, democratic parliament'
100; dreaming happens in 7–9;
functions, purposes 8; has censor
(Freud) 90, **91**, 93; 'natural
anarchy' 57; not same as 'brain' xii,
8; properties **22**
mind-body problem 7–8
mindfulness 157–160
minority groups 40
mirroring 20, 54
Mitchell, S. 46
monsters 94, 107, 111–113, 116,
126–128
moral defence (Fairburn) 96
mothers 95–97, 113, 166
Mozart, W. A. 121
muscle memory 60
music 125, 131, 153; creative dreams
121
*My own private Idaho* (film, 1991) 77
myth 10, 46–47; glossary 167

naked dancer dream 60, 122
narcissism 54, 109
narcolepsy 76–77
narratives 9–10, 13, 29; glossary 167
natural philosophy: sleep and dreams
67–83
nature 23, 144, 150
Navajo people (Arizona) 39

near predictions (Zadra and
Stickgold) 130
negative capability 13, 97, 118
neural Darwinism (Edelman) 9
neural networks 52; key concept 8
neural pathways 26, 52, 60; sleep *71*
neuroanatomy xii, 61, 67, 70, 97;
glossary 169–174
neurons 8–9, 16, 58–60, 65, 69–70,
74, 89, 169–170
neuroscience 52–53, 74, 77–78, 89,
102, 163
neurosis: definition 94
neurosurgeons 58, 75
neurotransmitters 70
new mammal brain 170
New York 48
newborns 54, 95; sleep about ten
hours 69
NEXTUP theory (Zadra and
Stickgold) 53, 64–65, 130
*Night my number came up* (film, 1955)
129
nightmares 13, 16, 41, 64, 76, 111,
121, 126–127; creativity 124–125
Nishitani, K. 41
Nolan, C.: *Dark Knight Rises* (film,
2012) 120; *Oppenheimer* (film,
2023) 120
non-REM sleep 73–74
null hypothesis 29

object relations theory 94–97
objective psyche (von Franz) 98
obsessive-compulsive disorder
(OCD) 82
occipital lobe 170; glossary 174
occultism 114, 154
old mammalian brain 170
oneirophrenia: etymology (Latin) 76;
*see also* schizophrenia
ontology 21, 30, 167
open-mindedness 16, 49, 54, 117

opiates 74, 76
orgone energy (Reich) 113
Orwell, G.: *1984* (2021 edition [1949]) 35
othering 41, 48–49
Ouroboros 122
oxygen 53, 77, 169

pain 74, 170
paradox 3, 8, 31, 68, 159
paranoia 17, 31; etymology (Greek) 49, 94
paranoid-schizoid position (Klein) 95
paranormal dreams: creativity 128–131
parents 105, 107–110, 125, 165
parietal lobe 74, 80, 170; glossary 173
parietal-temporal-occipital (PTO) junction 74–75, *75*; glossary 173
pattern recognition 55–56, 91, 104, 122, 152
Pauli, W. 119, 122
penny-in-hand technique 119
perception 6, 8, 16, 23, 26, 29, 57, 59, 86, **88**, 170; determined by expectation 62
Pereira, S. B. 4
periaqueductal grey matter' (PAG) 74, *75*, 75; definition 171
Perls, F. 110, 112–114
persona 18; glossary 167
personality disorders: glossary 167
person-centred therapy (Rogers) 110–112
Pharaoh's dream 47
philosopher's stone dream 123
philosophy 154–155, 168
physiology 4, **25**
pilots 71, 123, 129, 166
pineal gland 22, 69; glossary 174
planning 79, 115, 173
Plato 22–23, 38; *Republic* 45
play 14, 97, 117, 136, 150–163

playfulness 2–3, 5, 87; one of seven core emotions 153
playing with dreams 152–154
PM at Glastonbury festival dream 30
poems 9, 121, 153
political dreams: associate freely with religious dreams 44–47
politics 34–50, 153, 161–163
pons 169–170, 172
Popper, K. 29
Port Ban dream 12–14
post-traumatic stress disorder (PTSD) 55–56, 80, 97, 113, 127; nightmares 124
posterior cingulate cortex (PCC) *58*, 59, 63, 80–81, *81*; function 81; glossary 171
Potiphar 47
power 9–10, 13, 35, 43, 73, 110, 140, 161, 166
pre-thoughts 97, 173
precognition: play between 'material' and 'spiritual' 117
precognitive dream 118, 128–129
prefrontal cortex 76; glossary 173
Preiswerk, H. 93, 114
prejudice 39, 56, 86
premature closure 49, 113
Premonitions Bureau 129
prescience 147–148
presence and absence (luminous and non-luminous) **162**
present-moment awareness (Buddhist idea) 82, 97, 159, **160**
primary narcissism 54
*Princess Mononoke* (film, 1997) 41
princesses 4, 20, 94, 96, 153
projection 29, 41, 73, 91, 105, 160
psyche: etymology 7, 44, 98
psychiatrists 39, 93–94, 97–98, 107, 113–114, 126, 129
psychiatry 68, 167

psychoanalysis 1, 6, 11, 98, 152, 166; follows Freud 85, 89–92; listening to dreams 6; 'theory of everything' 93

psychoanalysts 83, 86, 111, 133

psychodynamics 110

psychology 7; *see also* transpersonal psychology

psychosynthesis (Assagioli) 110, 114–115, 151–152, 157

psychotherapists 133

quantum physics 123

questions: angels and spirits 42; boundaries of mind 38; capturing dream images by drawing 120; category errors 31; change 17, 103; consciousness (definition) 21; criticisms of Freud 92; cultural appropriation 41; cultural immersion 39; culture (influence on interpretation) 47; dead talking to us in dreams 131; depth psychology (two sides) 100; disaster dreams 130; dragon in supermarket dream 20; dream landscape (shaping by culture) 49; dream producing closure 18; dream symbols 37; dreaming (discriminating wisdom, better questions) 156; dreams (near predictions) 130; dreams (political and spiritual practice) 161; Easterners (projection onto Westerners) 41; ego and self (neuroanatomical basis) 68; flow states 160; Freud versus Jung 94; fundamentalists 13; identity symbols 18; mind versus body 3; mysticism versus science 85; myths of origin 10; neural pathways (reading) 60; politics of inner world 45; reflection 54–55; self 4, 35; Shadow 45; social and cultural dreaming 134; social dreaming 140; social values 35; therapists theories 116; unconscious choices 57

racism 47–49, 89, 146–147

rapid eye movement (REM) sleep 58, 64, 72, 76, 125–126, 151; 'abstract' dreams 75; improvement of implicit memory 61; 'sign of dreaming' 2

Rashevsky number 8

reality 3; changes across time 35–39

reality testing 24, 26, 65, 67–68, 71–72, 75–76, 94, 96, 114, 125, 153, 161, 166–167; science 'has no monopoly' 92

reconstructive imagination 56, 60–61

recreation 153

recreational drugs 59, 76

reflection 52–66, 148

refugees 99, 147

rehearsal dreams 60

Reich, W. 113

reification: definition 24

religion 34–50, 153, 161–163

religious dreams 42–44; associate freely with political dreams 44–47; complex emergent systems 43–44

remembering: what we predict rather than reality 62

repression 90, 93

reticular activating system (RAS) 70, 71, 74, 75, 77; glossary 171

retrograde amnesia 63

revision **91**

Richards, K. 121

right hemisphere 72–73, 171, 173; glossary 172

ritalin (amphetamine) 70

rock guitarist 121, 125

Rogers, C. 110–112

Rolling Stones: *Satisfaction* (1965) 121
Rome 48
Rovelli, C. 27
Rowling, J. K.: Harry Potter books 121
Rubin, R.: *Creative act* (2023) 117
ruminating 76, 158
Russell, B. 29
Russia 40, 141
Rutkowsky, K. 127
Ryle, G. 30

salience network 52, 57–58, 78–79, 79, 83, 123, 158, 170; risk assessment 79
Samuels, A. xv, 44, 99
San Roque, C. 135
schizophrenia 75–76, 88, 94, 171
school: starting time (of day) 69
science: creative dreams 122–123; 'no monopoly on reality testing' 92
scientific time (series of moments, Chronos) 27
self 4–6, 20, 26–27, 35–37, 40, 43, 49, 67, 78, 95–98, 111; creation (via dreams) 6; 'emerges patiently' 162; glossary 168
self-awareness 79, 155
semiotics 17; glossary 168
Senoi (Malaysia) 40–41, 47, 136
serotonin 59
Shadow 49, 109, 121
Shakespeare, W.: *Tempest* 74
shamanism 110, 126, 159
shame 41, 96, 130
sharp waves 58
Shone, T. 120
short-term memory 57–58, 172
signs 17–21, **19**; 'closed, simple system' 17; glossary 168
slavery 44, 48

sleep 59, 69–77; adults **74**; key concepts 83; memory improvement 61; natural philosophy 67–83; neural pathways 71, 71; 'patterns change throughout life' 69; stages 71–72
sleep deprivation 64, 71
sleep disorders 69, 76–77
sleep hygiene 76, 152
sleep laboratory 68, 70, 73, 128, 151
sleep on it (truth of saying) 61
slow-wave sleep 58, 61, 80
snakes 122, 145
social dreaming 133–149; applications **140**; examples 141–144; key concepts 149
social dreaming matrix 134, 142, 148, 151
social networks 8, 35, 37
Solms, M. 75, 89
song lines 136
soul 22–23, 26, 42, 98, 115
sound and vision 75, 174
South Africa 99, 113, 115
Sparta 45
spatial awareness 61, 68, 75
Speilrein, S. 86, 93
*Spirited Away* (film, 2001) 41
spirits 36, 130, 162
splitting (psychological defence) 128
squiggle game (Winnicott) 96–97
stereotypes 42, 48
Stevenson, R. L.: *Dr. Jekyll and Mr. Hyde* (1886) 121
Stewart, K. 40
Stickgold, R. 53
storytelling 1–7, 10–11
stress 54, 83, 125, 158
structural analysis 39, 42, 48
sub-personalities 20–21, 28, 40, 45, 107, 111; glossary 168
Sumer 45–46
*Sunday Times* 120

superego (Freud) 90, 93, 166
supply and demand 53, 90
survival 45, 53, 55, 89, 167
symbols 1, 17–21, **19**, 30, 90, 120, 131, 134, 155, 161; etymology (Greek) 18; glossary 168; meanings 'constantly change' 6; 'open, complex system' 17; situational meanings 12; 'spoken by unconscious to conscious' 15
synchronicity (Jung) 119, 122–123, 130
systems 16–17, 21; definition 16

Taj Mahal dream 129
'Tao of wisdom' (Rosen and Crouse, 2000) 156
teleology 115; etymology (Greek) 9; glossary 168
temporal lobe 58, 170–171; glossary 174
tennis 7, 86
thalamus ('bridal chamber') 57, 70–71, *71*, 74, *75*, *79*, 171; glossary 172; 'monitors incoming sensations' 78; 'vital part of sleep network' 69
The Dreaming 135–136
theories of everything 161
theosophy 114
therapists 157; Freudian 134; playing with dream symbols 115–116; theorising about dreams 110–115; work with dreams 108–110
therapy 102–116; joke definition 104
theta rhythm 72
theta waves 58
thinking: convergent versus divergent 65; primary and secondary processes (Freud) **90**
thought crime 35
thought processing: during sleep 68

three analysts dream 108, 113
three network model xiii, 68, 77–83, 97, 123, 125, 157–160, 170
Tibetan Buddhism 159
Tibetan dream yoga 126
timarchy (fascism) 45
time 103, 124; linear and nonlinear 139; two kinds 27–28
time perception 72, 80, 127
time sense 69
time-kaleidoscope 28
*Titanic* 129
transactional analysis (Berne) 107
transcendent function 28, 118, 154–156; glossary 168
transference 87, 97, 99, 104–108, 114; definition 91; glossary 168
transpersonal (beyond personal) 98, 162
transpersonal psychology (psychosynthesis) 114, 116; *see also* analytical psychology
triangle of conflict versus triangle of person 105, *106*
Trump, D. 146
trust 91, 111, 135, 151
truth 3, 54, 60, 97, 100, 110, 154, 167–168
Twain, M. 44
two-chair work 112–113

Ukraine 40, 141
uncertainty 13, 32, 43, 140
unconscious mind xii–xiii, 6–7, 21–22, **25**, 110, 128; 'collective' versus 'personal' 24; dreams 'gift' from 162; Freud 6, 85, 90; glossary 168; key concept 11; like an ocean 126; 'open system' 24; psychological map (iceberg model) *25*; trustworthiness 151
United States 36, 86, 113, 130, 137

vaginal candida 109
van Eeden, W. 126
van Sant, G. 77
van de Wetering, J. W. 41
Vedfelt, O. 2, 16
Virgil 143
von Franz, M.-L.: *Alchemical active imagination* (1997) 157; *Dreams* (1991) 98; *Way of dream* (film, 1987) 98

Wagner, R.: *Tristan and Isolde* (dream, 1854; opera, 1859) 121
wake-sleep cycle 69–70, 77, 174
waking dreams 72, 157
walk in park dream 68
Washington: attack on Capitol (2021) 147
weak associations 64, 68, 130
Webb, C. S.: *Dreams behind music* (2016) 121
whale dream 37
whale and ocean problem 38, 42
white zombie dream 48–49

Whitmont, E. C. 4
whole-brain memory 61
Wilde, O. 38
Will 110, 114–115; three parts 151–152
Winnicott, D. W. 96–97, 136
wisdom 16, 68; developing **156**
wise dwarf dream 152
wish fulfilment 92, 108, 120, 161
women 44, 48, 89, 143
wonder 87, 152
word association test 93
working memory 79, 126, 172
worldview 23, 36, 118

YouTube xiii, 98, 158

Zadra, A. 53
Zappa, F. 49
Zen Buddhism 87, 125, 158
Zinkin, L. 112
Zinn, J. K. 158
zombie apocalypse dream 105–106

Printed in the United States
by Baker & Taylor Publisher Services